The Writing Business

Business

A POETS & WRITERS HANDBOOK

**by the editors of
Coda: Poets & Writers Newsletter**

Poets & Writers, Inc., New York, NY
A Poets & Writers Book
Distributed by Pushcart Press / W. W. Norton & Co. Inc.

A Poets & Writers Book / Distributed by
Pushcart Press/W. W. Norton

Published by Poets & Writers, Inc., a publicly
supported, nonprofit, tax-exempt corporation
organized for educational and literary purposes. Donations to it are charitable contributions under section 170 of the Internal Revenue
Code. Please write or call for further information. Poets & Writers, Inc., 201 West 54 Street,
New York, NY 10019. (212) 757-1766.

Publication made possible by grants from The
J. M. Kaplan Fund and The New Hope Foundation.

Library of Congress Catalog Card Number
84-062411.
ISBN 0-916-366-27-8

Manufactured in the United States of America
by Ray Freiman and Company,
Stamford Connecticut.

Personal mail orders should be addressed to
Poets & Writers, Inc., 201 West 54 Street,
New York, NY 10019.

Bookstore and Agency orders should be
addressed to
Pushcart Press/W. W. Norton,
500 Fifth Avenue,
New York, NY 10110.

Contents

Introduction

As all writers know, there is more to writing than inviting the muse and getting the words on paper. There are also questions of negotiating a contract, getting publicity, preparing tax returns—problems similar to those of any business, but all with a particular twist for writers.

For twelve years, *Coda* has been delving into these issues for its readers. Now, with the help of a grant from The J. M. Kaplan Fund and additional assistance from The New Hope Foundation, the editors have collected those *Coda* articles unique to the newsletter. Here they are—the "best of *Coda*" compiled in a handbook for writers.

The articles, all of which deal with the business side of writing, cover a wide spectrum. They range from practical subjects, such as manuscript submission and book contracts, to investigative reporting on trends in paperback publishing. They answer questions such as what to do when your poem is ready for submission, what to expect once your manuscript has been accepted, and how to survive as a writer.

In most cases, the authors of these various articles are—or were—members of the staff of Poets & Writers, Inc. In a few cases, *Coda* used freelancers with particular expertise in the field for an article. A brief biography of each contributing writer and editor appears in the Appendix at the back of the book.

The articles we have chosen have all been carefully checked and updated. The date of the original publication of each is listed in the Appendix along with a list of addresses for the publishers whose books are recommended for further reading and a description of the services and other publications offered by Poets & Writers, Inc.

We have grouped these articles in six sections dealing with different areas of concern to a writer. We hope you'll find new insights and perspectives by exploring the experiences of other writers, as *Coda* readers have been doing for years. We also hope this handbook helps you to make the most of your writing career.

Lisa Merrill

Acknowledgments

Poets & Writers, Inc. wishes to thank The J. M. Kaplan Fund for the generous grant which allowed us to undertake publication of this book. We are grateful for the continuing support they have given our publications. We also want to thank The New Hope Foundation for an additional grant which has assisted publication.

The confidence expressed by these gifts from distinguished foundations is a source of encouragement to all of us at Poets & Writers.

Thanks also to the writers whose articles are reprinted here, to Daryln Brewer, Debby Mayer, and Lisa Merrill for editing the collection, to John Fox for proofreading, to Galen Williams for her interest and advice on the selections, and to the entire Poets & Writers staff for their enthusiastic support.

One

GETTING STARTED

Writer's Block: The Anxious Silence

I am fretting, scratching. What a heavy oar the pen is, and what a strong current ideas are to row in.

Flaubert

Kurt Vonnegut swims to get rid of it. Tom Wolfe orders custom-made suits, requiring many trips to the tailor for fittings—anything to get away from the typewriter. Few can explain writer's block or where it comes from, but most writers complain of it at one point or another. Whether it means not being able to write at all, or just not writing well, writer's block can be minor and cause a temporary setback, or debilitating and long lasting—and everything in between.

Following are some thoughts on the subject, and even a few tricks for unblocking.

Louise Glück (*Descending Figure,* Ecco Press): I question the assumption behind writer's block, which is that one should be writing all the time, that at any given time there is something worthwhile to be made into a poem. We become obsessed with silence then, and fail to cultivate patience. Of course I've experienced that anxious silence we call writer's block, but at times we simply have nothing to say. Then we need to get back in the world and put more life into ourselves—and hope we'll be vouchsafed some more poems. In fact, there aren't that many "real poems" to be written in any given year. Nevertheless, we set up a schedule—a set of habits that minimize the anxiety. But I find it scarier to sit down and write garbage. Then I do better not to write poetry at all—I write letters and cook.

Francine du Plessix Gray (*World Without End,* Simon & Schuster): There are two kinds of writer's block. One is when you can't write anything, and another is when you can't solve a technical problem in a novel or short story. I don't believe in the overall writer's block. You can always write something else—book reviews, or another genre. Then the pain of ceasing to write is not so present. I seek refuge in nonfiction. In the past—when I had longer spells between books and was less in demand for book reviews—I wrote letters.

Stanley Kunitz (*Poems of Stanley Kunitz 1928-1978,* Atlantic Monthly Press): Writer's block is a natural affliction. Writers who have never experienced it have something wrong with them. It means there isn't enough friction—that they aren't making enough of an effort to reconcile the contradictions of life. All you get is a sweet, monotonous flow. Writer's block is nothing to commit suicide over. It simply indicates some imbalance between your experience and your art, and I think that's constructive. You have to get in mesh again—better sit and think about it.

James Merrill (*The Changing Light at Sandover,* Atheneum): There's no such thing as a simple writer's block. You're usually in some other troubling predicament, whether you know it or not. Writer's block exists as an overt symptom of something else, not as its cause. The answer is to get away from your desk. You usually just weather it, wait for it to pass, go about your life—do anything to refresh you.

Tim O'Brien (*Going After Cacciato*, Delacorte): I've never had it—I'm not sure what it is. The only solution is to write and write and write. When I talk to students or others who've been blocked, I often find it was just an absence of thought. They didn't know what to write about. If you know what it is you care about, it's easy to write. Those who can't write probably shouldn't.

Lynne Sharon Schwartz (*Disturbances in the Field*, Harper & Row): I don't believe in any such thing. I'm very puritanical—you just have to sit down and do it. I haven't had writer's block since I began to write seriously, which was ten years ago. Before that, it wasn't that I sat down and tried to write and couldn't, I just didn't sit down. Now it is vital that I write, and I do it like a job. I can't afford writer's block. I started very late, and I hear time's winged chariot.

Daryln Brewer

How to Get Out of the Slush Pile

Slush: Confused and emotional, but unsubstantial, talk or writing; gush; drivel.

        —Webster's New International Dictionary

A year before her first novel was published, Sonia Gernes was an English professor at Nòtre Dame University in Indiana with no real connections to New York's literary community and little idea of what to do with her manuscript. Though Gernes had numerous poetry publications to her credit, she had never published any fiction.

Gernes assumed that in order to place her manuscript, she'd have to get a literary agent. So she asked for help from one of her colleagues, Elizabeth Christman, a former New York literary agent and the author of three novels. To her surprise, Christman said, "No one's ever heard of you, so no agent is going to take you on. You'll have to place the manuscript yourself."

"But no one will even read my manuscript if it comes in over the transom," said Gernes.

"Yes they will, if you do it right," said Christman, who set out to teach her the ropes.

Send a Good Query Letter

Sonia Gernes got out of the slush pile with a one-page query letter of four paragraphs:

1) a brief description of the book.

2) a brief identification of the novel's market—"a rite-of-passage novel of the mid-life woman," says Gernes. "I also mentioned its similarities to and differences from novels such as *Final Payments* and *The Women's Room*."

3) a request for permission to send the complete manuscript.

4) a brief description of herself—including her job and some of the journals which had published her poetry.

The letter (written on Notre Dame stationery) was neat, clean, and error free. Gernes also enclosed an envelope for the editor's reply.

Send an Enticing Synopsis

With the query letter, Gernes enclosed a 2½ page synopsis of her novel. That was the hardest part. "I spent a whole weekend on it, careful to include all major conflicts, themes, and characters," says Gernes. She showed it to Elizabeth Christman who said, "Sonia, this will never do. It reads like something you prepared for class. Remember, these are commercial houses—hype it up, make it exciting, make it sound like something people will want to buy."

Gernes did as she was told, although "hype doesn't come naturally to me," she says. "In fact, it's rather repugnant. I began to worry that I was parodying a book jacket." She went through the manuscript again, and selected the most enticing and suspenseful parts. This time Christman said, "Fine. Send it."

With the query and synopsis, Gernes sent a sample of the novel. She chose the first two chapters, which were typical of her writing. "Later chapters were too dependent on what came before," she says. (Gernes did not request the return of sample chapters.)

Make a List from *LMP*

Using the *Literary Market Place (LMP)* from her library, Gernes made a list of potential editors. She tended toward women editors because she felt they would be more receptive to the book. She usually wrote to those at the end of the publisher's listing; often these editors are younger, have fewer authors, and are on the lookout for new work. Gernes also had three friends who knew editors—one each at Norton, Putnam, and Andrews McNeel. She queried those editors first, mentioning her friends.

Don't confuse multiple queries with multiple submissions. A multiple submission is sending an entire manuscript to a number of different editors at the same time. This practice is frowned upon, perhaps for good reason: no editor likes to spend time reading a manuscript and talking it up within the house, only to find that another editor has done the same, and bought the book. Multiple queries, on the other hand, are less time-consuming, and many editors seem to take them for granted. But if you make multiple queries, it's a good idea to tell the editors you're doing so.

The Next Step

"Be patient," says Gernes. Norton, Putnam, and Andrews McNeel all responded within a month. Only Norton asked to see the complete manuscript. After a number of encouraging progress reports from Norton, the novel was rejected—three months after the full manuscript was mailed, and five months since the initial query.

"The editor from Norton wrote a long and complimentary letter saying she wanted to accept the book but couldn't because of the current state of the publishing industry. She also suggested cutting the novel," says Gernes, who took her advice. While shaving thirty pages from the 350-page manuscript, she queried five more publishers: Scribners, Doubleday, Harper & Row, Viking, and St. Martin's (where an editor had liked an earlier poetry manuscript of hers). Scribners and Viking responded promptly, asking to see the whole book. Harper & Row, Doubleday, and St. Martin's declined within a month. Gernes chose Scribners "because Susanne Kirk responded with a phone call, and then a note saying she loved the first two chapters."

Six weeks later, Kirk was Gernes' editor.

The Way to Susanne Kirk

Susanne Kirk was as pleased to find *The Way to St. Ives* as Gernes was to have her publish it. What made Kirk notice it? "Sonia presented herself and her idea in a literate, intriguing way, without any gimmicks," she says. "When telling the book's plot she wasn't too wordy. We get so many unsolicited manuscripts that the competition is tremendous. A writer has to prove immediately to an editor that he or she can write well."

Kirk's assistant read and liked the first two chapters of *The Way to St. Ives* and passed them on to Kirk. Assistants are often the first to read unsolicited manuscripts in a commercial house—either on a rotating basis for all editors or for the individual editor for whom they work. Kirk took the sample chapters home one night and came in the next morning worried. "It was very good," she says, "but I thought another house might have already grabbed it, because we'd had it for a month." She called Gernes to find that, in fact, another editor had expressed interest. Kirk had to wait until Gernes heard from that editor

9

(a rejection) before she was able to read the entire manuscript and, finally, to accept it.

Although Scribners doesn't publish poetry (they leave that to their sister house, Atheneum), they do publish several unsolicited fiction manuscripts a year. "People think we don't look at the slush pile, but we do," says Kirk, "precisely because of books such as *The Way to St. Ives*."

Nonetheless, there's a debate about whether the staff time spent reading unsolicited manuscripts is worthwhile. Because Scribners, like any commerical house, gets a lot of unsolicited material, Kirk stresses that a book must begin well. "If authors realized the amount of time it takes to read through the slush, they'd concentrate on the beginning of the manuscript. If a book doesn't begin well, a reader switches off and doesn't go on to page three. Authors are horrified to hear that an editor reads only a few pages of a manuscript, but unless a book grabs us right away, we can't make time for it. The notion that a manuscript gets better as it goes along just doesn't work."

Like Applying for a Job

Small presses have the reputation of being more willing to publish work by unknown writers, but because small presses *are* small—run by one or two people—they often don't have time to read unsolicited manuscripts either. Check *The International Directory of Little Magazines and Small Presses* for guidelines such as, "No new work will be considered between May 1 and September 1" or "Two to six poems per submission preferred." (Don't start off on the wrong foot by ignoring such details.) Some say simply, "No unsolicited manuscripts." Friends and friends of friends are helpful for entré to the small press world too.

What attracts a small press editor? It may be something different from what attracts a commercial editor. "I am most impressed with an author who cares about his work, and one who is concerned with the publishing process," says Gerald Lange of Bieler Press in St. Paul, Minnesota. Lange looks for a query letter that's not only professional but also friendly and generous. "By generous I mean if I get a dog-eared manuscript with a curt cover letter or none at all, or no SASE, I don't think that author cares much about me, the manuscript, or himself," says Lange.

"A writer should explain who he is and what he's published and should also show an interest in and an understanding of a publisher's goals," says Lange. In other words, study the particular press to which you're submitting a manuscript. "I don't like to feel that my press is one of a hundred an author is writing to," says Lange. "Mail from those who have actually seen a Bieler Press book interests me much more. This eliminates misunderstanding about what I'm doing as a publisher.

"An author's attitude is important too. Publishing is a personal thing between author and editor. The better I know the author, the better the publishing relationship is—and the happier we'll both be with the final publication. A lot of writers don't realize that submitting a manuscript is like applying for a job—they must put their best foot forward."

Study the Market

One writer who cares about his work is John Gilgun, Gerald Lange thought so too—Bieler Press published his first book, a collection of fables, called *Everything That Has Been Shall Be Again.*

Gilgun first learned of Bieler Press in 1978 through an announcement in *Coda.* Lange wanted animal stories for an anthology he was planning; Gilgun immediately sent him "Cow," a fable. "Lange loved it and asked me if I had more," says Gilgun. Eventually, Lange decided not to publish the anthology and just do a collection of Gilgun's fables. The book won an American Institute of Graphic Arts Award, the Chicago Book Show Award and The Midwestern Books Competition.

Gilgun's advice for getting out of the slush pile includes reading *Coda* announcements and studying *The International Directory of Little Magazines and Small Presses*.

"I read *Coda* announcements several times," says Gilgun. "I go through them with a magic marker and cross out entries that don't apply to me. Then I go back and read them again. A week later a manuscript in my file will remind me of a particular entry, and I'll send if off."

As a result of another *Coda* notice, Gilgun published a story in *Having Been There*, an anthology on alcoholism edited by Allan Luks. As it turned out, that book was published by Scribners, where Gilgun now says he'd feel confident to send a manuscript. He's met several editors there, including Susanne Kirk.

Young editors looking for fresh talent do exist—but writers have to do their own homework in order to find them.

Daryln Brewer

Do Your Research . . .

Literary Market Place (LMP)
R. R. Bowker

International Directory of Little Magazines and Small Presses
Dustbooks

Writer's Market
Writer's Digest Books

How to Get Happily Published—A Complete and Candid Guide by Judith Appelbaum and Nancy Evans

Harper & Row (hardbound), New American Library (paperback)

Finding an agent takes the same techniques as finding an editor: a query letter, synopsis, and writing sample. For more information see: *Literary Agents: A Writer's Guide.* Available from Poets & Writers, Inc.

Note: See Appendix for addresses of publishers.

How to Give an Unsolicited Manuscript Its Best Chance

In the survival of favoured individuals and races, the constantly-recurring Struggle for Existence, we see a powerful and ever-acting form of selection.

Charles Darwin

Charles Darwin's cardinal rule of the evolutionary sciences is popularly known as "the survival of the fittest." Substitute the term "unsolicited manuscripts" for the phrase "individuals and races," and it sounds like many writers' notion of what goes on in an editor's office.

In writing's natural world, fitness is ultimately determined by quality, or by an editor's judgment of it. The definition of survival is getting published. But as in all natural worlds, a number of characteristics can enhance survival, such as the way a manuscript looks and the way a writer presents it.

Be Neat

You're a step ahead if you think of your manuscript as a machine for reading. Follow the rule high-school theme teachers drum in: Be Neat.

Neatness starts with the typewriter. Use a black ribbon, and change it frequently. The film or carbon variety used in electric typewriters gives the clearest image. Try to avoid nylon fabric: it's long-wearing, but it runs out of ink before it wears out. And clean the keys. A used toothbrush works perfectly well.

An ideal manuscript arrives on an editor's desk like so: it has clear black type, whether it's an original or a photocopy. It's on opaque white, standard-sized (that's 8½″ x 11″) twenty-pound paper (the weight commercial photocopy centers use). It has a title page; if a book, a contents page. The pages are consecutively numbered and have the author's name in the upper-right-hand corner. It's been typed on a 12-pitch, serif machine, double-spaced, on one side of the paper only. Left-hand and top margins are 2¼ inches wide, right-hand and bottom margins one inch wide.

The manuscript has no handwritten inserts and corrections; strike-outs are blackened solidly with pen, and no more than three of those can be found on any one page. Poetry comes one poem to a page (if it's a two-page work or longer, "stanza break" or "no stanza break" is typed in the bottom-left-hand margin). As for prose, whether article/story or book/novel length, sections or chapters begin at the top of new pages; if the text ends in the middle of a page, "Please Go on to Next Page" is typed in. The end is unambiguously marked "The End."

Is All This Really Necessary?

A fair question. Editors read a great deal, however, and poorly typed, smudgy, or misnumbered copy tends to predispose even the mild-mannered and the sympathetic against a work. Actually, a whole day of that kind of reading can be painful.

So don't use onionskin, or carbon tissue paper, or

newsprint; they all rip and smudge (the smudge quotient of corrasible bond is so high this kind of paper is useless). And don't use paper that's too heavy or too thick—it's unwieldy. In these days of word processors, print-outs have become acceptable; however, some editors prefer not to have the right-hand margin justified. As for the typeface, sans-serif and italic or script faces can create difficulties for typesetters as well as editors: "a's" can look like "o's" and "t's" like "i's." Numbering and naming are simply common sense: who wants to try and recollate an unnumbered manuscript that's fallen off the edge of a desk, or separate two similarly prepared texts that somehow got interleaved?

The final point for neatness is that giving editors what makes them comfortable may help you out in more ways than one. Submission can be a rough-and-tumble affair, with repeated mailings, packing and unpacking; shuffling, stapling and unstapling, moisture damage (to say nothing of coffee rings), and marginal scribblings. If your manuscript isn't accepted the first time out of the box, presumably you'd rather have something returned that you can submit again elsewhere, without its costing a fortune in retyping or postage. (That's another reason twenty-pound paper is good—not too light, but not too heavy.)

At the Post Office

Your local Post Office will tell you all you need to know about postal classes and rates (they do change frequently). A few specifics, though, are worth bearing in mind. First of all, for local mail, there's little difference—except in cost—between Third and Fourth Class and First Class Mail. All require between one and ten days for delivery, but First Class can cost up to 50% more. Whatever class you choose for a manuscript, however, you must add a First Class stamp to the package and write First Class Mail Enclosed on packages to which you're adding a personal letter.

As useful as they sound, beware of "Special Fourth Class: Manuscripts" and "Special Fourth Class: Books." The former is for typed or handwritten originals only, not for photocopies; the latter works only if one of the items in the package is stapled and over 24 pages.

If you want to rush a package out, remember that Priority Mail is no more than First Class for packages over one pound. The only real speed insurance you can get is Special Handling or the very expensive Express Mail. Additional, smaller fees can buy insurance proper, though only enough to cover the cost of paper and typing or photocopying. (Nothing but a photographic memory can insure you against the loss of your only copy of a manuscript.) A few cents more can provide certified mail with a return receipt, which, when signed by the recipient and returned to you, gives proof that your manuscript was not only mailed but delivered.

Wrap Carefully

Except for certain mechanical details, book and magazine submission are quite different. These mechanics are simple enough: any manuscript should be wrapped in a manner that insures its arrival unbent and undog-eared. A rough rule of thumb—adhered to by the United States Postal Service—is that any collection of paper over one inch thick or one pound heavy should be mailed in a box, not an envelope (use the box your typewriter paper came in). Whether in box or envelope, the manuscript should fit snugly. Shake it before sending it off, and if necessary brace it with stiffeners. Binding the outside corners with tape doesn't hurt either. There end the similarities of magazine and book submission.

Magazine submission is relatively straightforward. Simply send off the manuscript with a letter stating that you're submitting it and including a brief list of your previous publications. Note that you'd prefer copyright notice to be printed in your name, and, if the periodical hasn't listed what rights it customarily buys in *Writers Market* or in the *International Directory of Little Magazines and Small Presses,* that you're reserving all rights, other than First North American Serial Rights, to yourself. Don't forget to enclose a stamped, self-addressed return envelope.

It's politic not to give a rigid deadline for acceptance or rejection of the manuscript, but rather to wait five weeks. One week is for the United States Postal Service, and the other four are the maximum waiting period the P.E.N. American Center recommends in its 1977 statement of authors' rights. Then decide whether to send a mild query or to withdraw the manuscript entirely. Which you do is really up to you. No one wants to be kept hanging, or be prevented from submitting an unwanted work elsewhere. But many magazines, and particularly their poetry and fiction sections, are edited with more love than modern management, and in between paying work. That means submission requires patience, even fortitude.

The Query: An Interview by Mail

As for books (and screenplays, both television and film), finding a publisher takes longer than five weeks. Practiced submitters cut down the waiting time by sending a query kit to the targeted publisher (or producer) well before the text is finished. Think of your query as an interview by mail, designed to impress upon people your best qualities—your writing and the financial return that can accrue to its publisher.

Be brief, business-like, and enticing in your covering letter. Give your past publication history and biographical data; in one tight paragraph, state the specifications—the length of the manuscript, and what illustrations, photographs, permissions, and indexes—publishing your work will entail; and, in the proverbial 25 words or less, tell what you think your book is about.

Then settle down to wait. After three months, send a query about the fate of the query, with a return postcard enclosed. This is a convenient way of reminding an editor that you'd like to know if the house wants to see more.

Editor-Writer Relations

Years—at least several of them—can elapse between submission and acceptance, especially if you're approaching one publishing house or periodical at a time. In a perfectly natural effort to save themselves time, anxiety, and frustration, writers often succumb to multiple submission. That is, they send off their queries, and even their manuscripts, to more than one editor at a time. If you're tempted, be forewarned that many editors abhor the practice and send back a manuscript unread if they suspect it's under consideration elsewhere. If you feel you must submit multiple manuscripts—if, say, your work is topical—tell the editors you're sending them to, and explain why. In publishing as in life, deception is no way to start a relationship.

And starting a professional relationship is what you hope to do, whether with several magazines or one book publisher. The numerical odds are against you, but in the long run, the fittest will survive.

Caroline Rand Herron

Publishing Market Guides

*International Directory of Little
Magazines and Small Presses*
Dustbooks

Literary Market Place (LMP)
R. R. Bowker Co.

Small Press Review
Dustbooks

Writer's Market
Writer's Digest Books

Note: See Appendix for addresses of publishers.

Self-Publishing: When a Writer Needs to Go Public

Self-publishing has a distinguished history: Virginia Woolf published her own work, as did Mark Twain, Upton Sinclair, Edgar Allan Poe, and Lord Byron. But that was before publishing as we now know it. What about self-publishing today?

Bill Henderson, editor of *The Publish-It-Yourself Handbook,* a primary source for self-publishers, thinks that it is still respectable. "As commercial publishers accept fewer and fewer first novels and books of poetry, more people in this country will take on the task themselves," he says.

David McCann, Director of Foundation Relations at Cornell University, has had poems published in *The Pushcart Prize III, Ploughshares, Poetry,* and *Greenfield Review.* He also published his own book, *Keeping Time* (Troubadour Press). Originally, he saw a stigma in self-publishing, until a series of rejections from university and small presses ("thanks, but we're booked for three years") changed his mind. Although some of his friends advised McCann not to self-publish and called it vanity publishing, he was tired of waiting. He was also encouraged by the realization that he could do the book any way he wanted.

McCann decided that a group of etchings by his mother-in-law would complement the poems. He laid the four etchings out on his living room floor and dealt the poems onto them, in four different piles. The book began to take shape.

Find a Printer You Can Talk to

Next McCann started looking for a printer, hoping to find someone he could get along with personally. Some months before, he had received a copy of *The Apple Anthology*, a collection of New York State Poets. He liked the book's printing, layout, and design, and called the printer, Stuart McCarty of Geryon Press in Tunnel, New York.

Within two weeks came McCarty's first estimate— $3.35 per book, for quality paper and if McCann was willing to bind the book himself. McCann agreed and began working with McCarty. "We spent an hour just looking at cover stock and typefaces," he says. "Stuart explained the subtle effects of different typefaces. I hadn't read any books on the subject and since I had edited only scholarly journals that called for plain, simple layouts, I was venturing into unknown territory. I talked about what my collection meant to me, and Stuart translated those ideas into production ideas. He wanted the paper, the type—everything— to reflect my feelings about the book."

McCann had a choice of two typefaces and McCarty made a sample of each. They decided on Times Roman, for a 5½" x 9" book, on white laid paper, 70-pound weight. McCarty suggested using a square spine which, says McCann, "adds a lot—it looks better on the shelf."

Added Color, Added Cost

The final estimate was more than the original— $3.98 per copy, for a print run of 250. Cost went up because McCann decided against binding the book himself. The book was also larger—48 pages instead of 44—because of the etchings, and with section titles on separate pages. McCarty had first planned to photocopy the etchings, but ultimately he used the more expensive offset lithography. Blue endpapers also cost more.

Color was a big consideration for McCann and McCarty. "Stuart explained the nuances of color," says McCann. They finally settled on Strathmore Pastelle Deep Tan for the cover, with Curtis Tweed-weave Royal Blue for the endpapers. McCann chose the simplest page design. Another $10 was added to the overall cost because McCann and McCarty went back and forth four or five times on cover design. The title page and acknowledgments were also changed, and the list of subscribers kept growing and needed to be reset.

Subscribers Help with Printing Costs

Subscribers? To a book? Actually not a new idea, if an unfamiliar one. Poets did this years ago in England and Jon Stallworthy of Cornell's English Department suggested McCann gather subscribers to help cover costs.

For $32, McCann had 250 postcards printed, announcing his subscription offer. He passed them out to family, friends, and colleagues, and mailed another fifty. For $3 plus postage, a subscriber could be listed at the back of the book and receive a copy upon publication. Although the retail price of the book was $5, McCann charged $3 to subscribers because he thought that was "what the traffic could bear." Next time though, he says he'd charge $5 and pay the postage himself—it got complicated when sending the book to many different places, as far away as Tokyo.

Before the book was printed, McCann also wrote a proposal to the Cornell Council of the Creative and Performing Arts, which helps non-academic employees of the college. He sent a sample of ten poems and was granted $300 toward the cost of finishing his book. With 130 subscribers at $3 each, he now had a total of $690 toward the $1,000 printing cost. Other contributors helped to make up the difference; McCann lost nothing out-of-pocket.

A final touch: at a reading, McCann met Dennis Brutus, a poet associated with Troubadour Press. The press allowed McCann to use the Troubadour imprint. This kind of association can help with publicity, since the more people connected with a book, the more it gets talked up, and the better chance it has for review.

Complete Control of Your Book?

Even a self-publisher doesn't have complete control of the process. McCann's book wasn't ready by Christmas, as anticipated, but was published in January—about four months after McCann first sent his manuscript to Stuart McCarty. That's a bit longer than the average two months promised by the Print Center in Brooklyn, New York, but much shorter than the typical nine-month gestation period of a book at a commercial house.

Self-publishers can't review their own books, either. "It's too bad," says Bob Hershon of the Print Center. "After all, Boswell reviewed *his* books, anonymously." McCann sent review copies to his college alumni magazine (for all books sold as a result of a review, he gave 40% to the alumni fund) and to literary magazines, such as *Greenfield Review, Poetry, Wood Ibis, New Letters, Ploughshares,* and *Epoch.*

Self-publishers are also self-distributors, and "distribution is the biggest problem with self-publishing," says poet Martha King. "Poets' ideas on distribution are either grandiose and vague or minimal and vague." King lost enthusiasm for distributing her book (*Women & Children First*, Two and Two Press) after walking the New York City streets with copies in a shopping bag, stopping at every bookstore.

McCann had a similar method: a book in his briefcase or in an envelope tucked under his arm—*at all times*. Ithaca bookstores and the Cornell campus bookstore sold his book on consignment: that is, McCann got 60% of the purchase price, and the store received 40%. "They didn't sell like hotcakes," he says, "but they did sell." McCann also sent books to friends who own bookstores.

Why Self-Publish?

While self-publishing won't bring national fame, it does get your book into the hands of those you like and respect. "A collection in book form is a different creature entirely from all those loose sheets of typing paper that littered my desk," says McCann. "It was direct and satisfying. I got positive comments, I broke even, and I probably sold as many books as most small presses," he says. Martha King summed it up: "There comes a time when a writer needs to go public."

McCann doubts that having self-published will make trade or even small press publication any easier for him. But he now knows what kind of manuscript best represents his work, and he learned to edit and organize his poems. "Editing an entire book is parallel to editing a single poem," he says. "The poem is a structure of words, the book a structure of poems."

McCann also had fun. And he's busy working on a new collection.

Daryln Brewer

Self-Publishing Tips

The following suggestions come from some printers and self-publishers. For further advice, consult one of the books listed.

Estimates. David McCann trusted Stuart McCarty of Geryon Press, so he didn't get estimates from other printers. In general though, it's a good idea to shop around for a printer. Get a few estimates.

Changes. Change a book during production, and the cost goes up. Early, minor changes may not amount to much, but later, more substantial ones will. Try to decide on everything *before* setting the type.

Subscribers. Subscribers are an instant distribution network, so make your subscription card attractive. As a friend told McCann, "If the book is anything like the card, what a book it will be!"

Permissions. Be sure to get permission to reprint a poem or story that has been previously published elsewhere. Even if the copyright has reverted back to the author, "it's a good idea to notify everyone," says McCann.

Copyright. McCann secured his own copyright by sending away for the TX copyright registration form for nondramatic literary work from the U.S. Copyright Office, Library of Congress, Washington, D.C. 20559. "The instructions are clear," he says. "You send in the form with $10 and two copies of the work. One month later, you get an official form back with a copyright stamp. It feels great. You have your own book."

ISBN. A self-publisher should get an ISBN. Request a "Title Output Information Request Form," a "User's Manual," and a "Bowker Products and Services" form from the International Standard Book Numbering Agency, c/o R. R. Bowker, 205 East 42 Street, New York, New York 10017.

Schedules. Christmas, spring, and fall are busy times for printers. Slow periods are summer and winter. Take this into consideration when publishing a book.

Press Name. Bob Hershon advises: "Make your publication look professional by putting a press name on the binding." Get permission to borrow an imprint, or make up a press name and use that.

Self-Help. At the Print Center, Bob Hershon lets authors

save money by doing certain things themselves, such as layout and typesetting. Martha King found a "paper jobber" where she got inexpensive paper, substantially cutting the cost of her book.

Invoicing. Martha King advises invoicing all book sales. When doing so, "make up letterhead with your press name and address," she says. "It's more professional and bookstores will take you more seriously."

Listing. Fill out an Advanced Book Information form to get your book listed in *Books In Print,* among other publications. Write ABI Department, R.R. Bowker, 205 East 42 Street, New York, New York 10017.

Promotion. The best selling tool for commercial and small press books is good old-fashioned word-of-mouth. "It's easy to get a book published; the hard part is getting rid of it." Bob Hershon says. "You have to be ruthless. Lean on your friends. Use any outlet available, from your club to the local butcher."

Vanity Publishing. Don't confuse self-publishing with vanity publishing. In vanity publishing, you turn over your manuscript to a subsidy publisher and pay them to do everything for you. You have no control over publicity, promotion, or distribution. (See the following chapter.)

Vanity Press: Stigma or Sesame?

Vanity presses are not to be confused with book manufacturers. Book manufacturers print and bind books for a fee and then hand them over to the author. Use of their services is part of self-publishing. Sometimes they use an author's imprint, but some book manufacturers have imprints of their own, such as Harlo, Sol III, RVK, J. Marks, Heritage, Hallmark, Thom Henricks, Nimrod, Port City Press, and Publication Press.

Vanity presses, on the other hand, not only manufacture, but also distribute books. In most cases, the author does not own the books and must buy them just like anyone else.

It is also important not to confuse vanity publishing with co-op and small press publishing, in which the author pays directly in cash or contributed labor or indirectly by foregoing advances and royalties. The difference lies in editorial control: co-ops and small presses exercise subjective literary judgment, while vanity presses leave literary decisions to the author.

Eight Possible Advantages of Vanity Presses

Despite their bad reputation, vanity presses offer eight possible advantages:

• Their books are usually bigger and better-produced than those of the small presses, co-ops, or hired manufacturers, and they are mainly hardcovers. Hardcover binding is essential for sales to libraries, and just as important as a reputable imprint for getting reviews. Furthermore, printing quality is often good.

• The chances of your manuscript being rejected are small. Unsolicited work is profitable to the vanity publisher and is welcomed. While a trade publisher usually wants to see only a summary or sample, the vanity publisher wants your whole manuscript right away—the cost can't be estimated without it.

• Vanity publishers work fast. A trade publisher or small press editor may hold a manuscript in limbo for over a year, but the vanity publisher can have it in book form in as little as three months after the contract is signed. If there is any editing to speak of, it certainly won't involve the massive rewriting or deletions that a traditional literary editor might demand.

• Promotion, distribution, bookkeeping, and royalty payment, though rarely used to the full, are nonetheless available. Ads can be purchased, flyers mailed.

• A minimum of $300 is usually spent on promotion and advertising, if only to fulfill the publisher's contract obligations. $300 is clearly inadequate, but it's about all a book of poetry ever gets—even from a top trade publisher. With cooperation from a knowledgeable author, it can be spent effectively.

• Royalties are an impressive 40% on the first printing of vanity books, contrasted with a 10% to 12% royalty from a trade publisher's books or payment in free copies of the book, which is customary from small presses. When a first printing sells out, the subsequent printings are published at the vanity house's expense. Royalties then go down to about 20%.

• Royalties are usually tax-free until the original investment is regained. Or, in some cases, losses may be deducted. Tax treatment varies with the Internal Revenue District in which the author lives, but it is usually favorable if an author can demonstrate a business motive.

• When vanity books are good they do get reviewed. This has happened frequently for books on technical subjects; reviews have been extremely rare for poetry and fiction, however, largely because these books are generally a vanity press' worst.

Contracts: What to Look for

If quality writing and vanity publishing ever make friends, part of the process will be learning how to avoid treacherous contracts. The points below are summarized from several sources, including the *Writer's Digest* reprint, "Does It Pay to Pay to Have It Published?", comments by vanity publishers, and warnings from poets. It would be wise to go over these points carefully with a lawyer before signing any vanity contract.

• What does the contract mean by the term, "first edition"? Make sure that binding and jacketing are included, not just printing. A minimum number of completed copies is usually made available for sale by a certain date. As with most publishers, the remaining copies are not bound and jacketed until more orders are received.

• How many free copies do you get?

• Can you resell your copies? (You may wish to assign them to a class you are giving or sell them at readings.)

• Or, can you get copies to sell at readings or in classrooms on a commission basis?

• After the first printing is sold out, make sure additional copies will be produced at the publisher's expense. Or will you have to invest your money again?

• Exactly how much promotion and advertising will your book receive?

• Can you direct the advertising and promotion yourself? This is a crucial question not just for vanity but for all types of publishing. With vanity publishing, however, you are paying for these services yourself and ought to have some say in the matter. If you leave it up to the vanity house, they may do a bad job. But even if they do a good job, the stigma attached to the imprint may hurt your book rather than help it.

Why Not Replace the Vanity Imprint with Your Own?

The most frequently cited drawback of vanity houses is the stigma. To reduce it, why couldn't the vanity house substitute a writer's own imprint? The new imprint could be used on the book and promotional literature. The vanity imprint would still appear on invoices and labels used in fulfillment, to save the cost of reprinting these, but only as the book's "distributor."

Perhaps we will see more imprint substitutions in the future. With publishing outlets shrinking, this and other concessions to authors may win the vanity presses a new clientele among authors of quality poetry and fiction.

Nelson Richardson

Suggested Reading

The Publish-It-Yourself Handbook, Literary Tradition and How-To, edited by Bill Henderson
Pushcart Press

The Self-Publishing Manual, How to Write, Print and Sell Your Own Book, by Dan Poynter
Para Publishing

Publish It Yourself, The Complete Guide to Self-Publishing Your Own Book, by Charles Chickadel
Trinity Press

How to Publish Your Own Book, A Guide for Authors Who Wish to Publish a Book at Their Own Expense, by L.W. Mueller
Harlo Press

Note: See Appendix for addresses of publishers.

The Chapbook: Quality and Substance in Twenty-five Pages

Ask Steve Miller, founder of Red Ozier Press, what a chapbook is, and he opens his arms as if he is wearing a coat lined with hot watches, and says, "Small books of poetry you can slip in a coat." Miller's accurate, if oblique, answer refers to a tradition that dates back to the eighteenth century, and to the origins of the word "chapbook." Chap is derived from an Old English word for bargain, price, or more precisely, cheap. Chapmen were itinerant salesmen; some hawked small books of poetry, others sold books of rhyming riddles.

The economics of poetry publishing today may make poets think they'd be better off selling their wares like a chap named D.H. McConnell. He was a door-to-door bookseller who ultimately made his fortune in cosmetics. You'd know him better as the original "Avon Lady."

A Competitive Market

Although chapbooks today come in a variety of shapes, sizes, and qualities, their one common denominator is the number of pages, which rarely exceeds twenty-five. At the Gotham Book Mart in New

York City, two random selections were a mimeographed book, covered in construction paper, dedicated to the author's grandmother, and filled with poetry sacred in its reverence for profanity, and an elegant, finely illustrated, handsewn volume by a well-known poet—a collector's item. Although not the case at the Gotham, which welcomes the unusual, chapbooks are generally unpopular in bookstores. Because they are usually spineless, chapbooks are easily overlooked on a shelf, if stocked at all.

Chapbooks do not fend well in competition for library space either. Those without a spine make cataloguing impossible. For this reason, a boxed set of a chapbook series, each containing a chapbook by a different writer, does have a distinct advantage over a single chapbook. Still, a librarian would probably chose an anthology over a boxed set of chapbooks.

Chapbooks are also overlooked, and ignored, by most reviewers. Competition for review space is so enormous that hardcover books of poetry seldom get the attention they deserve, not to mention a pamphlet which is a fraction of the size of a full-length volume. The irony, however, is that the publication of a chapbook may disqualify a poet from entering a competition open only to poets who have yet to publish their first book.

With such things against them, why publish a chapbook? What does it achieve for the poet? Ezra Pound started with one, suggesting that from acorns mighty reputations grow. And since selling full-length volumes of poetry to commercial publishers is increasingly difficult, a young poet with a newly published chapbook will at least have a first collection of poetry. A chapbook also allows several poems to be read and considered together, which can promote a poet's career.

A Psychological Advantage

"It gives you confidence," says Nancy Schoenberger, who had her chapbook, *The Taxidermist's Daughter,* published three years ago by Calliopea Press in California. "When I apply for jobs or to go to an artists' colony, I feel that a chapbook gives my application more substance. I always urge my friends to try to get one published because it can be the first small step toward getting your work to the public. If your chapbook comes from the right press, the chance of having your work noticed is very good. And since the major presses only do five books of poetry a year, it may be the only chance for a poet to get a collection of work published."

Schoenberger does see some problems with publishing a chapbook, however. "Their advantage is mostly psychological," she says. "They do not make a poet well-established. My chapbook did not change my life. I couldn't even tell my friends where to buy it. I still feel unpublished." What's more, Schoenberger received a royalty check for only sixty dollars, and credits half those sales to her mother. Still, she encourages others to publish chapbooks. "It is satisfying to see one's work in print, and they are a real boon to people whose work is off the beaten track."

Testing the Waters

"Chapbooks are a good way for a young poet to test the waters," says poet and critic Robert Peters. "They are much better than starting with a full-length book padded with weak poems. When reviewing poetry for the *American Book Review* or *Small Press Review,* I almost prefer to review chapbooks."

Peters has published nine of his own chapbooks. "Chapbooks are a sub-genre of poetry representing a wonderful mix of work which contributes to the enormous poetry activity going on today," he says. "For young publishers as well as poets, they are a good way to get started."

240 Manuscripts Sent to an Unknown Press

When State Street Press in Pittsford, New York announced a chapbook competition by running an announcement in *Coda,* they received 240 manuscripts, some from as far away as Alaska, Ireland, Germany, and Greece. "It was a staggering amount of poetry looking to be published," says editor Judy Kitchen, "and all of it coming to an unknown press." The competition for chapbook publication today seems almost as tough as that in commercial publishing.

The editors at State Street Press believe a chapbook should be treated even better than a full-length volume. "Because they're short, they demand a unity a longer book does not," says Kitchen. "To validate a new writer's worth, we work closely with the writer. We suggest which poems to print and which to drop, always trying to produce a top quality chapbook. Chapbooks are an art form in themselves," she says. The State Street Press chapbook series is beautifully produced, each jacket designed with a linoleum cut that purposefully harkens back to the woodcuts on the original chapbooks sold by those itinerant peddlers.

A Product That Amplifies the Writer's Words

Red Ozier Press in New York City also brings out beautiful books. Most of the work is done by hand, occasionally even down to the making of typeface. At Red Ozier, a fine edition chapbook may be illustrated by artist Barry Moser, or covered in silk from Tokyo. "The fun part of our work is the continuing relation to the writer's text," says Ken Botnick, Steve Miller's partner and co-publisher of Red Ozier. "Evocations from the poet's work will instruct the texture of the paper, the design of the watermarks, the choice of print, and the illustrator." The resulting product is one that "amplifies and expands upon the writer's words." Their publications, however, do not come without a price: a limited edition chapbook of poems by Charles Henri Ford, illustrated by Japanese sculptor, Isamu Noguchi, and signed by them both, sells for $100.

Can Chapbooks Work for Fiction?

What about chapbooks of fiction? Eighteen pages of poetry can show the strength of a poet, but eighteen pages of fiction amounts to one very short story. Still, fiction chapbooks do exist. The Treacle Story Series was started by Bruce McPherson of McPherson & Company (formerly Treacle Press) in New Paltz, New York. These slim, squareback "chapbooks" ranged from 32 to 64 pages and contained one or two stories with original illustrations. "You might consider them an advancement of the chapbook idea," says McPherson, who also suggests that chapbooks are the ancestor to today's paperback. "We wanted to introduce a forum for the appreciation of the short story as a singular experience. Chapbooks can do this; magazines can't. People don't have as much time to read anymore, and our chapbooks were designed so that something of quality and substance could be read in an hour."

Unfortunately, the series lasted only four years, from 1976 to 1980. "It was hard to get booksellers to take them," says McPherson, "and some journals took three years to review them." While McPherson himself prefers non-traditional literary forms, he believes chapbooks are an ideal way to publish conventional long stories, or novellas, those orphans in the world of literature.

Top Stories Appeals to Art Market

Anne Turyn, who publishes Top Stories, an eclectic series of chapbooks by women writers, proves that the chapbook can be an excellent way to publish other genres of writing—those difficult to define, and difficult to publish in mainstream publications. For instance, she successfully published the text of a piece by performance artist Laurie Anderson. "I started Top Stories because the writers I liked seemed to be the hardest to find," she says. "None of the writers I've worked with can be described as traditional. Each issue has a different style and nearly every one is designed by the author herself."

Top Stories is categorized by Turyn and her granting agencies, the National Endowment for the Arts, the New York State Council on the Arts, and the Coordinating Council of Literary Magazines, as a "Prose Periodical," but unlike magazines, Top Stories stays on the bookshelves for a long time. And unlike books, these chapbooks are not returned to the publisher if unsold. The philosophy behind Top Stories is different from many of the expensively produced chapbook series; Turyn keeps production costs low so she can publish more writers. "I didn't want the price of the chapbooks to keep anyone from buying them," she says. Since many of her authors are also artists, she has two markets. Because of the cross-over in the art market, "I'm even getting orders from Europe," she says. "The sale of Top Stories is up and the newer volumes generate enough income to keep past titles in print."

A Foot in The Door

What is the future of chapbooks? Diane Smeltzer, an editor at David Godine in Boston, says, "The economics of poetry publishing have caught up with us. We have no future plans for our chapbook series. People just don't buy them." Chapbooks average about three dollars in price, which makes them only slightly less expensive than a full-length paperback, weakening their already precarious position on bookstore shelves. Chapbooks may be doomed by an economy that does not support poetry, or they may flourish as they fill the vacuum caused by major presses turning their backs on poetry altogether.

Those poets who find themselves hawking their poetry door-to-door might want to employ D. H. McConnell's device: he gave the lady of the house a free bottle of perfume before she had a chance to slam the door in his face.

Allen Barnett

Word Processors: Do They Help Writers?

I never used to mind all the typing I did. But now I resent the time it takes from really writing. All that typing has nothing to do with the act of writing. It's just being your own secretary.

Eudora Welty

"A word processor is to a writer what a turbo drill is to a modern dentist," says Franklin Russell (*The Secret Islands,* W. W. Norton), a writer of both fiction and nonfiction. Russell began using a word processor in 1981, after several years of a serious writer's block. "The word processor was a result of pure desperation," says Russell. "I tried yoga, exercise, drinking, doing nothing—just about everything, but I couldn't get at what was bothering me," he says.

At the time, Russell was working on a number of different writing projects, which is how he makes his living. "I was hung up on a nonfiction book—it was all written, but I couldn't put it together," he says. "I'd gone through it six times—disorganization was impairing my ability. I could see the power of the word processor."

Retyping Is Passé

A distinction must be made between a word processor, designed only for the purpose of word processing, and a computer, which can perform many functions, only one of which is word processing. Russell has an Atari 800 computer, and loves it, for three basic reasons. "The machine results in perfect typing," he says. "The time I save not having to retype everything justifies my machine on those grounds alone." Secondly, the word processor does what file cards cannot: list, index, and cross-reference, all at the press of a button. Russell, who's also working on a novel, says, "I can outline the novel on the computer and then list certain conditions, themes, situations or names, and put them in the same indices. With a word processor you get insight into how you're operating, without destroying the creative process.

"Many people's knee-jerk reaction is that a writer who uses a computer is a bad writer," he says. "I have a slightly different attitude because I'm lucky enough to be both creative and to like things technical."

Don't Buy Hastily

For Russell, the third advantage of the computer is its capability to do taxes and figure a budget. Russell also wanted his children to learn computer games for fun and for the educational benefits, which is why he bought an Atari.

He would have preferred an IBM or a Xerox—both of which can handle a wide range of business and technical programs. But his local store only sold Atari, Radio Shack, Commodore, and the Apple.

Russell advises buying a computer which can be serviced nearby. "Go to your local computer store and see what they stock. Order by mail only if you're sure your local store will service it. The computer magazines will give you better deals, but service is spotty in this country. Ask yourself: 'Will the local store lend me another computer if mine breaks down?' 'Do I feel comfortable with the person who's selling it to me?'

"Be wary of high-volume city stores where the sales people have little time to help," he cautions. "New hardware and software are coming out all the time. Buying a computer can be confusing, so impose on the salesperson's time and ask a lot of questions before buying."

He suggests reading the articles in computer magazines, as well as the ads. "Get a sense of where the action is," he says. "Then sit down and try the computer at the store—see if you like the keyboard. Some are disturbingly slow at putting up the graphic."

Russell doesn't believe a course in word processing is necessary. "A book that will teach you everything comes with the machine—there's nothing to be scared of, unless you go to it with the kind of prejudice many writers had against the electric typewriter."

Russell estimates one month to learn how to use a word processor, and five months to be completely comfortable and effective with it. Most important, he says, "is to learn to think with the machine, not against it."

Low Failure Rate

A computer sometimes has a mind of its own, however. "The computer will seize up occasionally and betray you," says Russell. "I lost a whole day's work because the electricity went off for a second. My printer had broken down, and was being repaired, and I was writing away, storing everything on the disk drive. At that time, I was only using one floppy disk for storage, and toward the end of the day, a power surge turned everything on the disk into graphics, which I couldn't translate back into print."

The trick is never to have too much material in a "state of vulnerability"—when it is contained in the computer's memory but has not yet been transferred for storage to the disk drive. "Now I transfer my writing from the computer to the disk drive as often as possible—about every three pages," he says. "But even when the material is in the disk drive, it is not invulnerable. Voltage drops, power surges, electrical storms, or other glitches, can get into the disk drive and play hell there."

Russell now copies everything he writes on to two disks which "practically obviates the risk of losing what's on an entire disk—as many as 10,000 words of copy," he says. Still, he believes that the failure rate in the word processing equipment is low.

Russell's Atari, along with one disk drive and an Epson matrix printer, cost $3,000. He uses three main programs: Letter Perfect (word processing), FileManager 800 (file management system), and Visicalc (an electronic bookkeeping system). "My life has been arbitrarily divided into before and after I got my computer. If I were starting all over again, I'd have one from the beginning. Word processing is becoming part of the competitive market for writers. We're at the tail end of those who hunt and peck at the typewriter."

Not only does Russell think word processing is a fabulous new tool, but he never gets tired of using his machine—and he thinks anything that makes a writer sit down and write is worth it.

Sharing a Computer

A poet who knows the benefits of a word processor is Siv Cedering, who has published fifteen books, including two novels, in eight years. Since 1974 she has used a computer to write all her poetry, prose, and books for children. For three of those years she used a system called BOWNE Time-sharing; now she uses an IBM Selectric Typewriter with a 10-page memory. With BOWNE, she tied into, via phone, a computer center in Manhattan where she could store an unlimited amount of information.

Cedering learned the system in an hour and was completely comfortable with it in a week. It was easy—she typed her manuscript on a terminal in her home, there were no disks for her to worry about, and since the terminal printed out immediately whatever she asked for, she had the printed page as well. She has no horror stories about her use of the computer (except that telephone rates from her home in Westchester to New York City made using it increasingly expensive). At the time, her system had much more capability than a home computer. Now, she says, "As soon as I get a good advance, I'll buy myself a word processor.

"Asking if the word processor is the wave of the future is like having been asked in the '40's if the automobile or the washing machine is the wave of the future," she says. "Who wants to walk twelve miles to school or beat our clothes clean down by the river? A word processor simplifies a writer's work to that degree. It is a necessary tool of the trade," she says.

"I like things that are efficient and a computer is supremely efficient," says Cedering. "It numbers your pages automatically, sets margins, chooses a typeface and the thickness of characters, and does it all so fast. It's also very considerate. If you press 'delete', the computer comes back and makes sure that's what you intended, asking, "Do you want me to delete?" Cedering admits there's a margin of error when using a computer, but says "there's always a risk with an unpublished manuscript—it could get burned up or lost or stolen."

"I Hate Gadgets but I Must Have a Word Processor"

Computers also produce sparkling clean copy. "A writer is responsible for giving a publisher clean copy," says Cedering. "When you send poems to a magazine or to a contest, they should be easy to read."

Cedering has also published more as a result of using her word processor. "I did a 'How-to' book in six weeks. There was so much to keep track of that I never could have done it without a word processor. But perfection, even more than speed, is the biggest reward of using a word processor. The worst thing a writer can do is not to polish something because of laziness. We don't realize how much time all that housekeeping takes—fiddling with paper, erasing, re-typing—and after a while you get so tired of whatever you're working on. A word processor frees a writer from that."

A word processor isn't for everyone, however. "If you write only one poem a month, and your writing doesn't take that much time, a word processor is not worth it. But if you must produce page after page of a book which might take as long as four years to write, it's vital. My work is greatly facilitated by having a computer," says Cedering.

"I hate gadgets," she adds. "I don't want a new camera. I don't have a Cuisinart and I don't want one. But as a writer, I must have a word processor."

From Longhand to a Lanier

John Hersey was one of the first writers ever to use a word processor. In 1972, he had just finished the first draft of *My Petition for More Space,* when some people at Yale who were writing a sophisticated word processing program wanted to study whether or not it would be useful for creative work. "I typed my second draft using it," says Hersey, "and I was sold. After thirty years of writing longhand, I now work exclusively on a Lanier."

The word processor has helped Hersey in two ways. First, the machine is "an incredible time-saver. For instance, if you want to change the name of a character in a manuscript, the machine will go through the copy and change it everywhere it appears, saving the writer from having to fumble through and look for it." Secondly, it's easier to make all revisions. "The commitment in labor used to make me reluctant to go back into a manuscript and make certain kinds of changes. With the word processor, no labor is lost."

Hersey warns, though, that a word processor "doesn't write for you. You still have to do the work," he says. He refers to it as a "wonderfully versatile typewriter—one which also has the ability to sort, file and index research."

Hersey thinks learning how to use the machine is easy. "I was instructed at Yale by the man inventing the program and was also self-taught. My present machine comes with very clear instructions. Anyone with reasonable intelligence can learn fairly quickly how to use it. The first thing you learn is how to avoid serious mistakes. After you make two or three, you seldom make them again."

Hersey sees a day when publishers will find it economical to provide their authors with word processors. "The whole process of writing, editing and composition will be unified. A writer's machine will be connected to the publisher's machine by telephone, and they can converse about the manuscript through them. When the price goes down, more people will use them. It took many people a long time to go from the standard to the electric typewriter—a word processor is simply the next step."

Daryln Brewer

Two

THE WRITER AS BUSINESS PERSON

Writers on Revision: Is Perfection the Death of Energy?

When asked how many drafts of a story he wrote, S. J. Perelman said, "Thirty-seven. I once tried doing thirty-three, but something was lacking. . . . On another occasion I tried forty-two versions, but the final effect was too lapidary."

Few writers know exactly how many revisions they do of a poem, short story, or novel. But each has a method and a madness, and all agree there is no right or wrong way. Some, in fact, revise one way and teach another. Others go so far as to recommend not doing it their way.

Perelman went on to say in that *Paris Review* interview,* "What are you trying to extort—my trade secrets?" *Coda* would never do that, but following are some poets' and fiction writers' thoughts on revision.

Walter Abish (*How German Is It?* New Directions): I don't number my pages until at least fifty are finished. I start by writing brief notes by hand, and after four, five, or six drafts on different colored papers, I end up with the manuscript typed on expensive twenty-pound paper.

Paris Review, #30, Summer-Fall 1963, by William Cole and George Plimpton.

I would discourage revising sentence by sentence—that's a terrible obstacle to writing. I would not strive for that kind of perfection because the transition from one perfect page to the next is startling and profound. Then you have a lot of perfect pages, but not a perfect book. In a way, I strive for imperfection, for that rawness, clumsiness, an awkwardness—which retains an energy—so hard to do. Perfection is the death of energy.

Alice Adams (*To See You Again,* Knopf): I revise sentence by sentence, page by page, but not in a fine-tuned way. People who can't write another sentence until the last is perfect are constipated. I write a first draft quickly, in longhand, on yellow paper. Both my novels and short stories need at least three more drafts. I type the next on yellow paper, the third on pink, then blue and so on, which helps me to know what stage I'm in.

Ann Beattie (*The Burning House,* Random House): I only revise minor detail. If I get to page three or four and the material hasn't shown me the way, I don't revise, I throw it out.

Carolyn Forché (*The Country Between Us,* Harper & Row): It's hard to separate writing and revising, because both happen simultaneously, and one inspires the other. I retype a poem each time I make a change, even if it's only one word. Otherwise it doesn't look right. I've done as many as eighty drafts of one poem. Good lines give me the next ones, bad lines can't do that. A young poet's unwillingness to revise always surprises me—as if the way a poem first came out is sacred. Yet I've found students shocked to learn that it can take me three years to finish a poem.

Celia Gittleson (*Saving Grace,* Knopf): I rewrote the first twenty-five pages of my novel at least sixty times. Not that the first twenty-five pages are my favorite, but as a reader I know that if the first 25-30 pages aren't interesting—if they're slow or sluggish—I often won't read on. I rewrite in chunks, maybe one or two scenes, 5-15 pages. At the end, when I finally know what I've been writing about and have discovered all the things wrong with it, I rewrite the whole thing.

Robert Hass (*Field Guide,* Yale University Press): I don't recognize any process called revision. It is based on the notion that the inspired product is the *real* poem and that revision is when the conscious mind tinkers with it. Except in the smallest ways, revision doesn't exist. I simply work on poems a long time.

Sandra McPherson (*Elegies for the Hot Season,* Ecco Press): I like to put a draft away for a long time. Then I start the poem all over again, sometimes pulling out the first draft, sometimes not. Occasionally I notice the top of a poem has nothing to do with the bottom, so I cut off the top. I like to get the first three or four lines good, because they are the seed from which the rest of the poem grows.

Leonard Michaels (*The Men's Club,* Farrar, Straus & Giroux): I sometimes think I'm not a writer but a reviser, the worst example in the country of a compulsive revisionist. I'm the kind of writer who calls things back from editors, with the despairing apprehension that it could go on forever. If I were writing in a world without pressure to finish, I probably never would.

What's amazing to me is that we have so many selves within us who tend not to approve of each other. One day I am profoundly dissatisfied with what I was satisfied with the day before. Shame and horror begin to accumulate if the writing isn't close to what I recognize as good. That's why I can't go on to page two until page one is perfect. I do not recommend writing like this. In fact, I tell my students to get it all down on paper.

Steve Orlen (*A Place at the Table,* Holt, Rinehart & Winston): Too much revision can end up dulling the original material, taking out its freshness and spirit. I like words that don't seem poetic—those that just come out when talking, unrehearsed. Colloquialisms like that are spontaneous and can't be revised into a poem. You have to take advantage of what's already in a poem, not look for what should be there. I like imperfection in poetry—it tells me it was written by a human being.

Mary Lee Settle (*The Killing Ground,* Farrar, Straus & Giroux): I write a first draft quickly, in longhand, on thick 20″ × 30 ″ art paper, 3,000 words to a side. Then I do rewrites and inserts on the other side. Rewriting is always heavier at the beginning because each book has a voice of its own, and you have to find out what that voice is. I don't believe in rewriting sentence by sentence because the first draft is written in an almost trance-like state, from the gut. Stopping that flow by being your own critic shows insecurity. As James Thurber said, 'Don't get it right, get it written.' I agree.

Scott Spencer (*Endless Love,* Knopf): I usually revise the first chapter of a book four, five, or six times. When that's right, I finish the book. Then I write the whole book over again. Finally I do a very detailed, word-by-word edit. I have yet to write a perfect page. If I had to do that before going on, I'd still be on the first page of my first novel.

Daryln Brewer

Starting Your Own Small Press

"This has become my life's work and I love it," says Jennifer Dossin, who established the Elizabeth Street Press three years ago in New York's Little Italy. In that time she has only published two books; unlike many small press entrepreneurs, Dossin did not rush into production. She dealt first with the many details involved in starting a press.

Dossin realized early on that a desire to start a press wasn't enough. "You must decide the need for your press," she says. She publishes "commercially unattractive works"—books by unpublished writers and those which require unique production. They use the best materials, fine craftsmanship, and print limited editions (50-75 copies) of books bound by a master bookbinder.

Dossin started by collecting type. "It's a logical first step because it doesn't take up much space," she says. Then she found a printer who was going out of business and bought an 1,800-lb. Vandercook Universal III press for $500. "Printers who make their livelihood from the letter press are losing money now," says Dossin. "They are selling the old equipment and reinvesting in photocomposition or retiring to Florida."

She saved thousands of dollars (a new press costs around $20,000) and says others who know printing can do the same. But Dossin says to check out a secondhand press very thoroughly, because printers treat them badly. "If the bed of a press is damaged, it can't be repaired. You have to know what to look for," she says.

Not a Business, a Commitment

"I'm a good printer and type composer, but not a good editor or bookbinder," says Dossin, who set out to find a small group whose talents complemented hers and who would share the responsibility. She found Jack Galef, a teacher and poet who has been published in *The New Yorker* and *Esquire,* and John Stadler, a children's book writer and illustrator.

They decided to set up their press as a not-for-profit corporation before they published anything. They hired a lawyer who helped them define their goals in language acceptable to government agencies. Federal and state approval took a year and a half. "By declaring ourselves a not-for-profit press at the beginning, we crystallized our integrity and formal intention," says Dossin. "We're not a business, but a commitment."

Dossin also recommends hiring a good accountant at an early stage. "Such details weigh down the spiritual thrust of a press," she says. Dossin keeps accurate files, too. "We're nearing the end of our three-year probationary period. At the end of that time, the IRS reviews our records. If all is in order, the Elizabeth Street Press will have permanent tax-exempt status." Although they can now accept private contributions to the press, they cannot apply for state or federal grants until the probationary period ends. "At last, the press will exist independently of the three of us; it will have a life of it's own."

Dossin believes a fair contract should be offered by a small press. "Under no circumstances should a book be published from a verbal agreement," she says. "A small press like ours can't be expected to offer an advance, but we do have a contract which offers a royalty at a fair percentage.

"After all we've been through, finding manuscripts and producing beautiful, long-lasting books will be the simplest job of all," says Dossin.

Know More than I Did

If you don't want to wait a few years or actually own a press, you might consider starting an offset press. Doug Messerli, publisher of *Sun & Moon* magazine, did just that, without knowing anything about offset printing when he started. "I would advise anyone to know a lot more than I did before beginning," he says. What Messerli did know was that "our most exciting young writers, left high and dry by conglomerate publishers, are unable to get work published. I wanted to help alleviate that," he says.

Messerli, who is also a professor of literature and a writer, quickly learned typesetting and layout at the Writer's Center in Glen Echo, Maryland where he produced the first two issues of *Sun & Moon*. Then he moved the magazine to a bigger printer in Washington which had facilities to produce high-quality artwork.

After Messerli received grants from the Coordinating Council of Literary Magazines (CCLM) and the National Endowment for the Arts (NEA), he decided he wanted to publish books as well. He started by doing side-stapled books, either mimeographed or typed, and then offset. After publishing ten books in this way, he was dissatisfied with their looks and applied for another NEA grant. The money enabled him to print handsome books, perfect bound and typeset.

Messerli's philosophy is different from Jennifer Dossin's. "Nothing is wrong with limited-edition, beautifully produced books, but my dream is to be an updated New Directions," says Messerli. "If I'm going to change literature, I must be serious about distribution and get the largest possible audience. I want to make the books beautiful, but I also want people to buy them. A book shouldn't say 'for a special audience only'—it should say, 'this is good literature and you'll enjoy it.' Distribution is almost as important as printing," he says.

Messerli's advice to those who wish to start a small press is to have a clear idea of what you want to do. "That idea will change and grow, but don't be vague," he says. "It's also necessary to have a substantial amount of money in order to do handsome books which, in turn, will help to get grants."

Messerli teaches at Temple University in Philadelphia, runs Sun & Moon Press in College Park, Maryland and still finds time to write his own poetry. "If you want to run a small press seriously, it takes tremendous time and energy," he says. "*Sun & Moon* receives approximately 200 manuscripts a week. The press alone is a full-time job. Luckily, I have a high energy level."

Explore Funding Possibilities

CCLM is a unique organization which helps small magazines and presses. Its director, Jennifer Moyer, has some advice for those starting their own press.

"The first thing to do is to think the whole thing out from beginning to end," says Moyer. "Most people think of themselves solely as editors, not publishers. An editor acquires the material, makes the deal, and edits. But a publisher must concern himself with copyediting, proofreading, finding a typesetter, a printer and binder, worrying about finances, legal issues, contracts, defining a market, getting books reviewed, advertising, and deciding the most effective means of distribution." Before starting, Moyer suggests the would-be publisher talk to other small press publishers to learn the tricks of the trade. "A little homework will save a lot of time and money," she says.

"Government support, both federal and state, is drying up," she says. "Explore your funding possibilities—government, private, and individual. Ask yourself, 'Do I have enough money for one year?'" Most foundations don't give seed grants or endowments. "If they give grants at all, they expect you to have at least one year under your belt," says Moyer.

Moyer advises going to the Foundation Center and using *The Foundation Directory* for local sources. She also suggests getting things free and cheap from anyone you can. "Use friends and relatives shamelessly," says Moyer, slightly tongue in cheek. "For instance, if you have a friend who writes for the local newspaper, try to get a feature on your press. Many local businesses also provide 'in kind' donations—such as free paper or typesetting—instead of money." Moyer feels strongly that you have to do more than just love books to start your own press.

Aspiring small press publishers are also advised not to start a magazine like every other. Many new magazines are often a mixture of poetry, fiction, and whatever else comes in over the transom; they don't distinguish themselves from those already established. Magazines wishing to survive must have a focus, character and some style. And editors should avoid only publishing their friends.

You Can Always Go Back to Press

Planning a sensible print run is also important. "So many small press publishers have no idea how large their audience is. They'll publish 3,000 copies and only sell 500. Warehousing extra copies is expensive," says Moyer who encourages smaller print runs. "You can always go back to press," she says. Even though smaller runs are more expensive at the initial stages, she believes they save time and money in the long run.

"Only 4% of the people in this country are book buyers, which makes for stiff competition," says Moyer. "Commercial magazines and book publishers are having a hard time, so small press publishers must know their competition and decide the best outlets for selling their books. Walden and B. Dalton book chains control 30% of the books in this country, which means fewer independent bookstores with individual buyers." Still, Moyer says not to underestimate local bookstores. "Make an appointment with the store's buyer. You'd be surprised how many are receptive to local publishers.

"The market will determine how your books look," says Moyer. "If books will be sold from a bookstore shelf, don't make your books spineless. Always put the title on the top of a book (as well as on the binding) so it can be read if books are placed on a rack. And why is the price never to be found on a small press book?" she asks. "If you want to sell the book, put the price on it. Otherwise, leave the price off and just give it away. Try to attract attention to your book—that doesn't mean being traditional, aver-age, or standard, just well-done and presentable. Look like a responsible book."

Moyer emphasizes the importance of small press publishing, "especially in an era when conglomerate publishers are less interested in serious fiction and poetry. If we are to have a future generation of published writers," she says, "we must have small press publishers."

Daryln Brewer

Print Centers

Some Print Centers/Literary Centers which offer printing services and/or courses on printing:

The Print Center
Box 1050
Brooklyn, New York 11202

The West Coast Print Center
1915 Essex Street
Berkeley, California 94703

Open Studio, Inc.
(typesetting and design only)
Station Hill Road
Barrytown, New York 12504

Beyond Baroque
681 Venice Boulevard
Box 806
Venice, California 90291

The Visual Studies Workshop
31 Prince Street
Rochester, New York 14607

The Center For Book Arts
15 Bleeker Street
New York, New York 10012

The Writer's Center
McArthur Boulevard and
Goldsboro Road
Glen Echo, Maryland 20812

The Loft
3200 Chicago Avenue South
Minneapolis, Minnesota
55407

Suggested Reading

The Publish It Yourself Hand-book, Literary Tradition and How-To, edited by Bill Henderson
Pushcart Press

Printing It, by Clifford Burke
Wingbow Press

How To Start and Sustain a Literary Magazine, by Joseph Bruchac
Provision House

Note: See Appendix for addresses of publishers.

What a Writer Should Know About Book Design

A book is not a manuscript. Like all the great truths, this one combines absolute obviousness and almost endless ramifications. It hits many writers when their first book is already in the works, be it a tiny chapbook or a 400-page work produced by a major trade house. The writer, heretofore concerned only with writing, realizes the impact a new physical form will have on the work.

"And trouble starts," says Suzanne Zavrian, with the wry view of someone with a foot in two camps. A poet published by both independent and commercial presses, and a veteran organizer of the New York Small Press Book Fair, she's also worked most of her life in commercial publishing.

Design Is a Specialized Art

"Ideally, a writer should be involved in his book's production at every stage," she says. "But it's impossible, even for independent publishers. Editors in commercial houses dread the writer's input on production. Too often a writer's ideas are quirky, wildly expensive, or technically impossible. In fact, the writer with the most ideas on the subject is likely to be absolutely uninformed about what is or isn't feasible. I've been on the editor's side of the desk trying to deal with angry, hurt, and suspicious writers. It's awful.

"On the other hand, I recently read the proofs of a new work by a well-known literary writer. About ¾'s of the changes he'd made on his set of galleys related to production and design, about which he is extremely well-informed and sensitive. His suggestions were totally usable. For example, he insisted that each page contain 27, not 28, lines. His ideas on page design are based not only on a general aesthetic but on hard knowledge of the traditional page/text proportions, the effects produced by specific typefaces, printers' requirements, and so on. He is equipped by constitution and information to be fully involved in this end of his work."

How many writers can say the same? Book design is a special and complex art in its own right. Should a writer take the time and trouble to learn the particulars? Can a writer, even with the inclination, learn enough to be useful?

Zavrian says, "A grounding in technical information might hurt more than it would help. Many writers have no eye for design. Not every writer can carry a tune either. How much can a person with no native talent learn about an art? Then there's the time involved. I think I have a good eye, but I've picked up what I know about design through years of work. There's no way to take in quickly what I acquired over seven years as managing editor at Pocket Books."

Book Jackets Can Lead to Battles

Simply staying out of what one isn't specifically trained for isn't a good enough answer, however. Independent publishers may expect input from their writers—or, frankly, they may need it badly. Commercially published books have been defaced by professional design decisions that were inappropriate, or foolish, or ugly. Horror stories aren't hard to find, especially about jacket design, over which real battles are fought, not just between writer and editor, but among editorial, production, and sales departments.

In Hettie Jones' young-adult novel *I Hate to Talk About Your Mother* (Delacorte), a mulatto teenager frets throughout about how to fix her wildly frizzy hair. This is, of course, not only the normal teenage obsession with appearance but the outward sign of the protagonist's difficulty placing herself, the book's central theme. Jones was given a jacket design picturing her heroine with a smooth red bob. Her agent went to bat for her. "But suppose," Jones says, "jacket consultation hadn't been written into my contract!"

Even Without a Clause, Be Sure to Ask

"I try to get jacket consultation in all my contracts," says agent Elaine Markson. "Otherwise, it may be harder to persuade a publisher to change something. Many publishers don't want such a clause—but that shouldn't persuade a writer to back away.

"Contract or no, a writer should always ask to see the jacket rough [the design plan]. A good house will show it willingly. An editor will show samples of proposed type faces, paper, and talk over other design particulars, if the writer is interested. And writers should be.

"Writers should know they can ask to be informed. They should talk that over with their editors early in the relationship. After all," Markson points out, "both writer and editor want to be proud of the book and both urgently want it to sell. Don't be timid or assume the publisher won't listen. One of my writers mentioned to me how very much she disliked the jacket for her new book—as if it were something she had no right to complain of. The jackets had already been printed, but I insisted she tell her editor. The finished jackets were thrown away, and a new one designed."

Markson believes firmly that a "nonprofessional" opinion has a place in book design, especially in choice of jacket art, because even writers with no sense of design know their own book best and deserve to be consulted about the cover art that will represent it.

Learn Book-Production Basics

Before worrying about how to acquire that elusive eye for design, writers whose work is being published ought to inform themselves about the basics of the production process itself—the steps that will turn a hand-typed manuscript into a finished book. Hard cash could be saved and needless pain prevented if every writer understood that the first proofs, the galleys, are the last chance to make corrections. The second-stage page proofs are used only to check the position of text on the page—not to change words or correct errors. Composition (setting the type) is a major production expense, and galleys are run off to catch any errors that occur. Because composition is so expensive, standard book contracts limit AA's (author's alterations) to 10% of the text and insist that excess changes be paid for by the writer. Only the PE's (printer's errors) will be changed without an additional charge by the typesetter.

To expect all writers to become sensitive to, let alone skilled in, production/design is silly, but certainly a writer ought to know enough about standard practice to protest if a publisher neglects to put the book title on both the front cover and the spine.

The basic facts of book production can be self-taught. And they should be acquired. A number of excellent references, including the classic *Words Into Type* or the *Chicago Manual of Style,* with its thorough chapter on production, are worth careful reading. (They can be found in library reference sections.)

Those who want to know more, those who want to sharpen their sense about the art of book making, should seek out exhibitions of fine books and take advantage of courses, workshops, or seminars on book design offered at literary centers or by colleges and universities across the country. At the very least, one might learn something about one's own personal limitations in the field of book design for such an effort. At best, one might become as sensitive as the writer Suzanne Zavrian found so delightful to work with.

Martha King

Fiction Writer as Publicist

Most writers are uneasy about hustling for their books; they feel it's undignified or that it's not their job to act as a salesman. But for writers who believe in the value of their work, there's nothing undignified in making sure that as many people know about it as possible. I have discovered how with a little ingenuity, a lot of enthusiasm, and a great deal of spare time, any writer can make a difference in the selling of his book. I have.

In 1978 I got my first book contract with Taplinger, a New York commercial publisher, for a short story collection called *With Hitler in New York and Other Stories*. I'd had a hundred stories published in literary magazines over eight years, but I never expected to be published by a trade house, because I knew the huge odds against any poet or short story writer succeeding outside the small press scene. But once I had my $500 advance, I began to dream of literary success—even though I still knew the chances of it were almost nonexistent.

As my book went through production, I learned more about the New York publishing world, where books are no longer literature but products to be marketed. A valuable resource was *How to Get Happily*

Published by Judith Appelbaum and Nancy Evans. (I learned of this book when Judith Appelbaum appeared on a TV talk show.) The authors led me through the maze of publishing; most important was the chapter on "How to Be Your Own Best Salesman," which inspired me to begin a promotion campaign for my book. Meeting a young novelist who didn't get a single review for her first book also helped. I didn't want to join the legion of writers who swap horror stories about their books.

I also remembered something I'd realized when I worked earlier as a volunteer for the Fiction Collective in Brooklyn. Discovering a thick file of clippings, I saw articles about the Collective that had appeared as "news" in almost every major periodical in the U.S. This publicity had, in effect, legitimized the writers' cooperative; what might have been misunderstood as a kind of vanity press was instead perceived, rightly, as an innovative alternative to the inhospitable world of commercial publishing. Almost everyone I met had heard of the Fiction Collective "somewhere."

My publisher, Taplinger, was a small, independent house which had a promotion department of two highly capable professionals. But these people didn't (and couldn't) know my book better than I did, and besides, they had to spread their time among the forty titles Taplinger brought out along with mine. I could concentrate all my efforts on spreading the word about *Hitler*.

An extremely helpful tool was Richard O'Brien's *Publicity: How to Get It*. This book gave me the forms for an author's press release, using specific examples of different kinds of publicity. As my publication date neared, I began sending out news releases and personal letters—about 300 altogether—to newspaper columnists, radio commentators, book critics, and reviewers, all of whom I found listed in *Literary Market Place*.

When a favorable advance review came out in *Publishers Weekly*, I made dozens of photocopies and included these with about 200 more press releases. Each letter I wrote was tailored to the individual columnist's needs. I lived in Brooklyn, so of course I didn't overlook the weekly papers there. They helped by mentioning my book as local news.

By June 1979, when *Hitler* came out, I'd made my decision. I took off the whole summer and devoted my time and money (at least $200 in postage and stationery) to promotion. My first break came when Liz Smith, a New York *Daily News* columnist, responded to my letter by printing a "baby rave" of my book, comparing it to *Cruel Shoes* by Steve Martin, a bestseller at the time. Following that, Taplinger's phones began to ring: calls came in from magazines, newspapers, individuals, and even a movie producer who was interested in film rights.

With Liz Smith's column photocopied and included with my letters, I had further ammunition in my battle for publicity. I sent *Village Voice* columnist Arthur Bell a story from the book that featured celebrities he often wrote about, and he liked it. His next column included a wry plug for *Hitler* which ended, "Beware of Richard Grayson, but read the book." [Ed. note: Arthur Bell died in June, 1984.]

Humor—A Must

I found humor another basic tool. When a furor arose about book editors selling review copies to New York City's Strand Book Store, I sent out fifteen more press releases, stating that Taplinger had decided to send all review copies of my book directly to the Strand Book Store, bypassing critics and saving them bothersome postage and packaging costs. This story was picked up by *Publishers Weekly*, which ran it as a "news" item.

All the news items in the world won't do any good, however, if readers can't find books in the stores. So I culled a list of 75 stores from Bowker's *Book Trade Directory* and Poets & Writers' booklet, *Literary Bookstores in the U.S.* To these I sent a letter featuring the publicity I had received. Most stores didn't respond to this plea from an unknown writer, but about half-a-dozen did, saying they had ordered the book, or would. And I know from friends or from my own checking that several New York City stores stocked *Hitler,* even though they never answered my letter. One of these put the book in their window with a card—"Highly recommended by the author."

Knowing that the large chain bookstores were tough on books and authors without track records, I sent personal letters, Special Delivery, to the presidents of the Waldenbooks and B. Dalton chains. The replies from their adult trade directors were friendly. Walden said they were "sorry" they had "overlooked" my book; both chains promised to stock it in "metropolitan areas" where they had found "experimental literature sold well"—about 15-20% of their stores nationwide. Friends reported sightings of my book in Cleveland and Washington, D.C.

Little Luck with Book Reviews

I also wrote local libraries, both in Brooklyn and in neighboring places which are settings for stories in the book. Most of them ordered copies from one of the distributors which carried *Hitler.* Figuring the book would appeal to college students, I wrote to the editors of about forty campus newspapers all over the country. I got their addresses—and many more— from *Ayer's Directory of Publications.* Tear sheets of their reviews are still coming in. A note to New York

69

talk show host Stanley Siegel led to an invitation to come down for a taping. I kept thinking of new angles, and I found myself enjoying hustling.

The least effective strategy was writing book reviewers. Most of them apparently don't appreciate letters from eager authors. Greil Marcus of *Rolling Stone* gave my book a brief mention after I called it to his attention, but letters to over a hundred newspaper book reviewers led to only eight reviews. Six of those reviewers knew me, my work, or my family. The other two didn't, nor did three additional reviewers who reviewed the book on their own. Months passed before these few reviews were published. So authors writing to reviewers should think up an angle, or a hook—and be patient.

Because you can help sell your book. I did—about 1,500 in the first six months after publication, which almost earned back my advance. Several New York bookstores sold out their original orders of *With Hitler in New York*—not an easy feat with a book of short stories by an unknown author. I don't know how many sales I was directly responsible for, but by taking matters into my own hands, I now have clippings I wouldn't have had otherwise, I learned a new skill—public relations—and I had a lot of fun.

Richard Grayson

Help for the Writer-Publicist:

How to Get Happily Published, by Judith Appelbaum and Nancy Evans
Harper & Row (hardbound), New American Library (paperback)

Publicity—How to Get It, by Richard O'Brien
Harper & Row

American Book Trade Directory
R.R. Bowker

Ayer Directory of Publications
IMS Press

Book Contracts: How to Negotiate One by Yourself

The telephone rings, and the caller is an editor offering a contract for your book of poems, short stories, or a novel. This isn't the first editor who's read the work—you may have sent it out ten or more times before getting a genuine nibble (this happens to agents, too, especially with a writer's first book). Months or years may have passed and by now you may be perfectly willing to sign any document, sight unseen, as long as it assures publication. This creates a kind of fever that does not set the appropriate atmosphere for negotiating a book contract.

The most suitable response, then, to such delightful news is to welcome it enthusiastically but try diplomatically to avoid any substantive discussion of the details of the agreement. No editor is likely to be unsympathetic to a writer who makes it clear that since the news is so marvelous, he/she would like to take a day or two to let it sink in before talking over the details.

Then what? Few realistic guidelines are available for writers about to sign a contract. Although several books discuss contracts, their usefulness is restricted by the blunt reality of the situation: most writers negotiate a contract from a weak position. They are unfamiliar with and likely to be intimidated by the language, meaning, and conventions of such agreements (unlike the publisher), and they are probably aware that the current market—that is, the potential audience for their book—is shaky at best, at least in the trade commercial publisher's view. Editors know that nine out of ten books fail even to recover the cost of producing and launching them. The publisher is therefore not disposed to be generous, accommodating, and flexible in the contract negotiation, and the writer is inclined to be passive, accepting, or resigned to whatever terms are offered.

Small and university presses whose publishing operations are geared to break even with lower sales figures, or who are supported by grants and are not governed or constrained by bottom-line motivations, may be more receptive to a writer's contractual requests. And today these publishers are most likely to publish literary fiction and poetry. But most writers would prefer the opportunity for wide exposure and substantial sales and royalties which are generally only possible with trade book publication. They usually approach such houses first, so my emphasis here will be on trade book publishing.

Most writers negotiate their first contracts on their own. Very few literary agents will represent a writer for a book of short stories; scarcely any will consider representing a poet; an agent's commission is generally 10%, and poetry and stories just don't pay. Most agents will consider a literary novel, even a first book, but are very cautious about taking one on unless someone is already willing to publish it.

There are myriad contracts in trade publishing, ranging in length from about 15 to 103 clauses (a 28-pager issued by one of the biggest houses which intimidates many agents, too). Since even a superficial examination of the clauses and their implications would require book-length treatment, let us zero in on a few key provisions that are generally negotiable. Most of the contract provisions are standard, even though the phrasing may vary, and many publishers are inflexible about modifying more than a few of them, even for agents.

How Much Is My Book Worth?

Back to the editor on the phone. A day or two has passed, and you are returning the call. The editor is likely to discuss only two provisions with you: the advance against royalties and the royalty rate. For a writer, the former appears to be the stickiest and most uncertain element in a negotiation, as the question seems to boil down to: "What is my book worth?" In fact the question really is: "How much is the publisher willing to pay for it?"

With nonfiction a traditional rule of thumb is to begin by estimating the cost of producing the first printing (including royalties), and then affixing a tentative list price that allows the publisher to make a 20% pretax profit, provided most of the first printing actually sells. If the list price, for argument's sake, is $10, the first printing 7,500 copies, and the royalty rate 10% of list price (i.e. $1 per copy), presumably the publisher is willing to pay an advance up to $7,500—the amount the book would earn in royalties for the first printing. However, as trade books returned (unsold) from bookstores average 20% in the industry for hardcovers (35% for mass-market paperbacks), the publisher's maximum offer would probably be about $6,000. Potential subsidiary-rights income from book club or paperback reprint sales, etc., particularly for literary fiction or poetry, is so far away at this point that it generally won't be calculated into an offer unless the auhor has a track record or is a celebrity.

Unfortunately, literary fiction and poetry don't

lend themselves to this rule of thumb, since most don't earn their keep. For example, only one out of ten novels will earn substantial revenues for the publisher in sales and subsidiary rights, and who knows if yours will be that one? Most first novels sell an average of 2,500 copies, though the minimum first printing is usually 5,000, so the house is more than likely to lose on the book. Poetry and short stories are printed in smaller quantities, averaging between 2,500 and 4,000 copies, but here too, sales over a two-year period frequently fall far short of the first printing.

Nevertheless advances are customarily given, and the ranges for trade publishing are as follows: novels—between $2,500 and $6,000; short stories—between $500 and $2,500; poetry—between $250 and $1,000. Your editor will probably offer a figure in the lower part of the range, but generally has the leeway to go a bit higher. (Remember that in trade publishing this negotiation is a "business deal;" whatever attitude toward or commitment to literature your editor has, the house is governed by less lofty principles.)

I suggest you ask for double what is offered, especially if it is in the lower range, and then be prepared to compromise. I do not recommend agreeing to no advance, whatever argument is offered (there are several common ones). With each book, the publisher must lay out from $7,500 to $15,000 just to produce and set it afloat. Even though publishing fiction and poetry is a gamble (as it is with all books), it stands to reason that, having donated so much of your own blood for this project, you are justified in expecting a publisher to compensate you, even modestly, and to include that in the cost of the gamble.

Royalty Rates

At 95% of trade houses, royalty rates for hardcover books are 10% of the list price for the first 5,000 copies; 12½% for the next 5,000 copies, and 15% thereafter. You should accept no less.

After discussing advances and royalties, your editor will mumble something about sending you "our standard contract." You might then want to ask for a "boilerplate" contract (the printed form with no figures filled in), since "I have done some reading up on contracts and I may want to request a few minor changes." Some will agree; others will say they have to send a "final" contract. Don't be intimidated; you will want politely but firmly to indicate that whatever they send, you feel there are going to be some changes even though you are sure "we can work things out."

When you get the contract, read it. The legalese may at first seem opaque, but a second or third reading will usually render up the meaning. And while scrutiny may be tedious, or provoke vague anxieties, it certainly is worth the time and effort. How long did it take to write your book? Isn't the contract worth as much as half a day? The effort is not merely to get more money from the publisher or to safeguard against being taken, but to understand some of the long-term ramifications, to assure that your rights are protected, and to see that you participate at least minimally in decisions that affect the substance, sales, and lifetime of the book (fifty years after the author's death!).

Clauses and Provisions

Here are some of the clauses or provisions you may want to work out:

The Territory. Since you do not have an agent, your contract will "grant, convey and transfer" to the publisher the "world rights." British or translation rights may be sold or licensed at a later date by your publisher, who will in essence be acting as your agent. Your "share" of these rights is negotiable. But let's take up this and other subsidiary rights further on, as they are generally listed later in the contract.

The Copyright. Brook no arguments; it should be taken out in your name, not the publisher's, as some few stipulate.

"Acceptable" Manuscript. Somewhere in the clause giving the delivery date, a phrase about delivering the manuscript "in form and content satisfactory to the publisher" will appear. Since most poetry and fiction is completed when contracted, this provision may cause no problems (as it might for a nonfiction book signed up on the basis of an outline or sample). It does imply, especially with a novel, that unless your editor is satisfied that you have successfully made the changes requested, he or she can reject the book and retrieve the advance (usually paid half on signing the contract and half on delivery of an "acceptable," i.e., revised, manuscript). Therefore it would be prudent to elicit from your editor a clear notion of what substantive changes, if any, are wanted, before signing the contract. If you are at loggerheads about this, it may be better to part company now, before you have spent part of your advance.

Royalties. In addition to the standard 10%-12½%-15% hardcover rate, the quality or trade paperback edition, if one is issued, should pay a royalty of between 6% to 7½% of the list price (ask for the higher rate or accept an escalation to it after the sale of 15,000 or 20,000 copies). Both hardcover and paperback royalties for sales made outside of "normal channels," such as Canadian or mail-order, are conventionally reduced by one-half.

Subsidiary Rights. Your publisher will usually attempt to sell or license book club and paperback reprint rights. Conventionally the split on these rights is 50/50. Your share is deducted from any "unearned advance;" that is, the portion of the advance not yet earned back by book sales, and is then paid to you when your royalty statement is due.

The share of some other rights is negotiable; namely first serial (publication of an excerpt in a magazine prior to book publication), performance (radio, TV, film and dramatic), British, and foreign translation. On the first two you ought to receive 90% of the proceeds; on the latter two you will want to ask for 80%; be prepared to accept 75%. Many contracts lump all these sub-rights together and designate a 50/50 share. Don't accept it. The splits I have suggested are customary and fair. On other rights the income is usually shared equally, and they are rarely worth fussing over.

Warranty and Indemnification. An unfair and complex clause that deserves book-length treatment, it basically indemnifies the publisher against suits based on libel, obscenity, etc., and defends them at your expense. If you have plagiarized, this suit may haunt your career as a writer. If you have any doubts at all about the potential for a suit, such as if you've written a *roman à clef,* discuss the matter with an attorney before signing the contract, as some slight modifications are negotiable.

Termination Clause. Properly cast, this clause will permit you to retrieve all the rights if the publisher lets the book go out of print. Make sure that if the book is no longer available for sale from the publisher and is not listed in its backlist catalogue, upon your written request the rights will automatically revert to you if the publisher fails to reprint the book within six months (or settle for twelve) of receipt of your letter.

If the book is in print under a licensing agreement, say in a mass-market edition, you cannot invoke this provision. But you should strike from the clause a phrase that indicates the rights don't revert if "the book is under option"—it's too vague and open-ended. Retrieving the rights sometimes requires persistence, but if and when the opportunity arises, you should do it.

Option Clause. Since publishing literary fiction and poetry is such a gamble, publishers will expect an option on your next book. What you want to ensure is that the option extends only to that genre based on an outline and sample (for a novel), at terms mutually agreed on, and to be exercised within sixty days of submission. Most option clauses are more restrictive, but these changes are fair, generally accepted by publishers and should be insisted on.

Editing by Publisher. In a separate clause or embedded in one or more other clauses will be a statement to the effect that the book will be subject to editing and alteration by the publisher. You should not conclude that this merely means copyediting, unless the clause further states that such editing "will not materially change the meaning or otherwise materially alter the text of the work." Magazines are notorious for such shenanigans; book publishers generally don't engage in them. Nevertheless you will want to insert a phrase similar to the above, perhaps also adding "or the book's title" and "without the consent of the author."

University Press Contracts

University Press contracts are very similar to trade book contracts, though they are generally shorter and less complicated. The two main differences are in advances and royalty rates. The larger, more prestigious and well-known presses will give advances, albeit smaller ones. No matter the genre, about $2,000 is tops, $1,000 reasonable, $500 common. For the smaller and lesser-known presses, no advance is conventional, but some can be persuaded to part with $500. Most of them pay royalties based on "net receipts" rather than list price. As their net averages about 65% to 75% of the list price (every publisher sells books to wholesalers and bookstores at a discount), the royalties are lower than for trade publishers, although 10% to 12½% to 15% of net is what you should expect or request.

Trade publishers generally give authors a 40% discount on copies of their own books; a university press may offer less, and then may be persuaded to increase the discount to 40%.

[For advice on small press contracts, see note at the end of this article.]

We have merely skimmed the surface of negotiating a trade or university press book contract, but if it is your first and you attempt to cover only the points I discuss, you will have accomplished more than 90% of what most writers do when representing themselves. Negotiating can be nerve-wracking not only because writers are unfamiliar with contracts in general, but because few are willing to risk losing an offer over contractual details. However, consider two points: if one publisher wants your book, another probably would too. If you feel you are not getting a fair shake, it might be worth the trouble to look elsewhere. Secondly, this is a "negotiation;" your editor should be as prepared to compromise as you are. Trade publishers in particular commonly work with agents and experienced authors, and are accustomed to compromising and negotiating.

Perhaps you won't insist on that extra 10% of British rights or you won't get that additional $1,000 advance you might have if you had stone-walled it, but the experience of taking the time and effort to understand the contract, familiarizing yourself with the ground rules and meanings of clauses by reading some of the sources mentioned here, and grappling with the negotiation, will prepare you for the next one. You can then negotiate a better deal for youself, or maybe you will get an agent. In any case, when it's over, you can congratulate yourself; you are no longer a writer . . . you are now an author.

Richard A. Balkin

Editor's Note: A Standard Small Press Contract

In writing about book contracts, Richard Balkin noted that contracts in the small press world ranged "from a handshake to a one-page letter to a formal contract." Finding that a standard form was "sorely lacking," Balkin consulted with several alternative press editors and drew one up. Published by Dustbooks, it's now available for 60¢ a copy.

"I tried to write a contract that protects both the writer and the publisher, equally and fairly," says Balkin, "and to avoid all jargon and legalisms, so a poet without legal experience can read and understand it."

The result is thorough and comprehensible, covering, in a sensible way, nearly everything in a typical trade book contract. Blanks are left for negotiating royalty rates, subsidiary rights proceeds, and other amounts and deadlines. When an author's royalties consist of copies only (often the case in small press publishing), the percentage is stated: 10% of the first run, and 10% of each subsequent reprinting. Since authors are frequently responsible for a hefty percentage of the book sales—via readings and lectures— Balkin also suggests they ask for a 50% discount on "author's copies" instead of the standard 40%, so that in selling their own book they will realize a better royalty.

Balkin has used the contract twice, with a Canadian publisher and with a West Coast publisher of computer books. Dustbooks which distributes the contract, reports that it sells steadily, for the most part, to publishers.

Writers publishing with alternative presses may want to suggest Balkin's "Book Publishing Agreement" to their editor, particularly if the press has no contract of its own. But even if an agent is negotiating your trade book contract, you should know the basic terms and standard practices of publishing, and the "Agreement" which includes "Guidelines for Publishers and Authors," presents them in understandable language seldom found in trade book contracts.

Does a Writer Need a Lawyer?

Probably not. Consulting a lawyer about a book contract will cost anywhere from $250 to $500. If it doesn't deter you, try to select a lawyer who specializes in literary and publishing law, even though the fees are generally higher than those of general practice lawyers. Lawyers not thoroughly familiar with book contracts and conventions are often dismayed by a number of seemingly unfair provisions that are standard in such contracts. The legal wrangles they can provoke might unnecessarily cloud up your relationship with your editor, or even jeopardize the offer.

Suggested Additional Reading

A Writer's Guide to Book Publishing, by Richard Balkin
Hawthorn/Dutton

The Writer's Legal Guide, by Tad Crawford
Hawthorn/Dutton

How To Be Your Own Literary Agent, by Richard Curtis
Houghton-Mifflin

Note: See Appendix for addresses of publishers.

Five Thorns in the Standard Book Contract

The Authors Guild and the Society of Authors' Representatives have both drawn up a model book contract. The Guild's "Recommended Trade Book Contract" is for members only (a resourceful writer could borrow one from a member) and the SAR sample contract is reprinted in *The Writer's Legal Guide,* by Tad Crawford.

Only one publisher is known to have used either of these "ideal" contracts. Nevertheless, they are worth studying for specific clauses, provisions, or modifications that common sense says are reasonable, and fairer than the corresponding clauses in a publisher's standard contract.

In a seminar on book publishing contracts held at New York University, five panelists discussed the Authors Guild model contract clause by clause. The panelists at this seminar were: Jeremiah Kaplan, chairman of Macmillan Publishing Company; Irwin Karp, counsel for the Authors League; Perry Knowlton, president of the Curtis, Brown, Ltd. literary agency; Martin Levin, president of the Times Mirror Company Book Division; and science fiction writer Frederik Pohl. Kenneth S. Giniger of the K. S. Giniger Company, Inc. was moderator.

Following are five sections that sparked the most heated debate among the panelists, presented in the order in which they generally appear in a standard publishing contract. This discussion expands on Richard Balkin's in the previous chapter. Sponsored by NYU's Center for Publishing, the seminar was attended for the most part by publishing company employees. What they know, writers should know.

The Satisfactory Manuscript

An early clause in the standard book contract requires the author to turn in a manuscript "satisfactory" to the publisher "in style, content, length and form." If the publisher does not find the manuscript "satisfactory," it has sole discretion to terminate the contract then and there or request changes from the author, and then, if the manuscript is still not "satisfactory," to terminate the contract. Usually the publisher will require the repayment of any advance, either from the future sale of the work, or out of the author's pocket.

But if an author can then resell the manuscript to another publisher, who publishes it and markets it to readers, is that not a "satisfactory" manuscript? Not for novelist Herbert Gold, who had a four-book contract with Random House. His first two books in the contract did not sell well, and Random House turned down the third as "unsatisfactory." Gold sold the manuscript to another publisher, who brought it out to critical, though not popular, acclaim. Random House sued to retrieve *all* its advance money, for all four books (less royalties paid for actual sales). Gold countersued, saying that obviously his manuscript had been "satisfactory." The court ruled against him, saying that according to the contract he had signed, the publisher had sole discretion to turn down his book. The court did rule that Gold owed Random House only one quarter of the four-book advance (less royalties paid).

The Authors Guild contract requires "a manuscript which, in style and content, is professionally competent and fit for publication." It also provides for termination of the contract by the publisher if, after revisions, the manuscript is still deemed unfit for publication. The Guild clause does not give the publisher sole discretion in ending the contract for that reason, however; it lets the author challenge the termination in court and introduce evidence as to the publishability of the manuscript.

The publishers on the panel objected to the Authors Guild wording, saying it precluded making editorial changes or turning down a book because it was not the book they signed for. Literary agent, Perry Knowlton, also seemed to find it too general. "We all ought to admit," he said, "that there are other reasons than 'satisfactory' for wanting to get out of a contract—for both publisher and writer. An author's editor may have left the house, or the author may no longer want to write that particular book. Both author and publisher should be able to buy their way out of an unsatisfactory contract, and the contract should provide for those situations."

Irwin Karp defended the clause, saying that it did not preclude editing; that it simply makes a publisher say *why* a manuscript is not "satisfactory," if it is turning it down for that reason. He pointed out that the Guild model contract is meant as a general guideline for literary fiction and nonfiction, and that in special situations the parties may want to spell out the terms of this clause. And finally, why should an author be paid for a manuscript that is unsatisfactory? Because, said Karp, like the publisher, the author has made an investment.

Since most poetry and fiction is contracted for only after it has been written, this provision may not cause problems; however, if an editor wants revisions in your manuscript, be sure to know exactly what they are before signing a contract.

Warranties and Indemnities

This is a complicated clause present in all trade publishing contracts that basically requires an author first to guarantee the originality of his manuscript, and then to indemnify the publisher—that is, hold the publisher harmless, financially—in lawsuits involving copyright infringement, libel, invasion of privacy, and obscenity. It requires the writer to pay for any judgments against him and the publisher *and* to pay for the publisher's legal defense. Even if the court decision is in the writer's favor, most clauses require the writer to pay for a portion of the publisher's defense.

A case in this area was that of Gwen Davis Mitchell, who was sued for libel after Doubleday published her novel *Touching*. Davis and Doubleday lost the suit, and then Doubleday sued Davis under the indemnity clause. They settled out of court, for an unknown sum.

Some publishers will change this clause in varying degrees, a few not at all, said Perry Knowlton. In the meantime, over a dozen publishing imprints now offer libel insurance for their writers. This is a new trend, however, and does not cover pre-existing contracts.

The Authors Guild contract limits a writer's financial responsibility, to the amount received under the publishing contract, and only if the decision goes against the writer/publisher.

Martin Levin objected to increasing the publisher's share of the possible burden, saying it was a risk the publisher should not have to take, since "a publisher doesn't know what's in an author's head."

Irwin Karp responded that the warranty clause in current publishing contracts requires, in essence, an author to write an insurance policy for his publisher—something only insurance companies are, by law, qualified to do. Further, the threat of defending a publisher in libel suits and paying the publisher's legal costs even after a book is judged not libelous can lead to self-censorship—a contradiction of First Amendment rights.

Most publishers are tough when it comes to the warranty/indemnity clause; if you've written a *roman à clef*, best check with an attorney before signing a contract.

Royalties

In general, royalty rates for hardcover books are 10% of the book's retail price for the first 5,000 copies; 12½% for the next 5,000 copies, and 15% thereafter; and in general the Authors Guild model contract tries to raise these rates. The standard book contract also allows larger-than-usual discounts for quantity sales to booksellers and reduces the author's royalty on these sales. The Authors Guild contract limits this royalty reduction.

The publishers on the panel objected to higher royalties for authors, saying that because of the economic hard times in publishing (still applicable at this writing), authors should be prepared to accept lower royalties. Martin Levin described the great increase in his company's overhead expenses; for example, they would have had to pay $650,000 to store 32 million books in 1983, but they couldn't afford it—so they planned to destroy half those books. Their monthly

35-book publishing lists have been cut down to 30, and, he said, these lists will be reduced to 25 unless authors accept lower royalties.

Perry Knowlton objected to publishers asking authors, once again, to shoulder the burden of hard times. In the 1920's, he said, royalties were commonly 15% of a book's retail price and often rose to 20%. During the Depression royalty rates were lowered—and they were never raised again, even in the economic boom that followed World War II. He believes publishers can find other ways to do necessary cost-cutting, other than reducing author royalties.

Part of the retail price of a book—as much as 45%—goes toward the publisher's overhead costs, everything from office space to staff salaries. Irwin Karp noted that although many books do not pay their share of the publisher's overhead—publishers estimate three or four out of every five books don't sell well enough to do so—the overhead charge remains on a book even after it has paid for itself. So a bestseller pays its share of overhead time and time again—yet publishers don't take that into account in their royalty formulas.

To sum up: don't accept less than the percentages outlined above for your first trade book, but don't expect more.

Accounting and Payment

Royalties are usually computed semi-annually, but most publishers don't send a royalty statement—and payment, if due—until three to five months after the royalty period. Royalties due on sales between January and July, for example, would not actually be paid before October. The Authors Guild model contract requires a statement and payment within thirty days after the close of the royalty period. It also asks for more information than most royalty statements provide, particularly during the first twelve months after publication: such as the number of copies given away and the number of saleable copies on hand.

Jeremiah Kaplan thought authors might be confused by an array of numbers recording the first printing, the stock on hand, copies sold, the desk and promotional copies given away. Perry Knowlton disagreed, saying "authors are adults," and they could both understand and accept a readable royalty statement, if only they were given all the information. He added that the Guild's royalty statement clause was the kind of "ideal" agents fought for and didn't get; that the clause calls for only a minimum amount of information and publishers won't even give that.

Further discussion revolved around the Guild's "reserves against returns" clause. Standard publishing practice withholds some of an author's royalty income as a reserve against books returned as unsold by bookstores. The Authors Guild contract provides for this practice, but tries to limit the amount (in one case, a best-selling author had 85% of a book's income withheld, even though returns were well below 10%) and the time during which the reserve may be held. The publishers objected to these limits.

Option Clause

Another standard part of the trade book contract is the option clause, in which the publisher gets first bid on the author's next book. As Martin Levin said, "A publisher has an investment in an author and naturally wants to keep that author as he develops. The books we do best with are those whose authors have been with us the longest. This isn't a predatory clause."

On the other hand, the Authors Guild contract has no option clause because it is considered unfair to writers. "It's unacceptable to a professional freelance writer," said Frederik Pohl, who's also been an editor and a literary agent, "especially one who wants to work on two books at once." One book might be best marketed by one publisher, another by a second publisher; a professional freelancer doesn't want to get stuck with the wrong book at the wrong house because of the option clause.

"If you have a good relationship with a publisher, neither side needs an option clause," said Perry Knowlton. "If you have a bad relationship, only the publisher wants it. And in the absence of an option clause, the publisher is more likely to make the relationship a good one." Knowlton cited the example of Ernest Hemingway, who, in order to get out of an option with Liveright, wrote *Torrents of Spring,* a parody of Sherwood Anderson, another Liveright author. Liverwright released him from the contract and he went to Scribners, his publisher for the rest of his life.

Few writers have the time and dexterity to write a terrible book just to get out of the option clause in their contract. And the option clause, though still imposed, is usually negotiable. For example, it should extend only to the same genre of work as the book under contract and should be based on an outline and sample (for fiction).

These contractual clauses (and others) are discussed at greater length in the references listed at the end of this chapter. They're worth further study—they're important to every book, and they may be negotiable.

Debby Mayer

Suggested Reading

A Writer's Guide to Book Publishing, by Richard Balkin
Hawthorn/Dutton

The Writer's Legal Guide, by Tad Crawford
Hawthorn/ Dutton

Note: See Appendix for addresses of publishers.

A Writer's Guide to Federal Income Taxes

Give us day by day our Real
Taxed Substantial Money
bought Bread; deliver from the
Holy Ghost whatever cannot be
Taxed; for all is debts & Taxes
between Caesar & us & one an-
other; . . .

> *William Blake's parody*
> *of Dr. Thornton's version*
> *of the Lord's Prayer, 1827*

Your passions about God and Caesar may not match Blake's. But as April 15th moves closer, and somewhere about the house lies a packet from the Internal Revenue Service labelled "1040: U.S. Individual Income Tax Form" you may be having trouble thinking about it rationally. And no wonder. As the Volunteer Lawyers for the Arts' excellent tax handbook, *Fear of Filing*, points out, "in order to take advantage of the provisions of the Federal Tax Code, you must learn to think of yourself as three . . . separate personalities." That's not commonly considered a rational enterprise. The fact is, to the Internal Revenue Service, writers can be three people:

• Private individuals like all others, who eat, clothe, and amuse themselves, and occasionally go to doctors and dentists;

• Employees who get paychecks from employers from which taxes are generally withheld;

• Self-employed professionals, working to produce products—pieces of writing—from which they intend to make a profit.

What follows is about the tax life of the Third You—the self-employed writer: how to keep track of it, and how to fill out your Federal return with less pain, and with the possibility of more tax savings— with or without an accountant. Though as you'll see, paying for competent professional help can be one of the sounder business investments you make.

First Things First

You do have to file. For one thing, it's the law. In 1982 if your income from all sources, including your writing, totalled more than $3,300 a year, you had to send Washington a fully filled out tax return. That is, if you were single; if you were married the figure was $5,400. (Be sure to check with the IRS; the taxable base is likely to change.) For another thing, unless you do file a tax return, you won't get refunds that might be coming to you. Finally, putting your tax life in order can help put your real life in order by helping you see where your money comes from and where it goes. Doing your taxes properly may save you grief, not only in time lost in audits but money lost in interest on taxes due.

How Does the Tax System Work for Writers?

For the most part, very well.

That's because the Internal Revenue Service recognizes that the writing business is like any other. It entails legitimate business costs (you're used to thinking of them as deductions), and tax is paid on business income (in its most familiar form, royalties and reading fees) after those costs have been subtracted. In that regard, all businesses are equal; whether your product is poems, shoes, or matches, you're taxed on your profit.

The problem for writers is that some businesses are more equal than others. Writing ordinarily does not produce much profit. It can, in fact, require financial sacrifice. And that can cause trouble with the tax man. Al Shedler, of Shedler and Shedler, Certified Public Accountants, puts it as a fact of life: "People who characteristically show high expenses in relation to income, especially those in the beginning of their careers, may be subject to frequent audits."

That isn't persecution, though it may feel like it. Because business losses can help reduce personal income taxes—those you pay as an individual or employee—the IRS is quite naturally wary of enterprises that consistently lose money. It may want to determine that the business in question isn't merely a hobby. Hobby losses aren't deductible. A good accountant can help convince an audit agent that your true motive is not achieving a negative relation between receipts and expenditures to reduce your personal income taxes, but rather that your hope is ultimately to have your work recognized financially. According to tax specialist Burt Friedman, who works closely with Al Shedler, "Tax agents can and do understand this argument." If your income has been reported accurately, if your expenses are "ordinary and necessary"—that is, common practice in the writing profession—and if you've kept accurate records of them both, you'll probably be O.K.

What Is Taxable Income?

Income is any money you receive any time for any reason. Not all income, however, is taxable. Generally, taxable income is money paid you for a service you've performed or are about to perform, or for a product you've sold. Just as the salary you might get from teaching, or the tips you could get from waiting on tables, are taxable, so are:

• Royalties and advances from magazine and book publishers
• Fees for readings or lectures
• Prizes and grants (sometimes)

Prizes are not taxable, if they are, to use the IRS's terminology, "awarded in recognition of past accomplishments . . . (and) if the recipients are selected without action on their part and are not expected to render any future services." What that means in practice is that if a jury selects your work, either on its own or on the recommendation of others, for a prize or award, the money you get is probably not taxable. But if you submit your work to be considered for a prize, it is.

In terms of "future services," the operative word is substantial. An award that requires one reading a week for a year would probably be taxable; one that requires just a few, probably not. Ask the givers whether in the past their prizes have been considered taxable income. But to be absolutely safe, check yourself. Remember, the last word is the IRS's and the tax courts'.

As for grants, most are taxable, but not wholly. Often, $300 a month of grants which are not given as payment for past, present, or future services, or to help you get a degree, can be excluded from your taxable income. You should know, though, that you can take this exclusion for only 36 months of your life.

What's generally not taxable is most expense money that might go along with the grant—such as travel or clerical help—as long as you applied for it specifically, or the terms of the grant state specifically that's what the money is for. Here especially you should check with your accountant.

Finally, as a rule of thumb, expenses paid by others—such as travel to give a reading, or lodging at a conference or writers' colony—do not represent taxable income. Neither do *per diems,* or advances on living expenses, sent you by conference organizers, so long as the amount is less than $44 a day, and you can prove you actually spent that for lodging, laundry, phone calls, and taxis while you attended the conference. (Needless to say, the conference has to be related to your business as a writer: "Themes in Contemporary Poetry" would qualify; "Philately as an Income-Producing Sideline" would not.) That is the rule of thumb. The mechanics, which a careful recordkeeper would follow, are these: Report the expense money as income and take your actual expenses as deductions. Also note that the $44 figure is a variable one, depending on the area to which you traveled and the year in which you did the traveling. Check with your accountant or the IRS for the applicable amount.

What Are Legitimate Expenses?

As a self-employed professional, you have an office and office expenses; you attend meetings outside your office; you travel in connection with your work; and you entertain. Lest that list conjure up visions of Concorde flights to Paris to talk with French poets, remember that in writing, as in other businesses, only "ordinary and necessary" expenses are deductible.

Before deducting an expense, ask yourself a classic accountant's question: "Is this expense 'proximately related' to the business of being a writer?" Salesmen or corporate lawyers, for instance, might have to entertain at fancy restaurants exclusively; it's common practice in their business. It's hard to prove that serious writers have to. On the other hand, serious writers do have serious expenses. For what's legitimately deductible, read on.

Your Office. The Federal tax code establishes stringent rules for deducting the costs of an office at home. You are probably safe if your office area is: a) a separate room or separated by a room divider, b) used exclusively and regularly as your principal workplace (it shouldn't, that is, double as a guest room); and c) you produce more income in the office than you claim as a deduction for it. If your office space meets those three tests, you can deduct its share of your rent, or, if you own where you live, of the carrying charges on your house or loft or co-op, (including taxes, interest, utilities and so on). You can also pro-rate your office space's share of cleaning and insurance costs.

Office supplies—from paper clips to typing paper to erasers to staplers, and office equipment—typewriters, say—are clearly deductible the year you buy them.

On equipment, the usual treatment has been to "depreciate," or spread out the cost of the item over the life the tax code assigns it. In 1982, for instance typewriters were considered to have a life of five years. So for a $500 typewriter, you could deduct $75 the first year, $110 the second, and $105 the third, fourth and fifth years. Why those proportions? Something called accelerated depreciation is the rule now, by which you take 15%, 21%, 21%, etc.

But you might consider taking advantage of a wrinkle of the law called the investment credit. designed to stimulate business production. If you bought a word processor, for instance, you might be able to reduce your income tax by up to 10% of the word processor's cost. Here, however, you really do need professional advice. There are other complications. For instance, for the tax years 1982 and thereafter, you can choose not to depreciate equipment and instead deduct up to $5,000 outright—that is, write-off $5,000 worth of equipment purchases. But if you take that option, you lose 10% of any investment tax credits you might take.

Back to straight deductions. Equipment repairs and equipment rental (say you needed an italic typeface for a month) also qualify. So do secretarial services, such as typing.

Postage, photocopying, and telephone and telegraph expenses related to your work are deductible too. On the telephone, try to figure out a "reasonable use" standard—a third, or whatever—of your regular bill.

Travel, Transportation, and Meetings. Deductible travel and transportation comes in two forms: local and away from home. Local transportation includes subway, bus, and taxi fare, or the cost of operating your own car, to and from business meetings, with your agent or publisher or with colleagues in a professional association—with two exceptions. "Commutation" is not deductible. So your first run of the day, from home to office, doesn't count. Neither does your last run home. Expenses connected with such meetings— say you pick up the tab for lunch, or pay to have the agenda photocopied—are also deductible. (As for how much to deduct for the cost of operating your car, check with your accountant or the IRS. There is a standard mileage rate that you might want to use. But it does change occasionally.)

Travel away from home can be more complicated.

A clearly deductible trip would look like this: you are paid a fee to give a reading or lead sessions at a writers' conference in another city. You drive or pay your own airfare and transportation to and from airports, and pick up your own hotel bill, all your meals, telephone bills, and have your reading suit drycleaned at the hotel. All those expenses are legitimate business costs. But if any one of these items is paid for by someone else, you must include the payment in income and deduct the expense. Remember, you can't do one without the other. (Foreign travel is subject to new restrictions; check with an accountant before deciding what and whether to deduct.)

Suppose you're not giving the reading, or participating in the conference, but simply go to listen. To deduct your expenses, you need to demonstrate that your attendance is a necessary part of your professional life. Remember that accountant's question: "Is what you're doing 'proximately related' to the business of being a writer?"

Ask that question twice if you're thinking of deducting travel for research. If you can demonstrate that you couldn't write your novel on the compulsive gambler's soul without spending a week in Las Vegas, O.K. But be prepared for an argument.

Other Professional Expenses. Legal fees, agents' commissions, publicity and promotion expenses (within reason) are generally deductible. So are gifts for business purposes, up to $25 per gift per person per year. Permissions fees you pay to quote someone else's work and copyright fees you pay to register your own are tax deductible, as are dues to professional associations (PEN, for instance), subscriptions to professional journals, and books. Not all books, of course, but books in your field.

Entertainment is like travel—sometimes straightforward, sometimes not. In general, food and drink, whether at home or in a restaurant, is personal, not a business expense. But if the eating and drinking was done with present or prospective business associates—such as publishers—from whom you could reasonably expect to receive income or good will, and you paid for their fare, the cost could be considered deductible. Here, even more than elsewhere, the rule of reasonableness applies. Any self-respecting tax auditor would raise an eyebrow at a series of $75 dinners in a year in which you didn't sign a contract, didn't have a book coming out, and didn't have one scheduled for 22 months.

Be alert to two features of the recent tax changes that might benefit you. Both began in 1982. One is a tax credit for child care, 'though it's applicable only in certain situations and family combinations. The other is the revised Individual Retirement Account (familiarly known as IRA), under which you can set aside up to $2,000 of your gross earnings a year and for your spouse if he/she isn't working, and not pay any tax on them until you're 59½ or older, when you draw on them. But beware of penalties for early withdrawal. Consult a tax adviser to figure your best advantage. There is another kind of retirement fund, called a Keogh, which might work for you.

Good Records: All Important

You can't fill out tax forms unless you know where your money came from and where it went. If you're audited, you'll need what's called "substantiation," or proof, that expenses you deducted were real, and that you didn't make more money than you said you did.

Here's a relatively simple recordkeeping system that should meet those needs and also not drive you crazy.

Keep a Checking Account. Deposit all your income in it, even cash you get for a reading fee. Most checkbooks come with a little ledger for keeping track of deposits. Use it to write down the source of every dollar you put in the bank—"Harper & Row, 'Prelude' royalty;" "Lesley College, reading." If you want to deposit earnings in a savings account, fine. But rather than keep two ledgers, just deposit what you want to save in checking, record it, and then transfer it to savings.

Whenever possible, pay by check. Most checks have a space for noting what the check is being drawn for. Use it—"June rent;" "Ten copies, 'Prelude';" "Office supplies, paper." Write the same thing on the check stub too.

Keep Receipts. You can't pay for everything by check. When you can't, get a receipt and write on it what you would have written on the check—"Office supplies, paper clips;" "Lunch with agent to discuss 'Prelude' publication;" "Wine for publication party." The same goes for credit card slips. To be extra sure, keep receipts even for items you've paid for by check, attached to the cancelled check.

Keep a Diary. Business people have diaries in which they keep track of their appointments. You should too. It doesn't have to be an enormous daybook, in which every minute is accounted for, but it should include professional meetings and professional dinners and lunches and a note on what was discussed. For one thing, the Internal Revenue Service sets great store on diaries. For another, your diary can help remind you of deductible expenses you couldn't get receipts for (let alone pay for by check)—your subway or taxi fare to a meeting, for example.

When it comes time to get your tax affairs in order for your accountant, all you have to do is run through your deposit records and make an itemized list of your income. For your expenses, do the same with your cancelled checks, your receipts, and your diary.

Itemize by category—royalties, fees, office expenses, travel, and so on. Remember, the less time you spend with your accountant, the lower the accountant's fee.

Finally, keep all your records for any given year for three years after you've filed your return. The statute of limitations on audits is three years. Some accountants advise keeping all your records a little longer—say, five years—in case you're called upon to verify that over the longer haul, your income justifies your expenses, and that writing is more than a hobby to you. (Certain key records, such as receipts for purchase of a typewriter or other capital equipment, you should keep as long as you keep the equipment. If you resell the item, you could be subject to tax on any profit you might make.)

The Forms You Have to File

1040 and Schedule C. As an individual and as an employee, you probably use Form 1040; U.S. Individual Income Tax Return* to pay your taxes due or to claim a refund. If you have large medical expenses, make large charitable contributions, or pay interest on a mortgage, you might itemize your deductions on Schedule A, rather than use what's now called the zero bracket amount (that's the old standard deduction), and so reduce your tax. But that's personal taxes.

The Third You, the self-employed professional writer, must file Schedule C: Profit or Loss From Business or Profession—whether you itemize personal deductions on Schedule A or not. Schedule C is what you use to report professional income (royalties and reading fees) and professional expenses (office costs, travel, and so on). You'll be taxed on your profit; your loss can reduce your personal tax. Like Schedule A, Schedule C attaches to Form 1040.

*Form 1040 and the other forms referred to here are available from the IRS; check the phone book for your district office's address.

If you live abroad, check IRS publication 54 "Tax Guide for U.S. Citizens Abroad"; use form 2555 to adjust for certain foreign living costs.

Estimated Tax. Under the law, 80% of the tax you owe every year must be paid before the end of the year. If you owe more than 20% of your total tax on April 15, you may have to pay a penalty. That's why a spokesman in the IRS's New York office calls Estimated Tax one of the more important things a writer—or anyone else who has income an employer doesn't withhold taxes from—should know about.

To be safe in 1984, for example, if you thought you were going to owe the IRS more than $500 on your 1985 return, you had to file form 1040-ES Declaration Voucher every three months. (Every year, check out the bottom line; it may change.) 1040-ES is a simple form on which you estimate your income, deductions, and taxes already paid through withholding by your employer, and then pay a deposit on the balance due. If you weren't filing estimated taxes and suddenly got an unexpected windfall late in the year, don't worry; you can start estimating then.

Income Averaging. Windfalls are wonderful, except when it comes to paying taxes on them. Just one large advance on a book can jump you up three tax brackets. Schedule G (Form 1040) to the rescue! You'll probably need an accountant's help to figure out the complicated eligibility requirements. But if you meet them, you can use Schedule G to pull you back down into a lower tax bracket. So again, it's a help to save your records for five years back!

Self-Employment Tax. If you don't have a job yielding a paycheck from which your employer withholds Social Security tax (often designated as F.I.C.A. on your paystub), you will have to go through yet another computation every year. The purpose is to determine

101

whether you owe Social Security tax, which everyone who works, including people like writers who are self-employed, is required to pay—but only up to a point. There's a limit on how much of your income is subject to Social Security tax, that like all limits changes every year.

How do you know if you owe? Here's a workbook example constructed in 1982, when the limit was $32,400. Because the 1982 limit on Social Security-taxable income was $32,400, if you made more than that in salary and F.I.C.A. was withheld from your paycheck, you were O.K. But if you didn't and you cleared $400 or more from your writing, you owed. You would have had to file form SE (computation of Social Security Self-Employment tax) and with it a check for 9.35% of up to $32,400 of your net earnings. If you made more than $32,400 the balance was Social Security tax-free.

Suppose your income came from both a salary and your writing, say $20,000 in salary from which F.I.C.A. was withheld and $20,000 net from writing. You'd have paid self-employment tax on $12,400 of that $20,000. $7,600 would have been Social Security tax-free. And so on.

The figures change annually; check for the year's levels on your Estimated Tax form (1040-ES). Also, if you have a regular employee, say a regular typist, you might owe employers' taxes; check with the IRS and your state and local tax offices.

State and Local Taxes. Some states and cities levy taxes on professional income. In New York City, for example, writers with fairly large incomes may have to pay New York City Unincorporated Business Tax. Be sure to ask your accountant what taxes you are subject to; if you insist on doing your taxes yourself, double-check with your state and city income tax bureaus.

And if you do have to pay such state and city taxes on professional income, remember to deduct them on Schedule C the next year; they are a legitimate expense of doing business.

Foreign Income. Foreign royalties are like domestic royalties. You have to pay tax on them here. But you needn't be taxed twice. If your foreign income has been taxed abroad, the amount you paid can reduce what you owe at home. Check with your accountant for the appropriate form.

Unlatching Catch-22

Doing your taxes properly for the first time is like getting published for the first time. Sometimes it's impossible unless you've done it before. That's one reason getting the help of a tax professional—an accountant—matters. Another reason is that no matter how carefully you read the Internal Revenue Service's forms and booklets, an accountant will still know more than you do about what is legitimately deductible and what is not. And accountants will disagree. There are, after all, gray areas. How to figure your expenses if you have a grant for example, is complicated, and so is how to handle your office equipment.

But that's the accountant's business. Your business is writing, and your time is money. Accountants, you say, cost money. So they do. But this isn't Catch-22—accountants' fees are deductible.

Caroline Rand Herron

Where to Get Help

First, get a good accountant. If you don't know a good one, or know anyone who lives and works the way you do and has a good accountant, check with your state Society of Certified Public Accountants. Remember, accountants' fees are deductible. In a few states, *pro bono* or reduced-rate accounting programs exist for people with complicated tax lives and low incomes. The state CPA society should know if there's such a group near you.

If you want to read more, the Volunteer Lawyers for the Arts' *Fear of Filing: A Beginners' Handbook on Record Keeping and Federal Taxes for Dancers, Other Performers, Writers, and Visual Artists* is highly recommended. It takes you through your tax life and the Federal tax forms, step by step and line by line. Many accountants recommend a solid commercial publication, written in plain English, that Simon & Schuster puts out every fall. It's called *Your Income Tax*, by J. K. Lasser.

And then there's the Internal Revenue Service's very own *Your Federal Income Tax*. Another IRS publication worth looking at, especially if you're involved with a small press or literary magazine, is *Tax Guide for Small Business*. Both are available through your local Federal Tax office, as are many more specialized pamphlets. You should also note that each IRS district office holds Small Business Tax Workshops that last for a half day or a full day.

The Writer's Will

Delmore Schwartz was known for both his poetry and short fiction when he died suddenly of a heart attack in 1966. Yet the literary world is fortunate to have his work still available. Schwartz died unknown in a cheap hotel in New York City. He had cut himself off from his friends, who didn't know where he was living. His body lay unclaimed in a morgue for two days. Only when a *New York Times* reporter who routinely covered the morgue recognized Schwartz's name, and a day later the *Times* published an obituary, did [the late] Dwight Macdonald and Schwartz's other friends learn of his death.

Macdonald called the hotel to ask about Schwartz's belongings. At that moment Schwartz's aunt and uncle—his only relatives in New York City—happened to be there, puzzling over, in Macdonald's words, "a room filled with heaps of newspapers, 'girlie' magazines and other miscellaneous junk, all mixed in with letters, dirty laundry, carbons of poems and stories, bills (unopened) and sixty or seventy books, everything crammed helter-skelter into bureau drawers or under the bed or in corner midden-heaps." Macdonald, then a writer at *The New Yorker*, coopted a colleague and an office boy, and with their help, retrieved from the jumble a carton of books and papers that seemed worth saving, storing them temporarily in his office.

Needed: A Fellow Writer

Because Schwartz died without a will, his brother Kenneth was automatically his heir, being the nearest surviving blood relation. Kenneth Schwartz, an engineer who works in the Southwest, is unfamiliar with the literary/publishing world. Macdonald wrote him suggesting Kenneth put him in charge of the estate's literary property, empowered to deal with the whole body of Delmore's work—past letters, journals, and manuscripts, published and unpublished—and any future payments for these, transmitting the cash to Kenneth. Not surprisingly, Kenneth agreed. In this way responsibility for the literary property was taken by someone who knew writing in general and Schwartz's in particular—by a fellow writer who cared.

The alternatives are terrible to contemplate for writers who care about their work or that of their friends. Not only might literary material in Schwartz's room have been thrown away, but also manuscripts and letters found later might never have been published and made available to critics and biographers. The royalties, not incidentally, are considerable. They all go to Kenneth Schwartz.

Any adult who is of sound mind can have a will. Those with dependents, real estate, insurance, or savings, should have a will. Only with a will can they be sure of dividing their estate the way they want to, providing for dependents, and reducing the impact of taxes on the estate.

A writer should have a will if for no other reason than the unique nature of written works. These are the writer's creation and have aesthetic qualities not found in the rest of the estate. The problems and

106

complications that arise when a writer doesn't have a will—or doesn't carefully think through a will—can make the stuff of comic opera. For families, friends, editors, and publishers mired in years of litigation, they are no joke.

Who would own the copyright on your unpublished work if you died tomorrow? Would 25-year-old copies of *Poetry* be bundled off to the nearest thrift shop? University libraries are often eager to acquire original manuscripts—plus letters, journals, notes—sometimes for substantial cash. But who would take the trouble to catalogue your files? And who would you want to see your journals and notes?

"It Doesn't Matter, I'm Not Famous"

In drawing up a will, it is customary to name an executor, a person who takes charge of and eventually distributes the estate's assets (almost always with the help of a lawyer). A writer should either name an executor who is familiar with the writer's work and the literary world, or name two executors, one to deal with the estate's general assets, another to handle the literary assets in particular. Executors are usually informed of their appointment as a will is being drafted, so they can refuse it if necessary, and someone else can be chosen—by the writer, not by a stranger.

Executors named in wills are paid for working on an estate. The laws on this vary; some states set a fee, others allow executors a certain percentage of the estate. If fees for two executors would be too expensive for your estate, you will have to decide on one person who could do everything.

For those who die without wills, the local probate court must assign their estate and name an administrator for it. The administrator must then imagine what the deceased would have wanted. A life's work—

no matter how short the life—means too much to writers and those who love them to be handled carelessly or ignorantly.

When Sylvia Plath died in 1963 she had published only one book of poetry, *Colossus,* in her own name. Respected by other poets, she was unknown outside of a small literary circle. Sylvia Plath had written voluminously, however, and since her death, eight different poetry collections by her have been published as well as a novel, a radio play, and collections of her correspondence and short prose. Her work is published in both the United States and England, is reprinted frequently in anthologies, and is occasionally still published in magazines.

Whether you have a file full of unpublished poems or just one short story and the first act of a play, it is important to stipulate in a will who you wish to take charge of them and, if you can, what should be done with them.

"I'm Safe, My Family Knows My Work"

When Walter Lowenfels, poet, essayist, and anthologist, died, he left a will that named Manna Lowenfels-Perpelitt, one of his daughters, as executrix in charge of his literary property. She knew his will named her, but they had never discussed what her specific responsibilities would be. Perpelitt is a poet herself, was close to her father, and felt that she knew his work well. But her duties as executrix brought her an overwhelming amount of work for which she was unprepared in many ways.

"I knew that my father had left his manuscripts to Yale and that for my work as executrix I would receive 10% of all royalties and advances," says Perpelitt. "But I knew almost nothing about what I was actually supposed to do."

Lowenfels had published seventeen collections of

poetry in his life and seven books of prose. He had also edited nine anthologies. The first thing Perpelitt realized she didn't know was how to give permission to reprint poems from those anthologies. Did the rights belong to her or to the individual poet? Must she try to reach each poet for every request? Early on Perpelitt gave reprint permission for a poem, believing its author had died. Later she found out he had not. She does not want to infringe upon anyone's copyright, but she gets many reprint requests from textbook publishers, and altogether the amount of correspondence is tremendous.

Eighty Cartons of Books to Sort

Walter Lowenfels' library filled eighty cartons. "They took over my life and my house for a year," says Perpelitt. "I spent three months just sorting magazines." In among the hundreds of books were 200 signed by writers such as Gwendolyn Brooks, Langston Hughes, and Pablo Neruda—valuable editions for collectors. Lowenfels' will made no provision for the library, and what to do with it became a divisive problem for his family.

Lowenfels' will also left no instructions for sorting and packing his manuscripts and files. For example, he had card files of addresses for the poets in each anthology, and Perpelitt, recognizing them, brought them home with her. She feels she was lucky to get them—even though many addresses were out of date—since she didn't know about them and no specific provision had been made for them. They could have easily been thrown away, making her job of permissions editor even more difficult.

In all, Perpelitt has worked hundreds of hours as a combined editor, literary agent, librarian, and secretary. Although she earns 10% of all advances and royalties, this income is very small. A less concerned executor could have done the work in fewer hours, but the estate would have suffered. For example, if textbook publishers got no answer to their reprint queries, they would not use the poems. Or an executor unwilling or unable to sort through eighty cartons of books might have sold the lot without looking at them, and lost irreplaceable items.

Even if your spouse has edited your manuscripts and set up your filing system, you may want to leave instructions about reprint permissions and fees or to suggest someone to consult on unfamiliar subjects. Such advice does not have to be given formally in a will, but may be left in a letter for your executor. Or you may want to name two executors so that experience as well as work can be shared. Walter Lowenfels actually did this, but the second executor lives too far from upstate New York, where Perpelitt lives, for working together to be practical. If your best friend lives in Baton Rouge and your editor lives in Boston, a joint executorship may not work out the way you would want it to; another system might be better for your estate and those who will administer it.

See a Lawyer

In order to make a will binding—so that it cannot be challenged in court, or, if it is, so that your wishes will stand—it is almost always necessary to draw it up in consultation with a lawyer. Laws regarding wills vary from state to state, and even if your estate—all that you own, plus cash and insurance—is small, it may still be complex, since matters of copyright ownership will probably be ongoing. Writers who earn $6,000 a year or less may ask Volunteer Lawyers for the Arts to refer them to a lawyer. For the address of the VLA office nearest you, write Volunteer Lawyers for the Arts, 1560 Broadway, New York, N.Y. 10036.

W.H. Auden lived simply—indeed, frugally—all his life. But because he resided in both the United States and England, his estate owed taxes in both countries, and five years passed before the estate was settled. Although most people don't live in two countries, many keep homes in two states, and upon death their estates may owe taxes in both states. Consulting a lawyer will help avoid such problems. But even if you rent an apartment and have a relatively simple estate, settling it will probably require about a year. During this time, most assets will be frozen, unable to be sold or spent. One thing a lawyer will help you do is provide cash for dependents to live on while the estate is being settled.

William Meredith, poet and former consultant in poetry to the Library of Congress, was one of three executors for Auden's estate. Seeing the complexities of the Auden settlement spurred Meredith to revise his own will, which had become out of date. A will can always be changed, either by making additions called codicils, or by writing a new will. Again, a lawyer's help is necessary, so that the changes cannot be contested.

"It can be complicated," says Meredith of a writer's will, but in general he sees the literary part of a writer's estate as breaking down into three distinct parts: the manuscripts "as manuscripts—the Parke Bernet aspect;" copyright; and books, papers, and letters the writer has collected over a lifetime. "These things can be separated quite clearly," says Meredith, "and can be left to different people if you want."

Meredith emphasized making some provision for a writer's library. "Most people are unaware of how valuable the ordinary collection of books in a literary person's life has become in the last ten to fifteen years," he says. "But check any catalogue of modern first editions, and you'll see."

Thinking ahead to what your executor will actually have to do with your literary property can also help you draft a precise, workable will. In Manna Perpelitt's experience, an executor's literary duties break down into three categories: sorting manuscripts, books, letters, etc.; answering permissions requests; and finding publishers for unpublished works. Unless you choose an editor as executor, you may want to suggest consultants to help edit and market unpublished work.

Your Work Deserves Your Will

If you find yourself still thinking, "this is silly, I'm not famous" or "my family knows how I feel about my work, they would never do anything with it that I wouldn't want done," consider the following story reprinted from *The Writer's Legal Guide** by Tad Crawford:

> In 1945 Eugene O'Neill entrusted the original manuscript of *Long Day's Journey Into Night* to his editor, Bennett Cerf, at Random House. A written agreement between O'Neill and Random House provided that the play should only be published twenty-five years after O'Neill's death. Within two years of O'Neill's death in 1953, however, his widow, Carlotta, demanded that Random House publish the play. Cerf felt honor-bound not to do so, but his desire to follow O'Neill's wishes simply resulted in Carlotta withdrawing the manuscript from Random House and having it published by the Yale University Press. She had the power to do this as executrix under O'Neill's will.

Carlotta O'Neill certainly helped the world of letters with the early publication of *Long Day's Journey Into Night*. And it is difficult, if not impossible, for a writer to foresee everything in a will. But writers who want their wishes for their literary property followed after their death must have a specific, written will giving only those they trust power over that property.

*Reprinted with permission from *The Writer's Legal Guide*, by Tad Crawford (Hawthorn/Dutton). Copyright © 1978 by Tad Crawford.

The following questions, also suggested by Crawford in *The Writer's Legal Guide,** may help:

• Do you want unpublished works published after your death? Destroyed?

• If unpublished works are published, may they be edited and if so, by whom?

• If works are incomplete, can they be finished by someone else? Who? How should the author credits appear then?

• Do you want works published only in hardcover or paperback, or both?

• May your work be recorded, filmed, televised?

• Who may publish letters you wrote, and how? What about letters you received?

• Who do you want to see rough drafts, notebooks, diaries?

• If you want to name an official biographer, how will the estate then handle inquiries from other researchers and the general public?

No one wants the trouble and expense of consulting a lawyer—and, possibly, an accountant and an insurance agent—unless it's absolutely necessary. Any poet would rather write a poem than a list of financial assets, and facing the grim reaper can feel like tempting bad luck. But a will's cost in fees and annoyance is little compared to the expense in taxes and litigation, the time, and the heartache it could save your family and friends.

Debby Mayer

Suggested Reading

You and Your Will, by Paul P. Ashley
Mentor/New American Library

The Writer's Legal Guide, by Tad Crawford
Hawthorn/Dutton

Note: See Appendix for addresses of publishers.

Three

WRITING FICTION

Do Fiction Writers Read Fiction While They Write It?

Stories abound of writers who copy whole pages of someone else's fiction in order to imitate it; of writers who read *The Portrait of a Lady* and find themselves composing long, flowing sentences; and of those who become so immersed in the cadence of someone else's prose that they must stop reading fiction altogether while they work. Other writers say they still read while they write, but they limit themselves to certain kinds of fiction, such as murder mysteries. Some can't imagine writing—or living—without the nourishment of a good novel.

Coda asked nine writers to answer the question: Do you read fiction while you write it?

Linsey Abrams (*Charting by the Stars,* Harmony Books): I do read fiction while I'm writing it, although I tend to read fewer contemporary writers while in the middle of a novel. I read more nineteenth century novelists or contemporary writers whose style is very different from mine or who deal with subject matter different from my own. Reading doesn't affect my style, but when you're writing a novel, you're constructing a whole vision of the world

117

and you can't include everything. A writer tackling the same subject matter will bring up different aspects, which are interesting to read, but I don't want their vision coming in to rival mine while I'm writing. I want to keep my vision uppermost. At the same time, writers must read other contemporary writers. We're all trying to solve the same problems.

Donald Barthelme (*Overnight to Many Distant Cities*, Putnam): I keep reading while I write and I don't think it hurts me. My writing is sufficiently various that someone else's style doesn't take over. I don't suddenly turn into John Updike if I'm reading Updike. One can't just imitate another. Everybody is influenced by the people they read, but the pleasure in the situation is that usually there are so many influences—so many fathers—that they all get blended together. In the best case, no single influence dominates.

Harold Brodkey (*First Love and Other Sorrows*, Dial): I'm addicted to reading but I have to take vacations from writing to satisfy the addiction. Writing involves extra-complicated and very private mechanisms that claim to express the world in terms of common meaning. Of course, it is not yet common but you lie to yourself about that. Then to pick up a book and to discover—to rediscover—that others see and speak differently is an assault somewhat like being manhandled and interrogated by a foreign policeman who insists that you explain yourself to him although he knows little or nothing about the kind of man you are.

To risk being ugly for a moment: if I can read it while I'm working, then it's probably well-crafted and safely second-rate.

Writing is a bad life (or no life) in a number of ways, and this isolation for long periods of time from any sort of innocent or full-hearted reading and the inhuman snobbery in relation to reading is one of the worst parts of it.

Gail Godwin (*Mr. Bedford and The Muses*, Viking): I read constantly. If I don't have a good book, I'm beside myself. I'm now in the throes of writing a new novel and I've been reading Dickens' *A Tale of Two Cities* and some Ibsen plays. I like the mood of the Ibsen plays. I want to see if I can get anything out of them to use in my book. I also read a lot of contemporary writing. That doesn't really affect my writing one way or the other, not the way it used to, because now I'm more sure of the way I write. I'm not so easily influenced by another voice.

Shirley Hazzard (*Transit of Venus*, Viking): Yes, I read all the time. I couldn't imagine my life without its current of reading. One doesn't read in connection with one's work, but in connection with life. If someone else's writing seeps into my own style, I tend to apply an antidote: too much Evelyn Waugh, for instance, could be countered with Yeats. For too much Jane Austen, the remedy of Lord Rochester. We have the luck of endless choices, limitless diversity. Only an idiot would try to confine reading tastes to currently acceptable *isms*. Reading is a private, intimate act for which we are accountable to no one.

   Good writing—great writing—gives courage. After reading Shakespeare, Tolstoy, a writer might ask, why write another line—it has all been said. But the appetite comes back. Again, like life. You have your own view to bring to it, your own connections to make. Our individuality, which the era implies is valueless, is restored to us in art; in reading and writing.

Walker Percy (*Lost in the Cosmos: The Last Self-Help Book*, Farrar, Straus & Giroux): I go back and re-read some of my favorites. Lately, I've been reading *Don*

Quixote and Dostoyevsky, books I still find stimulating and exhilarating, those which make me feel good. I also receive manuscripts and galleys of new writing, so much of which is bad, and I get a certain perverse satisfaction out of that. Most novelists are depressed and reading writers who are worse than you makes you feel better. What a sorry lot we writers are. It makes me think maybe I'm not so bad a writer. So I read both the good and the bad—the bad makes me think 'I'm better than this.' The truly great writing steadies me and puts me on track to do the best I can.

Ellen Schwamm (*How He Saved Her*, Knopf): I read poetry, essays, letters, diaries, and murder mysteries—anything but novels—while I'm writing. I'm reluctant to lose myself in another person's fictional world when I'm in the process of imagining one myself. There are times, however, when nothing else will do. Then I re-read novels I know well.

Joan Silber (*Household Words*, Viking): It doesn't seem to affect my style. Sometimes I hope it will. I tend to read writers who seem to be solving a problem that I am having trouble with. When I began the book I'm working on now, I started reading a lot of books to see how they got going. Beginning a book suddenly seemed mysterious to me. I read as sort of a warm-up, but I don't use any of it directly. I feel safer reading old writers—I can't imitate George Eliot.

William Styron (*This Quiet Dust*, Random House): I do read fiction while I write, but not a lot of it. It doesn't seem to hurt. It's probably valuable for younger writers to read fiction while writing. I don't see how someone can write unless he or she reads a lot. If writers have quality, they will eventually develop their own style anyway.

Daryln Brewer

The Plight of the First Novel

When Marilynne Robinson finished her first novel, *Housekeeping*, she showed it to a friend, also a novelist, who said, "This is a lovely book, but you'll never get it published." He sent it to his agent, Ellen Levine, anyway, who said, "This is lovely, but it may be difficult to get it published." Nevertheless, Levine agreed to represent Robinson, and sent the book to Pat Strachan at Farrar, Straus & Giroux. Strachan said, "It's a lovely book, but we can't predict it will sell well." Regardless, Strachan signed up the book and Farrar, Straus & Giroux published it.

The hardcover edition of *Housekeeping* had multiple printings, was nominated for the PEN/Faulkner Award, and won the $7,500 Hemingway prize. Robinson also won the $3,000 Richard and Hinda Rosenthal Award from the American Academy and Institute of Arts and Letters. The book sold to England, Norway, France, Germany, Israel, Holland, Italy, Spain, Denmark and Sweden. Bantam published a paperback edition in this country and Penguin published one in England. *Housekeeping* spent several weeks on the *Washington Post* bestseller list.

An Avid and Charitable Readership

"It would be churlish of me to be cynical about publishing and the first novel," says Marilynne Robin-

121

son. "I had an amazing experience and people went out of their way for a book they considered a bad commercial risk." Robinson believes an avid and charitable readership awaits good fiction. "I've received many fan letters, some very emotional. It's odd how many say *Housekeeping* reads like poetry—as if that is the ultimate compliment—and yet publishers feel that poetic fiction won't sell. I think a market does exist for poetic fiction, in spite of the cynicism about public taste. Readers do exist who don't like being condescended to, catered to, or exploited," she says.

"We publish the fiction we want at Farrar, Straus & Giroux and we've been very successful," says Pat Strachan. "Editors at some houses may have problems signing up serious first novels, but we don't consciously limit ourselves to a certain number. We just try to find special ones, since exceptionally fine writing is rarely lost on reviewers or readers. Early praise from Doris Lessing, Walker Percy and John Hawkes certainly didn't hurt, but the overwhelming reaction to *Housekeeping* is attributable to the text," she says.

"It was very important that my book was published by Farrar, Straus & Giroux," says Robinson. "The title, for instance, turned out to be a curse on the book. Some men wouldn't have looked at it if it hadn't been published by such a fine house." Her one complaint was that "Farrar, Straus & Giroux didn't advertise the book very much. It never got into the Cleveland stores. I have the best spies there—my relatives," she says.

Robinson advises a first novelist to "write for yourself—stay close to what you feel is your compulsion for writing. Don't try to calculate—if you do, your writing will be false and tired. Getting published is a long shot, but it's easier if you speak with your own authentic voice."

Like Sending a Child Off

Lee Goerner, an editor at Alfred A. Knopf, has been the editor of many first novels. For him, the most exciting part of publishing is "to get in on the beginning of a career. I like to make noise and get attention for a writer. I hope their career builds and builds, and that they grow as writers. The first book is just a step in a career—and though that first book may not represent a writer's best work, it has something especially exciting for a publisher. It's like sending a child off.

"Of course you don't send it off alone and unprotected," says Goerner. "This means you write personal notes to people in the industry, you present it enthusiastically to the salespeople, and even give copies to strangers in the street. In general, you become a pest. I want to be obsessive about a book," he says. "If you can't be, maybe it's better for everyone involved not to publish it."

Sometimes it's tough for publishers to convince a salesperson to push a first novel, but not at Knopf. "Our salespeople are extremely helpful and have a tremendous respect for first novels," says Goerner.

"I'm optimistic about the writing of first novels and about publishing them," he says. "In fact, I'd like to accept more first novels than I do—the problem is, I just don't get as many good ones as I'd like."

.001% of the Population

Elisabeth Sifton, Editor-in-Chief of the Viking Press, agrees. Writing in the *Nation* she said, "The unpalatable truth is that most of the novels sent to us are no good . . . most are mad, bad, banal, derivative or imitative—and apparently purposeless." If there is a crisis in the publishing of first fiction, Sifton blames it on the reader. "The American people are not reading serious books the way they used to, and especially they are not reading novels. The average first novel sells only about 2,000 to 4,000 copies. This readership represents about .001 or .002 percent of the population." Publishers, she said, were not to blame. "If the books are not selling, the publishers will not have money to offer authors, much less to advance for a book not yet completed."

Gangland—Four Years in the Re-writing

Although a first novel may indeed be completed when signed up by an editor, that doesn't necessarily mean it's ready for publication. Lee Goerner signed a contract with David Winn for his first novel, *Gangland,* and worked with Winn on three versions of the novel before it was finally published. "Publishing is also about setting up a relationship," says Goerner. "Taking on a first novelist depends on the rapport between the author and editor."

Gangland began as a series of short stories which were published in tiny, not just little, magazines such as *Synapse, Big Breakfast,* and *Thrilling Janitor.* The stories were written while Winn was at the University of California at Irvine as a graduate student, at the University of Colorado as a writing fellow, and finally in 1977 at the Squaw Valley Writers Conference. In Squaw Valley, he met novelist and critic Francine du Plessix Gray, who liked his work, and subsequently mentioned him in a *New York Times Book Review* article on writers' conferences. Soon Winn began to receive mail from publishers and agents. For that reason, he advises a first novelist to make connections. "I know conferences often get laughed at," he says, "but many are very good and you do meet agents and editors who can help you." After reading the article in the *Book Review,* Maureen Howard, whom Winn had previously met at the Colorado Writers Conference,

124

called to congratulate him. She recommended Gloria Loomis, a literary agent who has her own agency in New York. "Good thing she called, because I was very impressed by the Little, Brown and Harper & Row stationery," says Winn. He might have succumbed and gone directly to a publisher without an agent—but he thinks writers need agents. "Publishing is a commercial business and a writer isn't able to look after his own interests."

A Persistent Agent and Lots of Luck

Loomis sold *Gangland* within three months. "You must have a persistent agent and a certain amount of luck," says Winn. Although he always felt that he would somehow get published, Winn cites a book by a friend, which he says is "somewhat better than mine," and still hadn't found a publisher after eighteen months.

"Lee Goerner was an extremely fortunate choice as an editor," says Winn. "His sympathetic wit and bedrock realism couldn't be found in all editors. What separates Knopf from other houses is that editors are encouraged to find first novelists."

Bob Gottlieb (Knopf's Editor-in-Chief) presented Winn's book at sales conferences, which helped to launch it. "Of course I'm concerned about sales," says Winn, "but there's little rhyme or reason to it—it's a hapless attitude to think you can affect sales.

"People are receptive to fiction," says Winn. "Go back to the *Library Journal* articles on first novelists and count how many there are (213 in 1983). There has to be an audience and a commitment from publishers if that many first novelists are being given an opportunity to publish. I'm at odds with the shop talk that says there's no market for new fiction. The novel isn't dead. It's changing, vital and alive."

Winn hasn't made a living from writing fiction,

though. To supplement his income, he teaches at Hunter College in New York City. "There is a generation and a half of illiterate Americans," he says. "I feel an obligation to teach people to read and write."

The Times: Searching Out First Novels

Gangland was reviewed at the *New York Times* by book review editor Le Anne Schreiber [who has since left the *New York Times Book Review*]. "The single most gratifying thing for me is finding a first novel and taking it on its way to a reviewer or reviewing it myself," says Schreiber. "I get more feedback from reviews I write of first novels than from anything else," she says. "People tell me they buy first novels because they've read my reviews. I don't know how large the market for first novels is, but these readers are certainly engaged and interested in new talent.

"The *Times Book Review* is very interested in reviewing first novels, but time is needed to ferret out a special one—so many are touted by the publishers," says Schreiber. "Sometimes you have to go through five first novels to find one you want to review."

Schreiber thinks fiction is taking a fascinating turn. "In the last ten to fifteen years, fiction has been dominated by sociological concerns. Changes wrought by the women's movement were the subject of the novel. People have been reading for therapy as well as literary pleasures. Maybe this is coming to an end—now there is more possibility for the publication of novels which are less socially narcissistic, more about the creation of imaginative reality or the metaphysical, such as *Housekeeping* and *Gangland*."

In New York, Thirty Editors Who Care

"The part of my job that gives me the most pleasure is opening the manuscript box, not knowing what's inside and finding a first novel like *Housekeeping*," says

New York literary agent, Ellen Levine. In addition to selling *Housekeeping,* Levine has sold many other first novels. "But fewer publishers are willing to take a risk today—it used to be easier," she says. "You must make the distinction between commercial and literary fiction, though. A first novel that's a horror story, mystery or a family saga, particularly one suitable for paperback publication, may not be as much of a problem to get published. Serious fiction is much harder.

"I have encountered situations in which a sponsoring editor wanted to acquire a first novel—one with an estimated sale of 2,000-5,000 copies—and had to struggle against editorial boards." Levine estimates New York has thirty editors who are really interested in serious first novels. But that doesn't tell the whole story: an editor may care about first fiction but be working for a house that doesn't. Levine believes that "a novel which is appealing, shows talent and promise in a writer, but is not necessarily a masterpiece or a little jewel, might in better times have been published just to introduce a writer to the reading public."

Levine agrees there is an audience for fiction, but is unhappy about the cost of hardcover fiction. "Good reviews attract a reader, but that reader might be a college student or someone who can't afford $13.95 or $14.95 for a first novel. We must re-think the format—perhaps first novels should be published in trade paperback, making these books available at $6.95 or $7.95. When paperbacks are reviewed regularly, perhaps mass-market paperback houses will think about consistently publishing original serious fiction. In fact, several houses such as Bantam and Avon have already begun to do so.

"Although there are more agents than ever, it's more difficult to find an agent for a first novel because it's so hard to place first novels," says Levine.

"Agents are more likely to take on nonfiction writers."

For first novelists having a difficult time, Levine recommends the small press. "The small press is a growing phenomenon fulfilling a need," she says. "The advances are more modest, the printings smaller, and distribution isn't the same, but it's worth a try. After twenty commercial publishing houses have turned down a book, I try the small press. When you love a book, you can't give up. If a writer gets a first book published by the small press, perhaps the bigger publishers will pay attention to the second novel." Levine cited small presses such as Madrona, North Point, Creative Arts, Capra, Ecco, and Persea, and university presses such as Pittsburgh, Louisiana State, and Illinois.

"I always tell a first novelist what I think his or her chances are at the beginning," says Levine. Still, she advises, "Don't be discouraged. The main thing is not to give up. More than a few houses will stay committed to first fiction. As long as people like us are around, first fiction will get published."

Daryln Brewer

The Second Novel and Beyond

Jay Neugeboren's eighth book, *The Stolen Jew*, was published by Holt, Rinehart & Winston. But Holt originally turned down the novel, as did fifteen other publishers.

Neugeboren didn't give up, however. He turned his book into short stories, sold eighteen of them to commercial and literary magazines, revised *The Stolen Jew*, and sent it back to Holt. This time they bought the book.

Why did this happen? Although a writer such as Neugeboren may have gotten good critical acclaim on previous books and may have a solid, albeit small, following, a publisher must look hard at the balance sheets of past books. How many copies did they sell? Was there a paperback sale, a book club sale, a movie sale? In these uncertain economic times, a lukewarm sales record will dampen the spirit of even the most committed publisher. A first novel, at least, has the advantage of a blank track record, allowing an optimistic publisher to take a chance on a new writer.

Not the Next *Garp*

"The editors who considered buying *The Stolen Jew* said they admired my previous works and that this

129

book was clearly my most ambitious, perhaps even my best," says Neugeboren. "But they weren't looking for a big, complex novel by a writer with a mediocre track record. Generally speaking, publishers won't publish a novelist's third, or eighth, book unless they believe it's that writer's 'breakthrough' book—the next *Garp*."

The Stolen Jew did better than any of Neugeboren's previous novels—it sold to Pinnacle Books for paperback, had a small book club sale, was optioned for a film, won the Present Tense Literary Award for Best Novel of 1981, and had extensive reviews—eighty or ninety—including a rave in the *New York Times*. The book came close to selling out its first printing of 8,000 copies.

"Publishers these days tend not to look at a writer's career, but at each individual book," says Neugeboren. "There was a time, I'm told, when publishers stuck with a writer, and believed in him, hoping he would eventually find an audience.

"My last few books had hard times finding publishers, and that wasn't easy on me," Neugeboren says. "I suppose I was naive. I used to believe that writers could live with the expectation that, if they wrote well and worked hard, they would eventually be published. Having your novel go begging is a distinctly unpleasant experience, and there were many years when I was angry and bitter and unhappy, even though I knew that nobody had ever promised me, or any other writer, that we would be published, or reviewed, or read."

Neugeboren believes that writers ought not to concern themselves with the literary marketplace. "Think about the good of the work itself—write as well as you can," he says. "Trying to control the marketplace—your book's fate once it's been written—can lead to madness."

The audience for fiction—first book or eighth—is limited. "People won't think twice about spending ten or fifteen dollars on a movie and pizza, but not on a novel—a book that can give hours and years of pleasure," he says. "People also seem to have a harder and harder time doing what fiction reading requires—being alone with the written word, in the privacy of one's mind and imagination.

"There's a Yiddish saying, 'Everything past seventy years of age is a gift,' and I've come in recent years to feel that way about my work. I do what I want to do every day of my life. I have the freedom to write the novels and the stories I want to write, and that is a great luxury, a true joy. And I do, despite hard times, work on with some assurance that what I write will eventually be published. Everything else, I tell myself, is a gift."

The Trade Paperback Solution

Neugeboren's editor, Donald Hutter, who is now at Simon & Schuster, says, "In the '60's, a publisher who believed in an author was willing to publish several books by that writer, even if the anticipated sales were only 3,000-5,000 copies. A publisher bought a writer's book because the author was too good *not* to be published. Now the economy has made it impossible for publishers to go beyond a certain point and they are less inclined to keep non-profitable writers going."

Hutter thinks the trade paperback may be the solution. "It's a less expensive format for serious fiction, and should, in turn, permit a wider readership. The risk is that trade paperbacks get less review attention and fewer library sales, but that seems to be changing," he says.

"You Owe It to Your Publisher to Help"

Carolyn See is a West Coast writer who was "stubbornly obscure, and didn't know one person in the publishing business" before her first novel came out

131

from Little, Brown. The book sold about 3,000 copies, did not have a paperback sale, got only a few reviews in California and "was savaged by the *New York Times*." Coward, McCann published her next novel, *Mothers, Daughters,* which was a Book-of-the-Month Club alternate.

Even with four novels published, See is not well-known in the East. "I'm not angry that more people don't buy my books, I'm always a little surprised that they buy them at all," she says. "It never occurred to me that one of my early books would be on the bestseller list."

She explains her small following, most of which is in California, by the fact that she lives in the West. "I want to keep my California point of view, but I realize that I have to start meeting people and doing my part of the promotional job.

"A writer can't expect a nervous, tired and economically harassed editor to do all the promotion," she says. "I should go east more often to talk to reviewers, address women's clubs, get on radio and television, and put my books into the stores—all the things I do out here. I've given over 100 speeches and I've spoken only once in the East. A writer owes it to the publisher to do everything possible to sell books.

"My favorite writers—E.M. Forster and Christopher Isherwood—never had a bestseller," says See. "I keep writing because it's the most fun in the world and I'll keep writing as long as my audience gets larger, my books sell enough to keep my publisher in the black, and I at least have a fighting chance to become an important American voice."

"Midlist Target Marketing"

Sensible Solutions, Inc. is a New York organization that helps market "books that fail to reach more than a small percentage of the people in their primary market"—what they call "Midlist Target Marketing." Sensible Solutions helps to find and tap markets for a book, get blurbs and reviews, and gives advice on how to get on radio and television. They offer guidance on where to place stories and help write press releases. At the end of the process, the writer receives a marketing kit for executing the plan.

Mostly nonfiction writers or their publishers have come to Sensible Solutions so far—because of the expense—although Sensible Solutions has handled one novel and one book of poetry. The base cost to the publisher is $3,000, and Sensible Solutions expects clients to have another $3,000-$4,000 budgeted to implement the program they propose. The group will, however, read a book without charge to see if they can help market it; an hour's consultation is $80.

The cost may be less for writers who convince their publishers to do some of the work. "The plan can become a cooperative venture between author, publisher and us," says Florence Janovic of Sensible Solutions. "The author pays a total hourly fee of $400-$600 tops, we give the publisher the lists and letters, and they do the mailing," she says. "We look for writers who are both able and eager to use their time and contacts to attract readers."

Russian Roulette

A well-known literary agent, who wishes to remain anonymous, believes that hardcover publishing is more depressed now than ever before.

"Publishers used to break even on a book if it sold 3,000-5,000 copies. Now they're lucky to break even on 10,000. Look at the price they have to put on books."

Though the agent agrees that $15 is a lot to pay for a book, she also thinks it's more of a bargain than people realize. "A Pac-Man game, one of the less expensive computer games, costs more than that," she says. "There's certainly money out there, but publishers have not been smart about educating the reading public and we're not breeding readers in our public schools."

Though she says some publishers continue to stick with a good writer simply because a book *should* be published, most no longer have access to their "research and development money. High interest rates make publishers, like everyone else, more cautious," she says.

She sees several reasons why good books go unnoticed and sell so few copies, leaving worthy writers struggling to find publishers. "The chain bookstores are one problem—they only stock sure-fire things. Also, at one time a publisher could count on a small reprint sale. Now, more reprint houses are doing their own fiction originals, not buying from other publishers, so there's less income from reprints. Further, everything costs more, from printing to shipping.

"The *New York Times Book Review* doesn't help the situation either. They're very influential and they're reviewing books later and later." She cites a client of hers, a well-known poet, whose most recent book didn't get reviewed by the *New York Times* until three months after publication. "By that time all her books were back in the warehouse."

The returns policy in book publishing is another horror story, she says. "When it comes to actually selling a book, publishing is filled with so many imponderables, it's like playing Russian Roulette. What works for one book may not work for another. And then something totally unexpected happens, like *The Confederacy of Dunces*—suddenly it won a Pulitzer Prize and sold like crazy."

An Ardor for the Novel

"We try to be welcoming toward a book when we consider it for review," says Art Seidenbaum of the *Los Angeles Times Book Review*. "We don't punish a writer for not having previously been a commercial success. In fact, we try hard not to let commercial success decide whether or not we review a book." He admits, however, that "a first novel may have a better chance of getting reviewed than the fourth novel, unless something has happened to the writer by that time.

"I worry about many writers I admire," says Seidenbaum. "Fay Weldon, for instance, is one of the best women novelists today, she gets published loyally and reviewed, but she hasn't sold many books. I don't know how you change a Fay Weldon into a Marilyn French."

The *Los Angeles Times* reviews about 3,000 of the 40,000 books published each year. Seidenbaum estimates that even though less fiction is published than nonfiction these days, the *Los Angeles Times* reviews a greater percentage of fiction submitted than nonfiction. "That's because of our overall bias," he says. "There's an ardor for the novel around here."

Supporting Other Novelists

Todd Walton's first novel, *Inside Moves* (Doubleday), did quite well—it sold 8,000 copies and had a movie sale. His second book, *Forgotten Impulses,* was published by Simon & Schuster. Walton's third novel was also accepted by Simon & Schuster, but when his editor there left, the new editor dropped the book. The book then went on to twelve other publishing houses, until Dutton finally bought *Louis and Women.*

"When my book was making the rounds, I did feel homeless—I truly believed the myth that publishing was easier once your first novel was published. But ultimately I don't write because someone is going to give me something for it," he says. "I write because I have to. I'm completely internally motivated—not by making lots of money or by reaching millions. I feel lucky when 500 people read something I write. I'm not concerned about the rest of the world knowing about me."

Walton thinks having a good editor is vital. "I've done some book reviewing and was appalled by the lack of editing and rewriting. When I was young and cocky, I thought I was a genius, and I didn't want anyone to touch my prose. No longer. I've been blessed with good editors—which a writer needs, because you get so close to a book that in order to be objective, you'd have to put it aside for five years."

A writer also needs an editor with in-house power, says Walton. "There's schizophrenia in publishing houses between the editorial and sales departments. 20,000 copies of *Forgotten Impulses* were printed, and all the editorial people were excited, but my book got no support from the publicity or sales departments." *Forgotten Impulses* eventually sold only 2,000 copies.

"I know writers who are angry and bitter that they haven't received more attention," says Walton. "But the irony is that many writers who have published a hardcover book won't buy hardcover books by others. If writers bought each other's novels, we'd do fine, be it our first, third or eighth book. If we can't support each other emotionally and financially, how can we expect others to?"

Daryln Brewer

A Renaissance for Short Fiction?

"There's a renaissance in the short story," says Raymond Carver, author of four collections of short fiction. Statistics bear him out: in 1983, for the first time in seventeen years, the *O. Henry Prize Stories* collection was taken as an alternate by the Book-of-the-Month Club. In 1982, at least five new prizes were initiated for short fiction. And the August issue of *Redbook* (base circulation: 3.8 million), which contains as many as seven short stories, regularly outsells every other issue of the magazine.

No Longer a Poor Stepchild

"I wouldn't discourage anyone from writing a short story," says Carver. "The short story used to be regarded as a poor stepchild to the novel, but a well-made story is worth any number of bad novels."

Carver first started publishing his short stories over twenty years ago in little magazines introduced to him in a writing course given by the late John Gardner. "I read the magazines and sent my work to them," he says. "I didn't have an agent." Gordon Lish, then an editor at *Esquire,* gave Carver his first national exposure.

"Not every editor of a large magazine will be as encouraging as Gordon was," says Carver, "but I think now's a good time to be a short story writer. Many are getting serious attention. I think immediately of Tobias Wolff, Bobbie Ann Mason, Mary Robison and Barry Hannah. Plenty of others. I think collections are more viable and attractive to publishers than they once were. More people are reading short stories."

Short Story Advances—$1,000-$1,500

"People *are* reading more short fiction than they used to," agrees Rob Cowley, an editor at Random House. "In the late '70's, when I was at Houghton-Mifflin, I can remember being told that short stories sold worse than poetry, so I never published them." Now, at Random House, he does "because I believe in them. Too many novels exist that shouldn't—many are just overgrown short stories or novellas that really should be a short story—the oldest and most honorable form in literature."

Why the sudden optimism about the short story? "People are writing more accessible short fiction that has much more of a narrative quality to it, which has added to the popularity of the short story," says Cowley.

He believes that Ann Beattie was one of the first writers to turn the tide with her book of short stories, *Secrets & Surprises* (Random House). Although short-story collections usually sell between 1,000 and 2,500 copies, on a par with poetry, Beattie's book sold 7,000 copies and sold to paperback. "Not a big sale, but a sale," says Cowley. Her new book, *The Burning House,* also sold extraordinarily well for a book of short stories—about 20,000 copies.

Where does Cowley find good stories? "I usually hear of writers from other writers," he says. Cowley seldom reads literary magazines because he finds "too many academic stories. Going through quarterlies is wasted effort," he says. "You might read one good story, but what's to guarantee that person can write a lot of other good stories?"

Cowley tends to publish short story collections by writers who have written or will write a novel. "If you take a risk on a short story collection and don't do well, you might recoup your money on a novel by that author," he says. "I hate talking like a businessman, but I can't get around it. An editor can't afford to have too many books showing red ink." For that reason, advances for short story collections are generally very low—$1,000 or $1,500 for a collection.

"The advances look like they're out of the '40's," says Cowley, "but we have no guarantee we'll even make that much back. You can't tell if people will warm to an ordinary collection of short stories," he says. Cowley also warns that not every group of stories makes a good collection. "A successful collection must have coherence. Some are simply uncollectable."

"Dallas" or "Dynasty," Not *Collier's*

William Abrahams, editor of the *O. Henry Prize Stories* collection, feels that even though there is an audience for short fiction, a writer can't make a living at it. The *O. Henry* collection sells over 10,000 copies a year, "but the market for short fiction is small," says Abrahams. "The most striking change is that a considerable group of little magazines—*Ploughshares, Kenyon Review* and *Shenandoah,* for instance—put out as high a quality story as the *New Yorker* or the *Atlantic,*" he says. "I don't see a marked difference between them." However, unlike the *New Yorker* and the *Atlantic,* the little magazines don't pay much.

University presses, which are partially subsidized, are also publishing more short fiction. Some good examples are the University of Illinois Press, Louisiana State University Press and the University of Iowa Press.

Abrahams feels it's hard for a short story writer to break in. "The notion of the commercial story has drastically changed. Once upon a time, in the 1930's and '40's, we had the *Saturday Evening Post,* which published three or four stories a week. The old *Cosmopolitan* had a circulation of one million, and so did *Collier's.* All published fiction with a middle-brow orientation," he says. "Writers were paid thousands of dollars, and a short story writer could make a living then. But that kind of slick story—formula fiction— doesn't exist anymore. Instead, people watch an installment of 'Dallas' or 'Dynasty'."

The New Yorker

"I imagine today is a total reversal of the situation in the '30's and '40's," says Charles McGrath, one of six fiction editors at the *New Yorker.* "Writers used to write stories to pay the bills and write novels on their own time. Now that's flip-flopped. Writers have to write novels to pay the bills.

"The short story is alive and well," says McGrath, "but at the same time, a lot of the regular markets have dried up. Ted Solotaroff's magazine *(New American Review)* is gone and many others don't seem to have the same commitment to the short story. That hurts a writer," he says. "As difficult as it is to publish a novel, at least one can count on some money from a novel, but not from stories. For many, short story writing is a luxury."

McGrath thinks the situation may be changing, though, with the arrival of new magazines such as *Grand Street* and *Vanity Fair.* "What a writer needs is more than one market," he says.

The *New Yorker* receives between 200 and 500 stories a week and publishes about two a week. "The odds of getting published in the *New Yorker* are astronomical," says McGrath, "and the vast majority of the stories we do publish are by writers either known to us or who we have published before. I wouldn't submit a story if I really thought about the statistics," he says. "But we do publish ten or twelve new writers a year." Out of those, one or two come out of the unsolicited pile.

More often, though, a writer comes out of that pile, not a particular story. "On the strength of the story submitted, an editor will establish a relationship with a writer and begin encouraging him or her," says McGrath. "If we have any bias here, it's in favor of the brand new or young writer. We are open and eager to find new writers," which is, he says, an editor's great joy.

"We Read Every Manuscript We Receive"

The *New Yorker* pays a word rate for its stories, with a minimum of about $1,000. Every writer gets paid the same amount, famous or not, with or without an agent. "With a few writers we do have a reading agreement—the right to the first look at a story," says McGrath.

"We read absolutely every manuscript we receive," he says. "An efficiency expert would say that's certainly not the practical way of proceeding, but we have a commitment." Having an agent doesn't matter at the *New Yorker*. What an agent can do for a young writer is to send a manuscript directly to a particular editor, bypassing the unsolicited pile and "the first reader." The *New Yorker* has one full time reader and three or four who read unsolicited manuscripts, in addition to secretarial duties. A first reader who thinks a manuscript has potential will pass it along to one of the fiction editors. "Our first readers are extremely reliable and dependable," says McGrath. "If they make a mistake, it's on the side of optimism."

McGrath, who also teaches at Columbia University, says he sees many writers with good technical skills, but that "writers seem to be more conservative than they were. I see a lot less experimental writing now." He blames that partly on the economy and also on the fact that writers tend to imitate the generation above them. "Donald Barthelme was the most imitated. Now students seem to have gone back to imitating more realistic writers," he says.

Twentieth Story Accepted

Short story writer Bobbie Ann Mason was encouraged by Roger Angell, an editor at the *New Yorker*. "I didn't have an agent and I presumptuously sent the *New Yorker* a story," says Mason. "Roger Angell wrote and asked to see more of my stories, and that relationship was my incentive to work hard. I owe a lot to his encouragement—it put things into focus and gave me a goal. Someone thought I had talent," she says. "I don't think I could have done it without that encouragement." The *New Yorker* finally accepted her twentieth story.

"I don't have ten or fifteen years worth of rejection slips because I took a ten-year break from writing," says Mason. She wrote while in college, but stopped while she got her Ph.D. in Literature from the University of Connecticut. "It doesn't seem to have mattered that I spent the last ten years not writing. I just waited until I got older and was ready."

Mason has been published in the *Atlantic, Redbook,* and a few little magazines, including *Virginia Quarterly Review, Bloodroot,* and the *North American Review.* Her collection, *Shiloh and Other Stories,* was published in 1982 by Harper & Row. "I'm embarrassed because getting published seemed so easy," she says.

Mason got an agent when Amanda Urban at International Creative Management came to her. "I don't think anyone needs an agent for getting short stories published in magazines, but I do think an agent is essential for publishing books," says Mason, who's now writing a novel. Mason's advice: "Don't be disappointed if you're not successful right out of college. It takes time."

How an Editor Feels That Day

"What happens to a short story is almost an accident," says a New York literary agent who wishes to remain anonymous. "Often when I think an editor will buy something he won't, and when I think he won't, he will. It's easy to sell short fiction by a big-name writer because it helps the magazine, but it's difficult to sell fiction by an unknown writer," she says. "Selling short fiction frequently depends on how an editor is feeling that particular day, what he or she is bringing to the piece."

The agent tells a little short story of her own, illustrating how important perseverance is for writers: "I submitted a story everywhere, to no avail. I put it away for four years. When I took it out again, I took the staples out of the cover, retyped the cover page, restapled it and sent the story out again. The first magazine editor who read it, bought it. The editor said he remembered reading it in an earlier version and remarked how the writer had grown. Word for word it was exactly the same story."

Daryln Brewer

Major Prizes in Short Fiction

Associated Writing Programs. An annual award in short fiction, for a book-length manuscript. The award includes publication and an invitation to read at the AWP annual spring meeting, for an honorarium of $1,000. Associated Writing Programs, Old Dominion University, Norfolk, Virginia 23508.

Chicago/Nelson Algren Award. $5,000 given annually for an outstanding unpublished short story between 2,500 and 10,000 words. Open to writers living in the United States. The winning story will be published in *Chicago* Magazine. The Nelson Algren Award, c/o *Chicago* Magazine, 3 Illinois Center, 303 East Wacker Drive, Chicago, Illinois 60601.

Drue Heinz Literature Prize. For a collection of short fiction: $5,000 cash award and publication by the University of Pittsburgh Press. Open to all writers who have published a book-length collection of short fiction or who have had three short stories or novellas published in commercial magazines. Drue Heinz Literature Prize, University of Pittsburgh Press, Pittsburgh, Pennsylvania 15260.

Iowa Short Fiction Award. $1,000 plus publication for a collection of short fiction at least 150 pages long. The Iowa School of Letters Award for Short Fiction, Department of English, English-Philosophy Building, University of Iowa, Iowa City, Iowa 52242.

The Aga Khan Fiction Prize. $1,000 and publication in the *Paris Review,* given annually for an unpublished story between 1,000 and 10,000 words. *The Paris Review,* 541 East 72 Street, New York, New York 10021.

Mademoiselle Fiction Contest. For a short story under 5,000 words. Open to writers 18-30 years of age whose work has not been previously published in a magazine with a circulation over 25,000. First prize: $750 plus publication in *Mademoiselle.* The Fiction Department, *Mademoiselle* Magazine, 350 Madison Avenue, New York, New York 10017.

The Flannery O'Connor Award Series. The University of Georgia Press publishes original short fiction in a series honoring Flannery O'Connor. Open to both published and unpublished writers.

Winners will receive a $500 cash award and publication by the University of Georgia Press under a standard publishing contract. The Flannery O'Connor Short Fiction Award Series, University of Georgia Press, Athens, Georgia 30602.

PEN Awards. The PEN/Nelson Algren Fiction Award. For the best uncompleted novel or short story collection by an American writer who needs financial assistance to complete the work. In addition to a $1,000 cash award, the winner will be given a month-long residency at "The Barn," the Edward Albee Foundation's summer residence for writers and artists in Montauk, Long Island, New York 11954.

PEN/Faulkner Award for Fiction. $5,000 for the best work of fiction (novel or short stories) published in the preceding year by an American writer.

The Ernest Hemingway Foundation Award. $7,500 for a published first novel or first collection of short stories published in the preceding year. PEN American Center, 568 Broadway, 4th floor, New York, New York 10012.

Redbook Short Short Story Contest. An award for short short fiction of not more than nine pages. In addition to a monetary award, the prize includes publication of the winning story in *Redbook* magazine. Open to men and women over eighteen who have not published (or had accepted for publication) fiction in a magazine with a circulation of over 25,000. *Redbook*'s Short Short Story Contest, Box S-S, 224 West 57 Street, New York, New York 10019.

The St. Lawrence Award for Fiction. $1,000 given annually to the author of an outstanding first collection of short fiction published in North America during the preceding year. *fiction international,* St. Lawrence Award for Fiction, English Department, St. Lawrence University, Canton, New York 13617.

Syndicated Fiction. Given by the NEA and PEN American Center. $250 and publication of a short story in one of ten participating newspapers across the country. An additional $150 will be awarded for each newspaper acceptance of a story. Unpublished short stories of 4,500 words or less may be submitted. Writers eligible to submit stories are recipients of individual grants for creative writing from the Literature Program of the NEA, recipients of a state arts agency or regional fellowship in literature, recipients of any national literary award, current members of PEN American Center, and writers currently listed in the *Directory of American Poets and Fiction Writers*. Stories will be chosen based on their literary quality and suitability for a general newspaper audience. PEN Syndicated Fiction Project, c/o the Writers Center, 4800 Sangamore Lane, Bethesda, Maryland 20816.

Writing for Young Adults

When Paul Zindel, playwright, screenwriter, and writer for young adults, first appeared on NBC's "Today Show," the TV show generally considered the most effective for promoting books and authors, he was not there to discuss his Pulitzer Prize-winning play, *The Effects of Gamma Rays on Man-in-the-Moon Marigolds,* or how it feels to earn $100,000 for writing a screenplay (he did for *Mame*). He was on TV to promote his novel for young adults, *Confessions of a Teenage Baboon,* for which Bantam had just given a minimum guarantee of $125,000 for paperback reprint rights. According to Zindel, his 1977 TV interview was not only the first time a writer for young adults had been on the "Today Show" to promote a novel, but also the first "adult" publicity tour Bantam had ever arranged for the author of a novel for teenagers. "They told me I was going to 'barnstorm' the country," says Zindel. "Young-adult novels could no longer be ignored."

Writing with Passion and Compassion

Although writers for young adults may have felt ignored by popular media and by paperback publishers until recently, there has always been a large hardcover market for "juveniles"—books for readers aged about thirteen to sixteen. The difference is that since the late 1960's the market's scope has broadened considerably, and now problems and ideas that used to remain unmentioned are the themes of popular books. The young-adult paperback market has grown, too, both in schools, where the books may be assigned reading, and in bookstores, where some of the novels are bought by adults as well as young people.

Two editors are usually given much of the credit for this change: Ursula Nordstrom, former publisher of Harper Junior Books, and Charlotte Zolotow, editorial consultant and editor of Harper Junior Books, and the author of over sixty books for children and teenagers. "The changes that have come about in children's books," Charlotte Zolotow wrote in *Prism,* "stem mainly from our acknowledging the intensity of a child's emotion and the ability and need of children to cope with the gruesome and tragic, the violent and hostile, as well as with the sweet and the lovely."

Charlotte Zolotow discovered Paul Zindel when she saw an NET adaptation of *Man-in-the-Moon Marigolds* in 1967, before it was ever on Broadway. "I was impressed by the compassion he showed for the teenagers in that play," she says. "I was sure he understood them." Zindel was in Houston at the time, on a Ford Foundation playwriting grant. He had taught high-school chemistry for ten years on Staten Island, had never heard of Charlotte Zolotow, and had no idea what a young-adult novel was. "I went off to the Houston Public Library to study it all," he says, "and I found nothing in those young-adult books that was from the real world." Encouraged by Zolotow, he wrote *The Pigman* (published in 1968), for which Harper's paid him a $1,000 advance and Dell paid a modest $9,000 for paperback rights. *The Pigman* also earned $40,000 for a one-year movie option.

Zindel has never stopped writing for adults. "The problem with writing is pacing yourself," he says. "Most writers need to do something different after they finish a play or novel. I couldn't do two young-adult novels back-to-back. I need variation, and I think other writers do, too."

Weren't there anything but mysteries and will-he-ask-me-to-the-prom books for teenagers before 1968? Charlotte Zolotow cites *Harriet the Spy* by Louise Fitzhugh (Harper & Row, 1965) as an earlier breakthrough for a slightly younger reader (ages 9-12). "It was the first time an adult drank a martini in a children's book. People were shocked." As with virtually all successful children's and teenager's books, it is still in print.

Perhaps the earliest honest novel for teenagers, one that is mentioned by almost every young-adult writer and editor as a seminal work in young-adult literature, is *The Catcher in the Rye* (Little, Brown, 1951). "J.D. Salinger was able to hit both audiences," says Paul Zindel. "He captured the mood and speech of kids, and yet there's a lot there that only adults would understand."

A Compulsive Theme

Paul Zindel is not the only successful writer for adults who has found himself writing for a younger audience and liking it. Robert Cormier is an award-winning journalist from Massachusetts who has published three novels for adults and over 75 short stories. Since 1974 he has also published five popular, highly respected young-adult novels, including *The Chocolate War* and *I Am the Cheese* (both Pantheon). Each was selected by the *New York Times* as an "Outstanding Book of the Year" and now has a teacher's guide available for it. Dell paid $100,000 for paper-back rights to *I Am the Cheese* before it was even out in hardcover.

Cormier's adult novels were well-reviewed too—the first one, *Now and At the Hour* (Coward McCann), was on *Time*'s "recommended" list for five weeks. The advances and print runs were small, however, and the books never made Cormier well-known or earned him much money. Now he's reviewed from coast to coast, his young-adult novels can be found in book-stores and libraries all over the country, and he gets mail every week from his readers. How did he hit this nerve?

"I didn't consciously set out to write about young people," he says, "but there came a time when my home was occupied by a son and two daughters in the throes of adolescence. Their lives see-sawed between ecstasy and despair, often during a single afternoon. They fell in and out of love as swiftly and flamboy-antly as the seasons change. I realized they were living a life far more exciting, more excruciating, more intriguing than mine. I began to write more and more about them, matching their comings and goings with memories of my own. But I did not set out to write for them but about them."

When Cormier was writing *The Chocolate War*, he didn't even know about the young-adult book market. "I wrote it the same way, with the same attention and passion that I had for my earlier books. Once again it was a matter of a compulsive theme."

The first publishers to read *The Chocolate War* thought it was too downbeat, with too many charac-ters. Cormier disagreed and refused to change it. Finally Pantheon accepted it as written and published it as a young-adult novel. It was the first time Cormier had ever heard of the category.

Pantheon paid him a $2,500 advance, and he still

receives hardcover royalties. The paperback sold for $36,000, which, like all paperback fees, was split with the hardcover publisher.

"You Can't 'Write Down' to Teenagers"

"When I finished *I Am the Cheese* I was afraid that this time I might have lost my young-adult audience," says Cormier—"that this ending really was too unhappy. But Pantheon respects teenage readers and knows they can absorb a downbeat ending." Again Pantheon published the book without changing it.

What if Pantheon had found *I Am the Cheese* too tough for teenagers—would Cormier have softened it? "No. I've never tailored a book to an audience. And you can't 'write down' to teenagers. If a book is written for teenagers, it's not written for me. I don't regard myself as a 'young-adult' author. Any story or novel, if written honestly and without regard for a specific audience, will set off shocks of recognition across a broad range of readers."

Cormier enjoys talking to high-school classes about his books, finding the students "eager, intelligent, and sharp. There is no audience so responsive, so caring, so quick to be passionate about a book, so innocently critical and so marvelously appreciative," he says.

You Can Explore an Idea Deeply

Who are these responsive, passionate readers? Officially they're boys and girls aged thirteen to sixteen, but actually they're probably any reader, aged ten and up, who likes a good story. "One difference between a very good young-adult novel and a good adult novel is weight," says Elaine Edelman, a poet and former editor at Harper Junior Books. "Storyline is important, so there are generally fewer characters in a young-adult novel and its focus is usually stronger and more cohesive."

Edelman pointed out several publishing crossovers, books such as *Sounder* and *Freaky Friday* which Harper & Row marketed for young adults but which are often read by adults. Or the reverse—a book such as *The Empty Chair* by Bess Kaplan, which came out in Canada as an adult book, but which Harper & Row published in the U.S. for teenagers.

"The young-adult novel is a wonderful place for an author to explore a new theme or idea more deeply," says Edelman, "because these books have a longer time to establish themselves. They get more reviews and more kinds of reviews."

Books for young adults get trade reviews (newspapers, magazines) and they get a full panoply of library (both public and school) reviews. Through sheer volume and variety of reviews, then, a book has a better chance to become known and approved. A book that doesn't do particularly well in trade reviews gets, in effect, a second chance in the trade world; paperback publishers, for example, now pay attention to both review systems. "In general, a book for teenagers isn't stopped so quickly by one bad review, the way an adult book may be," says Edelman. "All of this takes a certain pressure off the writer."

"You Use a Broad Brush . . ."

So a young-adult novel can be about anything, as long as it has a teenage protagonist or a subject that interests today's teenagers—right? Not quite.

"You are always aware that you have a teenage audience," says Marijane Meaker, who has published ten books for teenagers, including *Dinky Hocker Shoots Smack*, under the pseudonym M.E. Kerr. "The writing is not as subtle as for adults. You wouldn't put in a racial slur, for example, without immediately letting the reader know it's wrong. But although you use a broad brush and always write from a kid's point of view, I don't find that confining. I can just relax and tell a story."

Norma Klein, another prolific novelist for both adults and teenagers, is a little more discouraged. She let one of her books be "tailored" for teenagers and was sorry afterward. Klein's first novel for young adults, *Mom, the Wolfman and Me,* has an 11-year-old protagonist, but was considered strong stuff for teenagers because the girl lives happily with her mother, who has never married. When Klein brought the manuscript to Pantheon another publisher was already interested in the book but wanted to clean it up. Pantheon published *Wolfman* as Klein had written it, but some librarians objected to it. In some areas, students had to have written permission from their parents in order to borrow the book; in others, it was taken off the shelves.

When Klein brought in her second manuscript for young adults, *It's Not What You Expect,* Pantheon edited it to make it palatable to librarians. "I would never agree to that again," Klein says now. "A year later I was too angry." Dial Press found another answer for Klein's young-adult novel, *It's Okay If You Don't Love Me.* They marketed it as an adult novel, even though the book's two main characters are high-school students and it is probably read mostly by high-school students. But by calling it "adult," Dial avoided problems with libraries.

"I get a lot of positive feedback about my books, not just complaints," says Norma Klein, "and I think my reputation as a writer for young adults is good, so that editors and librarians should trust what I write." Klein stays with the field because she likes bringing realistic books into it. "Of course teenagers can and should read everything, but they enjoy reading about people their own age, like everyone else."

Alice Childress, a playwright and screenwriter, also

suffered library censorship when her young-adult novel, *A Hero Ain't Nothin But a Sandwich,* was one of several taken out of circulation in an Island Trees, New York school library. *Hero* treats a 14-year-old black boy's heroin addiction and its effect on him and his family. "You do meet with resistance," says Childress—"not from the kids, who can read adult books if they want, but from adults who see you as teaching their kids bad language and practices."

Study the Field: There's a Future

Charlotte Zolotow of Harper & Row believes that every writer has one good young-adult novel inside, based on experiences in his or her youth. Writers interested in trying out this field should first read widely in it. They should remember that hardcover advances are still relatively small. Norma Klein got only $4,000 from Dial Press for *It's Okay If You Don't Love Me,* her seventh young-adult novel. But Norma Klein can write a novel for young adults in two weeks. Paul Zindel needs a year—about six months for research, which includes everything from daydreaming to interviewing with a tape recorder, and six months for two drafts.

Once the book is out, it will most likely be bought by libraries, both school and public. It will be kept in stock by them, replaced when necessary because every year brings a new generation of readers to whom people like Paul Zindel, Alice Childress, and Norma Klein are brand-new discoveries. Since the hardcover advance was low to begin with, it is quickly earned back and then the author earns hardcover royalties.

Since paperback publishers have discovered that young-adult novels can be sold to both educational and trade markets, paperback fees are growing. There is increased movie interest in the books as well.

A pilot for a TV series was based on *If I Love You, Am I Trapped Forever?* by Marijane Meaker. A writer for young adults is still more likely to talk to teachers' and librarians' conventions than to TV talk-show hosts, but for the writer interested in young people, the conventions are more to the point.

Young-adult novels are almost always written in the first person, with the story seen through a teenager's eyes. The memoir-type novel is discouraged by editors in the field. The teenage narrator may limit a writer's language, but the humor and depth of feeling in the novel can be expansive. For many authors, writing for teenagers is satisfying and can offer variation from other work.

"Writers speak out our fears for us," says Alice Childress. "This is an especially important discovery for teenagers. They are so relieved to find out other people feel what they do. Then they don't feel so damned."

Debby Mayer

Underground Writing: Genre Fiction

In one mood, or in one crowd, the serious writer writes fairy tales; in another he writes ponderous novels; in still another, dirty limericks. A great writer is not great because he never writes dirty limericks but because, if he does write one, he tries to write a very good one.

John Gardner, Antaeus, Winter/Spring 1981

Survival is the key word, money the bottom line—the reason many poets and fiction writers use finely honed skills to produce romances, screenplays, adventure stories, novelizations, pornography, or other people's books. The following five chapters explore "underground" writing: the ways in which writers write to earn a living.

A Serious Writer, by any Other Name?

Martin Cruz Smith, whose *Gorky Park* (Random House) spent weeks on the *New York Times* bestseller list, resisted getting an office job while he worked on that book. "I figured any job I got would consist of some kind of writing, probably copy for something like *Cellophane Age*," he says. "The last thing I'd want to do after that is come home and write some more." Instead he freelanced on the side: 35 novels, most of them paperbacks—westerns, mysteries, and spy novels.

Smith got started in the '60's as a writer/editor at a company called Magazine Management, which churned out adventure magazines, confession and movie magazines, and comic books. He worked with Mario Puzo, Patricia Bosworth and Bruce Jay Friedman, among others. They worked hard. "Sometimes we had to do a 15-page story in an evening, but we thought nothing of it," says Smith.

He left Magazine Management in 1968 and went to work in Portugal. By chance, on his way back to the States, he met an American paperback editor in Paris who signed up his first paperback adventure. Only after a couple of years did his agent take over and begin to get paperback assignments for him.

Smith has used many pseudonyms to write paperbacks "of a fairly primeval order, but which kept me writing fiction. They're also a good learning ground, and with most writers earning so little, I was proud just to survive by writing."

Smith admits it was hard to work at both "underground" fiction and his own fiction simultaneously, but he still found it better than working for someone else. "Doing mind-numbing work for others is no good. For myself it was O.K."

Smith's advice: "If you're writing a book just for the money, always try and make it better than it has to be. It's important not to denigrate yourself, even if you're using the category."

No Time for Henry James

John Bowers, whose novel *The Colony* (E.P. Dutton) was well-received, worked with Smith on Magazine Management's adventure magazines while he wrote his own fiction. "One of the rewards of working there was learning narrative technique," he says. "We wasted no time getting someone through a door. We couldn't fool around with Jamesian language. We learned how to hold a reader's attention, and to move people and emotions quickly, something which often gives beginning writers a hard time.

"Martin Cruz Smith and Mario Puzo trained at Magazine Management," says Bowers. "They each gave *The Godfather* and *Gorky Park* an added dimension, but the technique—a fast, lively story, with resonant, easily understood characters—came straight from Magazine Management."

Bowers enjoyed letting his imagination run wild. "I could invent battles in World War II, crime waves on the East Coast that never happened, or any conflict between man and woman."

Magazine Management also paid well. Bowers made $150 a week as an editor there. Each 15-page article he wrote earned him about $400, and he could do "as many as my brain could take, usually one or two a month." He also rewrote pieces for about $150 each, and condensed books for $100 apiece.

"Beginning writers are now doomed to write for newspapers or literary magazines, which don't pay," he says. "Magazine Management no longer exists. It's gone, like the Bloomsbury Group."

Bodice Rippers

Another Magazine Management graduate is Mary Bringle *(Fortunes,* Putnam) who found such magazines as *Screen Stars, Movie Album,* and *Movie World* good training for her fiction. "One of the stories I wrote was 'The Night Elvis Presley and Ann-Margret Had a Blind Date.' It was complete fiction," she says. Much of Bringle's income has come from writing what she calls "Bodice Rippers," or "Burning Loins"—long, juicy romances.

Bringle has written up to 500 pages in 6-10 weeks, depending on the contract. Her first, an historical romance called *Mara,* sold 100,000 copies and earned her roughly $13,000, including bonuses for historical research and completing the manuscript on time. Her second was a contemporary romance called *An Elegant Affair.* A teenage gothic, *Don't Walk Alone,* was also published by Scholastic Book Club.

Bringle got her first "Bodice Ripper" assignment through "a friend of a friend" who put her in touch with Richard Gallen Associates, a book packager for historical and contemporary romances. Although Bringle didn't have to, a writer usually submits a three-page proposal and a writing sample to Gallen.

He hires and pays the writer, then negotiates with the paperback publisher—Dell, Pocket, and many others. Writers also receive a royalty.

If quickie paperbacks have a professional bonus, these writers agree it's in teaching discipline. "You have to throw yourself into a book and keep hundreds of threads going at once," says Bringle. "I learned a lot about novelistic skills such as structure, and that mystifying process when you can't see ahead, and then suddenly you find the key to a story and it takes shape."

Although Bringle won't do a "quickie" if it takes time from her own writing, she takes all her books seriously. Even after a "Bodice Ripper" is finished, she finds herself still "plotting, spitting it out, past the point of the ending. I get emotionally tied to my characters. Those books are hard to let go, especially when they tap into teenage fantasy, which is a strong and bittersweet memory. You'd think that would only happen to a novel you care about."

Nevertheless, there is one important difference— ideas for the romances originate with someone else. "An idea of my own is not necessarily more successful, but working on it does feel different—there's more ego investment and I put more care into it," says Bringle.

Hack Writers and Athletes

John Calvin Batchelor (*Birth of the People's Republic of Antarctica,* Dial) a novelist and a book reviewer, has also been what he calls a "bullyish editor" and has done some rewriting for romantic suspense novels such as *North Sea Mistress* and *Heart of the Harbor.* His name doesn't appear with the author's on any of the books, but he received 25% of the royalties. "At $1,250 per year, that was my major source of income for five years," says Batchelor.

Batchelor agrees with John Gardner that writers have within them many kinds of writing. "To my surprise, I have the gothic novel within me. It's a genre rich in history, a satire of Jane Austen. I'm pleased to have worked on them and to have made money doing so." Batchelor and his author, Katrinka Blickle, made a natural team. She had been reading gothics all her life and knew the format; he helped with the prose. Blickle had an old school friend at Doubleday who signed up their first book.

Batchelor and another friend have also written an off-beat thriller about a nuclear accident, as yet unpublished. But he warns against using writing skills on subjects that don't challenge the mind. "Hack writing can abuse one's natural gift. Like an athlete, a writer must train and practice every day. But playing in a pick-up game can hurt one's talent and sense of oneself. Such work can be draining, debilitating, and maddening."

Batchelor mistrusts the siren song of Hollywood, and as for pornography—"it ruined Jack London and didn't do Burroughs any good."

Daryln Brewer

Underground Writing: Screenwriting

In an age when many people see more films than they read books, screenwriting might seem a natural way for poets and fiction writers to use their skills and supplement their incomes. But how do you break in? Is it worth it when you do? Can a writer think for both print and screen?

A Good Track Record

"Some screenwriters write poetry, but very few poets write screenplays," says Mark Strand—poet, fiction writer, and part-time screenwriter. In 1969, Strand made a few thousand dollars writing a screenplay which was never produced. "I could have gone to Hollywood and tried to become a screenwriter," he says. "I thought all you needed were brains and desire—and brains, I thought, were not in long supply out there." Instead, Strand stayed east and concentrated on his poetry.

"Writing for the screen isn't easy," he says. "To start, they want a 15-page treatment. You might as well write a 15-page story and try to sell it to the *New Yorker*—it's a surer thing.

"And it's hard working in the industry from the

161

outside. You can eventually make a lot of money, but only if you connect with those on the inside. If one screenplay goes, that helps the second time around," says Strand. In screenwriting, like most anything else, a good track record helps.

Instant Deadlines, Fast Money

"Screenwriting is another experience for writers, and writers need all the experience they can get," says novelist Hilma Wolitzer (*In the Palomar Arms*, Farrar, Straus & Giroux) who has also written for feature films and television.

Although Wolitzer looks positively upon her screenwriting experience, she warns that it's much different from writing fiction. "As a screenwriter, you must concede that you have no real power over the script. A lot of other people are involved—producer, director, actors—who will reinterpret your script. All changes are left to them in the end, and this can be quite painful. Something you think is literate or funny is taken out, or something they like but you don't goes in."

The biggest advantage to writing for the screen seems to be the money. That's why Wolitzer did an episode for the old TV series "Family." "It's good, fast money—if you can work quickly and meet instant deadlines," she says.

Wolitzer was given a plot outline with the established characters. She spent one month on a one-hour script and earned about $10,000 plus residuals. "The Writers Guild contract protects your right to residual earnings any time a portion of your work is shown," she says.

Wolitzer also made good money, considering the time spent, writing two episodes for a PBS series, "Up and Coming." She was offered a flat writing fee of $3,000 for each episode, and if the films were produced, an additional $5,000. She wrote one of the two half-hour scripts in a weekend. The other was more difficult, required more revision, and took longer. Both were produced and she made $16,000.

Wolitzer also wrote a television screenplay of her first novel, *Ending,* and adapted her second novel, *In the Flesh,* for the screen. For *In the Flesh,* she wrote a narrative outlining the plot for which she was paid $1,250 on commencement and $1,250 on completion. A first draft of the screenplay paid an additional $12,500.

In the Flesh was never produced, however. In fact, many works optioned never make their way to the silver screen. "You're disappointed the first time, but then you get used to it. It's a pleasant surprise when something is produced," says Wolitzer.

Writing a screenplay from one's own novel poses particular problems. Although her third novel, *Hearts,* was quickly optioned, Wolitzer turned down the chance to write the screenplay. "Changes always have to be made when writing a screenplay from a novel, because fiction is introspective, not cinematic," she says. "I was still too close to the material and the characters to do that."

Screenwriting may delay her fiction slightly, but doesn't interfere with Wolitzer's creative process. "It takes time, like teaching, but it doesn't use the same kind of psychic energy. I wouldn't accept a script if I were actively writing a novel. But when I'm not engaged in fiction, I'm glad to be busy doing something productive."

Free to Starve

Al Young, a poet and novelist, who has also written for the screen, is less encouraging about film writing than Hilma Wolitzer. "In Hollywood, writers are the pariah of the industry. Producers, directors, and actors tend to feel that they'd be able to do what the writer does if they just had a few spare weekends."

Young was the second writer brought in on the Richard Pryor movie, "Bustin' Loose." He got paid, but didn't receive credit. The same thing happened to him on "A Piece of the Action," with Bill Cosby and Sidney Poitier. He also wrote an adaptation of Dick Gregory's autobiography. Again, he got paid, but producer/director Joseph Strick never made the film. "It even happens to people like Strick, who is a very literary-oriented producer," says Young. He wrote the screenplay for his own novel, *Sitting Pretty*, but the company, First Artists, went out of business. Young was also the "initial scenarist" on "Sparkle." It was produced, but Young still calls himself, "an uncredited, backroom writer in Hollywood." Even though he's been able to buy enough time to write novels from his earnings as a screenwriter, he hasn't been credited on a single film.

A writer may go uncredited when several writers work on the same screenplay; usually only the writer who contributed the most will get credit. When a screenplay is finished, each writer receives a "Notice of Tentative Credit" and may read the final script. A writer may protest lack of credit, sending the case into arbitration under the direction of the Writers Guild.

"I've usually been brought in to adapt someone else's idea," says Young. "From now on, I'll write only original screenplays—that's better both financially and psychologically. It's harder for others to tinker with your idea."

He agrees that screenwriting pays well, but finds it imaginatively unrewarding. He also finds many expensively produced films of "wretched quality" and is particularly disturbed by what he calls an unstated boycott on black material. "When times get tough, as they are now, the minorities get hurt," he says. "Films and television are backsliding in terms of racial equality."

Writing screenplays has had both positive and negative effects on Young's fiction. "It can be fun because you learn to think like a camera: no narrator, no voices jumping in, just action. Screenwriting made my fiction more lucid."

Yet friends of Young have been seduced by the money and never returned to fiction. "I also learned about being kicked around. I thought academic malice was bad until I went to Hollywood—it's scandalously inhumane."

Writing for the screen, then, can help fiction indirectly. "Screenwriting sends you back to your own writing feeling like the freest man in the world," he says. "Even if you're free to starve."

Selling Ideas

In 1977, novelist Rhoda Lerman and actress Jean Stapleton were working together on a charity function. Lerman wrote a monologue for Stapleton; Stapleton thought it was so good that she took Lerman straight to Norman Lear. Lerman subsequently wrote a two-hour teleplay about Eleanor Roosevelt for Norman Lear. She has also written an original screenplay for 20th-Century Fox, and her two novels have been optioned for the screen and for a musical. "Movie options are a nice amount of money for not having to do anything," says Lerman.

"It's fun to be in Hollywood," she says. "There's lots of action, power, and movement. And plenty of room for writers with good ideas." But Lerman says a writer must learn how to sell those ideas—and have the knowledge to back them up. "Expertise gets you in at a higher level, higher than writing for the soaps," she says. "There may have been better writers to do the teleplay of Roosevelt, but I knew a lot about her."

165

Got an idea? Lerman suggests writing it in two pages. "If it doesn't fit on two pages, it probably isn't a good idea," she says. "The simplest ideas are the best. Make those two pages pithy, well-written, fresh and clear. And don't be vague." Then, after researching agents who handle film and television, she suggests putting three or four ideas together and sending them to an agent. "Talent does win out," she says.

Another way to break in is to watch the credits on a television show. Try writing a script for that show, and send it directly to the producer with a good letter. And finally, Lerman advises to remember that "without a track record, you must have a good product."

"I Prefer Writing Books"

Writing for the screen hasn't hurt Lerman's fiction. "It helped structure my fiction, cut down on my wordage, and gave me a specificity I didn't have before," she says. "It forced me to think of one scene at a time, to use one line to get an idea across, and to think visually."

Lerman thinks the difference between writing fiction and writing for the screen is in the audience. "When screenwriting, you're working for an enormously large audience, so you must write for them," she says. "Sometimes when I go back to fiction, my work feels inaccessible, since I don't write fiction for an audience."

It's clear that all these writers write for the screen for one reason: money. Yet there is more to screenwriting than the money. Lerman praises the Writers Guild. "The union is good: you get free prescriptions, life insurance and medical care. It protects a writer, much more so than in the literary world." Only one hitch. "I prefer writing books," she says.

Daryln Brewer

Definitions for the Screenwriter

Initial Scenarist: First writer on any screenplay.

Option: Money paid to a writer for a book or other literary material which gives a producer rights to that material for a limited amount of time.

Screenplay: The final script with individual scenes, full dialogue and camera set-ups.

Story: Literary or dramatic material indicating principal characters and containing sequences and action suitable for use in a final script.

Teleplay: A script written for primary release on television.

Treatment: An adaptation of a story, book or other literary material for motion picture purposes in a form suitable for use as the basis of a screenplay. When a story is written specifically for the screen it is referred to as an *original treatment.*

For further reference:

Writers Guild of America, West, Inc.
8955 Beverly Boulevard
Los Angeles, California 90048
(213) 550-1000

Writers Guild of America, East, Inc.
555 West 57 Street
New York, New York 10019
(212) 245-6180

Underground Writing: Pornography

The telephone bill was unpaid. The net of economic difficulties was closing in . . . I did thirty pages of erotica.

Anais Nin
The Diary of Anais Nin, *Volume III*

Regardless of what a poet or fiction writer might think of pornography, can a serious writer earn a living writing it? Is the money worth the hackneyed phrases and formula plots? *Coda* found those who have written pornography generally unwilling to talk about it, with the following exceptions.

130 Books in Fourteen Months

Roy Campbell is a fiction writer with an MFA in Creative Writing from Wichita State University. While job-hunting in New York City, he did as so many unemployed writers do: he answered a classified ad in the *Village Voice* and took an office job. He worked an 8-hour day in a midtown-Manhattan office, for a firm named Corporate Design.

But Campbell's job was unlike most others: he wrote pornography, two books a week, 130 books in fourteen months. Corporate Design is the only pornographic book publisher in the country that employs full-time writers.

Campbell had seven co-workers, all of whom had higher aspirations to write serious fiction, poetry, or nonfiction. Both men and women were on the staff, several of whom had Ivy-League degrees.

On a typical workday (or night—the company runs sixteen hours with a day and a night shift, four writers per shift) Campbell checked an assignment sheet to find out what to write. "Each book belongs to a series that plays up a particular sex element," he says. "We might be given a title, such as *Cheerleader Sex Trio,* and if the art work was done in advance, we'd be shown that too." The most important guideline for the books, the editor told him, was "keep it hot, hot, hot."

Each Corporate Design book has 180 pages and eight to ten chapters. Half of each chapter is sex, the other half dialogue. "The book must also have some plot or it's terrible," says Campbell. "I rewrote my favorite novels, from *Huckleberry Finn* to *Ulysses.*"

A Corporate Design writer must be a good typist because the books are typed directly onto an IBM Selectric Compositer. The compositer is hooked up to a recording unit with magnetic tape and voilà, instant book. No time to revise; a motto in the pornography business is, "They don't want it good, they want it Tuesday."

If the writing isn't good, the pay isn't that good either—anywhere from $160-$300 a week, depending on output, with a minimum requirement of one-quarter book a day. Anais Nin earned more forty years ago at $1 a page. "It's a myth that the pay is good," says Campbell. The writer also earns no royalties, nor is his or her name on any of the books, adding no credits to the clip file.

The highest salary at Corporate Design went to a man who worked three days a week and produced half a book a day. He wrote without thinking, proving another porn motto: "Every time you stop to think, you lose money."

Although the pay is better for pornographic fiction written on a freelance basis, there's no weekly paycheck. Campbell has also written for magazines such as *Hustler* and *Chic,* which publishes what he calls "higher class porn." The competition, he warns, is as fierce as at mainstream magazines. "*Hustler* receives 750 fiction manuscripts a month. They publish one," he says.

At pornographic magazines, a writer must still conform to the editor's rules. "They tell you what they want. If the magazine caters to a blue-collar audience, and your hero went to college, the editors won't accept your story. They want a well-developed piece of fiction with some sex, but they want more than sex. They also care about style, setting, and character development. With the books, the rough draft gets published. At *Hustler* or *Chic,* it's the fourth, fifth, or sixth draft that finally gets into print."

Campbell has since left all this. Looking back, how did his experience affect his fiction? For one thing, porn disciplined him. He met his deadline on time. And porn allowed him to write rough drafts of later novels. "I'd had ideas for stories in my head for two or three years, but didn't know until I experimented with the porn if they'd work on paper. Years from now, I can take the gratuitous sex out of those books and turn the stories into something good," he says.

Sick of Sex

But writing porn hurt his fiction too. "It wrenched my style out of joint," he says. "My own style is bare bones—I cut a draft in half and that's my final story." The opposite is true for pornographic books. "You have to make things last as long as possible, with many adverbs and adjectives and as much dialogue as possible to fill up the book. Now that I'm back to my own fiction, I'm having terrible trouble getting rid of that padded style. And I can't write a sex scene in my novel."

Campbell advises those who think they might want to write porn to go another route. "The work is tiresome and not literary—just typing for fun and profit." Those who still want to try would be better off writing freelance, but Campbell warns that editors tend to reject one-shot deals. "Most pornographic publishers have a stable of writers they depend on, and will only accept a manuscript if they think you can churn out a lot.

"Pornographic books are a dying breed," says Campbell. "They don't sell today as they did ten years ago, and they won't sell as well ten years from today. Sex scenes are common now in mainstream fiction, and porn fans have video."

Porn writers don't last long either. Employees at Corporate Design generally stay from two months to two years. The novelty wears off, they "burn out" and run out of things to say. "The average is six months," says Campbell. "Freezing is when you just can't do it anymore. Perhaps that's just as well. The rule of thumb is, 'if you're still writing porn at thirty-five, you won't make it as a poet or fiction writer'."

Corporate Design protects its employees, both past and present. The company's "editorial director," who asked not to be identified, claims he's never heard of Roy Campbell.

The director describes Corporate Design as a literary sweatshop. "The factory atmosphere teaches you to produce prose on command whether or not you're in the mood," he says. "And you learn to write first drafts, fast.

"On the positive side, the job allows you to work with words instead of a gas pump or cash register," he says. "Although it's formula writing, it can help your fiction if you use it to toy with dialogue and style. Most of us are in our 20's or 30's—we treat this as a workshop experience."

But they don't expect one to write well. "Good writing gets in the way. You can't waste time laboring over images or making plots work. This is functional writing, and your reader has but one focus."

Unblocking Flaubert

Iris Owens is the author of *After Claude* (Farrar, Straus & Giroux) and *Hope Diamond Refuses* (Knopf). She hasn't written pornography since she lived in Paris years ago but her impetus then was the same: money.

"I did live off the money I made—one could then—in Paris. Now a writer can hardly live off published novels. We were a group of expatriates who were all writing for Maurice Girodius and the Olympia Press. At that point, it was a new genre, very avant-garde."

Owens is ambivalent about porn's effect on a writer's work. "A certain spontaneity exists in writing genre fiction of any kind. You learn to be free because you don't feel responsible for any kind of reality," she says. "Some who have written porn feel it was wonderfully liberating. Flaubert wrote porn when he was blocked.

"It only took me two months to write a book, which was another good experience. Most writers have a terrible confrontation with finishing something. At least a writer gets from start to finish when writing such books. I did five or six books and was paid a flat fee for each," she says. "It's also good for a writer to get used to being paid."

Writing porn has a destructive side too. "The writer has only one behavior in mind," says Owens. "Every twenty pages or so you're pushing to the next sex scene. Because of this built-in structure, the writing is very easy, which can make you careless. And naturally, you're not going for character.

"As I was writing, I'd often say, 'This is not literature.' But I didn't look back because I never thought those books would be widely distributed." When the books were pirated and brought to the United States, Owens was shocked. Her advice is, "Get a copyright—no matter how illegitimate you feel the material is."

Odd Ways of Staying Alive

Sybil Taylor has written nonfiction and is now working on a novel. She puts her porn writing under the general heading of "Odd Ways of Staying Alive." She and a friend who did erotic art decided to write porn because "we were both quietly starving to death."

Taylor presented an outline and a writing sample to *Variations*, a pornographic magazine. The editors liked her work and began to commission stories. "But it's hard to break in," says Taylor. "The editors are fussy and have their own formula."

The formula is distinct, restrictive, and not easy. "First you're handed a style sheet with a list of requirements," says Taylor. "Each story must have four sexual episodes. At the end of each book, two paragraphs have to give a socially redeeming reason for why the whole affair happened. You also get a list of about thirty possible subjects."

Taylor earned $400 for a ten-page story that took her four days to write. "I did ten overall, one a month, which almost paid my full rent."

She enjoyed it too. "It was fun and improved my writing. I relaxed, my imagination loosened up, and I discovered a lot about myself. You don't hold back when writing porn. You let your fantasies run wild, and you don't care, because it isn't serious—the more outrageous the situation, the better. The job tightened my prose. It was demanding and specific—good for me technically."

Daryln Brewer

Underground Writing:
Ghostwriting and Collaborating

Do you believe in ghosts? Not the kind that haunt old houses, but those who write other people's books: ghostwriters. A. E. Hotchner doesn't. He wrote the "autobiographies" of Doris Day and Sophia Loren and insisted his name be on both books. "A writer is a writer and should be listed as such," says Hotchner, who also writes fiction (*The Man Who Lived at the Ritz,* Putnam's).

Whatever you call it—ghostwriting or collaborating—there's a big market for stories of the famous and the infamous. For instance, *Fonda, My Life* as told to Howard Teichmann, *Inside and Out: Hostage to Iran, Hostage to Myself,* Richard Queen with Patricia Hass, or *Every Secret Thing,* Patricia Campbell Hearst with Alvin Moscow. Some of these books are written by poets and fiction writers to "buy time" for their own work.

Don't Write Down

Hotchner turned down the Day and Loren autobiographies at first. But then he became fascinated with each woman. "Doris Day gives the impression of being so happy-go-lucky," he says, "but she led a dreadful, rotten life. I reacted to that—and to the slums and squalor of Sophia's early life. I was interested in the obstacles each had to overcome."

Writers interested in a collaborative project with someone famous are advised by Hotchner to read everything on and by the person. Then comes the hardest part: getting a subject to open up. Don't ask regular "press line" questions, he says, or the subject will just give stock answers. "Trust must be established, and for that, the writer has got to care."

Writing someone else's autobiography can take up to two years, so money can't be the writer's only motivation, says Hotchner. "Begin by doing profiles for magazines. The women's magazines are a good market. Publishers are interested in a writer who's done celebrity profiles before. What's difficult is finding a celebrity who hasn't already been written about."

One of the pitfalls in collaboration is that serious fiction writers may "write down" to a level they consider a lesser art form. "With an attitude like that, the material won't be accepted. Writers must do their best no matter what they write."

Fiction writers who take this kind of writing seriously "can learn something about human spirit and emotion—something you don't get from sitting in a room and writing," says Hotchner. "It can also loosen you up. It's easier to write something you're not creating—and it keeps you writing."

Good Exercise

Yvonne Dunleavy doesn't like the term ghostwriter either, because it implies the writer is invisible. She generally advises a writer to use his or her name, as she did when she wrote *The Happy Hooker*. Xaviera Hollander got top billing on that book, but the credit further read: "with Robin Moore and Yvonne Dun-

176

leavy." Robin Moore didn't write any of the book. He took care of "editorial business," says Dunleavy. She did not use her name on a book about Elizabeth Ray, however, which she also wrote, "because it was changed in the editing process and it wasn't my style," she says. Her name did appear on an autobiography of Fanne Fox, also to her credit.

Dunleavy spends from three to six months ghosting or collaborating on a book. At first she saw the work as just another step to "the real thing"—her own fiction. Her novel (*Cumshaw,* Jove) took her four years to write. Now she thinks ghosting is good exercise. "It frees your concentration, buys time, and keeps your writing mind active and alert," she says. "You're less likely to get blocked or make as many false starts and ghosting can build confidence—it lets you know you have another skill." She thinks ghosting and fiction complement each other. "Fiction is art and comes from emotion; ghosting is craft and comes from information."

Dunleavy got started in 1970 when she met Robin Moore, a ghostwriting packager, through friends. For the less well-connected, she recommends getting an agent. "Too many landmines exist out there," she says. "An unprotected writer can have trouble. When you're in the talking stage of a book deal everyone is easy-going, but when the deal hardens into figures, the atmosphere can often become acrimonious."

The way to a good collaboration is through the specifics of the contract, says Dunleavy. "You need to spell out who does what and when you'll be available to each other. Friendship between the two of you is a bonus."

To break in, Dunleavy advises picking a celebrity who fascinates you. Before she wrote *The Happy Hooker,* Dunleavy had written a 5-page treatment for a nonfiction book on prostitution. "Get together with the person, prepare an outline, and send that to an agent. No reason why writers shouldn't have a good time and write about people they admire," she says.

Get Credit and a 50-50 Split

No standard contract exists for a ghostwriter or collaborator. Negotiation is left to the writer, agent, and publisher. "Payment for a collaborator—I prefer that word to ghostwriter—is a totally negotiable thing," says Owen Laster, a New York literary agent. He tries to get at least a 50-50 split on everything for his clients, but it varies—sometimes a writer will be paid an outright fee. Ghosts generally get paid less than collaborators, but it depends on the writer's track record, reputation, and the specific assignment. Most ghostwriters agree, however, that it's best to get a percentage of the royalty—that makes you care more about the book.

Vicki Lindner, a fiction writer (*Outlaw Games,* Dial) collaborated on a different sort of book: *Cheryl Tiegs: The Way to Natural Beauty.* Her previous experience included some nonfiction writing and collaboration on two books, *Facelift Without Surgery* and *Do-It-Yourself Shiatsu.* When Simon & Schuster was looking for a collaborator for the Tiegs book, Lindner's agent sent them some of her writing samples.

Lindner's contract called for half of the $40,000 advance and 10% of the hardcover royalties. Then came "six months of incredible tension."

Celebrities can be temperamental and their schedules are often complicated. They may also have no sense of a writer's skill. "They think all they have to do is provide the information. The writer is nothing more than a glorified secretary. Cheryl Tiegs called me, 'someone who did research for the book'," says Lindner.

"On the other hand, everyone knows Tiegs didn't

write the book," she says. "And I came into contact with a great many things I wouldn't have otherwise. New experiences gave me new metaphors and a new reality, revitalizing my fiction."

How and where a ghost's name appears on a book depends on a complicated hierarchy and the writer's clout. Some writers get a straight by-line, but others are listed after "as told to," "with," or "and," on the front jacket. If even less credit is given, a writer's name appears on the spine of the book. Last and least, a writer is thanked on the acknowledgments page.

Lindner's credit caused much debate, but because the book was worked on further by someone else, she agreed to have her name taken off the front jacket and put on the spine.

After the Tiegs book, Lindner did another beauty book—*Easy Glamour* with Barbara Walden. This time she tried splitting her energies between that and her fiction. "I didn't think I could do both," she says, "but they stimulated each other. The novel became my reward for working on *Easy Glamour*. The collaboration gave me incentive to work on my fiction. Three days a week I worked on the Walden book, three days on my novel. Switching back and forth kept me from getting bogged down. Most people say they can't do that kind of thing, but I think it's just snobbery that keeps them from trying."

A Cautionary Tale

"I was invisible and I liked it that way," says Kathrin Perutz, also a fiction writer (*Reigning Passions,* Lippincott) who ghosted two books on Polly Bergen. "The perks of ghostwriting can be attractive," says Perutz. "I wrote one of the Bergen books in a suite at the Waldorf." Later experiences discouraged her, however.

She worked on a biography of Topol, the Israeli actor and in a two-month period he cancelled eighteen appointments. "I couldn't plan anything, not even a dentist appointment," she says. "Ghosting can be a very masochistic situation because, basically, you are someone else's flunky." Then the project fell through. Perutz got an apology from the publisher and a kill fee of $1,500.

"Breaking in is difficult for novelists because some writers specialize in ghosting. The competition is tough," she says. "The quality of language is much less important—now editors just want juicy, sexy, scintillating language. It doesn't even have to be grammatical. A novelist usually won't get the job, even one willing to work for less money than a professional ghost."

No Time to Breathe

Shelby Hearon would not "ghost" *Barbara Jordan,* the biography of Barbara Jordan. "I spent long enough building up my name as a novelist," she says. Hearon and Jordan were introduced in Austin, Texas and liked each other. "You can't collaborate with someone unless the two of you agree completely on the project," says Hearon. "Collaboration is a matter of trust." She thinks writers looking for a compatible subject should not go through an editor or agent in the initial stages of the collaborative job. "Approach a famous person yourself," she says.

Most ghosts/collaborators record their clients' stories on tape. This way they pick up the vitality and subtleties of the individual. The challenge then is to retain the person's voice. Hearon used a special technique for the Jordan book. She alternated chapters, from Jordan's autobiographical voice to her voice, third person, filling in historical background. The *New York Times* reviewer said: "This rather awkward format could have been disastrous, but it works, thanks to Mrs. Hearon's delicate and empathetic touch."

The transition from fiction to collaborating can be tough. "I kept wanting to prove a point by inventing a scene that didn't take place," says Hearon.

Hearon split a $50,000 advance and all other subsidiary rights with Jordan—earning a total of $30,000. It was enough to live on while she wrote the book, but it didn't pay for her next work of fiction, as she had hoped. Hearon spent a year on the Jordan book, working 14-hour days for the last five months. "Obviously I didn't write any fiction—I hardly had time to breathe," she says.

Still, Hearon thinks writing every day is good for a writer. "If you can't make yourself write fiction every day, you must do it with another kind of writing."

Nonfiction sells more than fiction too. *Barbara Jordan* sold 25,000 copies, not a lot for nonfiction, but more than Hearon expects most of her novels to sell. *Barbara Jordan* was also syndicated by the *Los Angeles Times*, which helped to make Hearon better known. As a result, she was asked to give writing workshops, speeches, and readings. "If you just write fiction, you have a more limited *vita*, a more limited way to present yourself. I made a lot of contacts from the Jordan book."

Writers with the temperament for ghosting—those fascinated with a celebrity, willing to put up with someone else's erratic schedule, ready to divest themselves of ego and often take partial or no credit for something completely theirs—for those writers, the rewards of ghosting are many: decent pay, good contracts, better sales than poetry or fiction, a close look at how the famous live, and good practice. As Shelby Hearon says, "nothing helps writing like writing."

Daryln Brewer

Underground Writing: Novelizations

"Novelizations used to be much more in vogue," says Knox Burger, a New York literary agent. "Now they're a dying form of employment." Though the jobs are harder to get than they used to be, some poets and fiction writers still write novelizations—the paperback version of a movie—to make money.

$7,500 in Five weeks

Darcy O'Brien, whose novel *A Way of Life, Like Any Other*, won PEN's Ernest Hemingway Prize, agrees with Knox Burger. Yet when O'Brien wrote the Ballantine novelization of "Moment by Moment," the film starring John Travolta and Lily Tomlin, he earned $7,500 plus a 2% royalty. Since the paperback cost only $1.95, O'Brien earned about 4¢ on each book, or approximately $9,376. The book sold 469,000 copies—not a great number for a novelization, but a lot compared to poetry or literary fiction.

Novelizations have been written since the 1920's, "but I have the impression that book publishers are less interested in them right now," says O'Brien. "I don't think they're making money on them. Picture books of the movies sell better." According to O'Brien, the only people who read novelizations are teenage girls.

Still, he says, "I loved doing it once. I never made so much money in such a short time, and I've never written so many words in five weeks—50,000, with only a 90-page script as a guide. The idea of writer's block became absurd. It gave me confidence that I could make things up out of absolutely nothing."

Having a friend or an agent with Hollywood connections can help a writer find a novelization job. O'Brien went to Hollywood twice on the job, with both trips paid for by Ballantine. First he went to look at the sets and talk to the filmmakers. After finishing half the novelization, he went back, to see the film shot up to that point. Although he says he could tell the film was going to be a flop, he finished the book anyway. "I needed the money," he says.

O'Brien says he wouldn't do a novelization again unless it was "absolutely necessary." One problem he discovered was having "to convince yourself you believe in the project—it's like self-brainwashing—or you turn the copy into satire or parody."

Writing a novelization can also be time-consuming. "I was teaching, and my students kept asking me what was wrong. And once you get into it, it takes a while to get out. O'Brien needed a couple of months to recover—until he finally went back to his own fiction.

The Genre Is Dead

Leonore Fleischer, columnist and magazine writer, has written forty novelizations, several of which have been very successful, and welcomes them—when she can get the work. Even Fleischer, who wrote five novelizations in thirteen months and who wrote the novelization of "A Star Is Born" (one million copies) and "Benjy" (three million copies), thinks "the genre is dead." Fewer movies are being made, and paperback houses have lost money on recent novelizations. For example, Dell paid $400,000 for Sylvester Stallone's "Fist;" both the movie and the novelization bombed.

In fact, successes like Fleischer's hurt the genre. Prices for novelizations became inflated, and publishers couldn't afford them. Also, many screenwriters now do the novelizations of their own scripts, making competition for the jobs stiffer than ever. According to the standard Writers Guild contract, the screenwriter must be offered a novelization job first. So a novelist's publishing contacts may not help; a publisher who buys novelization rights to a script may have no say in who writes it.

$1,000 a Week for Four Weeks

Although Leonore Fleischer sees "no way for a young person to break into" novelizations, younger writers still occasionally get the jobs. Even when Avon simultaneously published two books by Paul Monette—*The Long Shot* (a novel) and *No Witnesses* (poetry)—Monette still wasn't making a living. "I was pleading for work from an editor at Avon, and he offered me the novelization of 'Nosferatu.'" Although Monette found the fee "low" ($4,000) and the schedule "crazy" (four weeks), he enjoyed writing it.

Monette had the "Nosferatu" screenplay from which to work and 200 production stills (photographs). *Nosferatu* became a Book-of-the-Month Club quality paperback selection, and rights were sold in Japan and England. "I also got a lot of publicity from the book, which is unusual," he says. That also helped him find more work. Although he says he wouldn't do another novelization, Monette has written six screenplays since *Nosferatu*.

Not the Writer's Creation

Another novelist who makes a good living from this dying genre writes under the pen name of Robert Alley. He wrote the novelization of films such as "Last Tango In Paris," "Shampoo," "The Front," and "Honeysuckle Rose." For "Last Tango," he made $40,000 plus a 2% royalty. The book sold three million copies.

Alley doesn't use his real name on novelizations because he doesn't consider them his creation. "Since they aren't my idea, I don't deserve to put my name on them. Novelizations are never the legitimate product of the writer," he says.

Alley advises those who want to write novelizations to do so "only if they have a strong control over their craft and are able to devote themselves intensely to a project and then forget about it." The success of a novelization also depends entirely on the success of the film. "If a writer's ego is involved, that can hurt," he says.

"I'd be surprised if a novelization job were offered to a young writer for a number of reasons," says Alley. "First, you have to sit still for six weeks." And novelizations always have to be done fast. Alley has done them in as little as three weeks, working twelve hours a day. "They also require a certain stylistic and structural facility and you must have some experience reading between the lines of a movie script. You have to do what a director does—interpret characters and discover what makes them tick. The writer does it through language. It takes a peculiar talent."

Writing novelizations has had little effect on Alley's own fiction, except for financing it. "Maybe if you're having trouble with another project, writing a novelization cleans you out, so you're clearer when you start something new. It hasn't helped my style, though," he says.

"I Really Had to Pad My Style"

Sonia Pilcer's first novel, *Teen Angel,* was published by Coward, McCann and Geoghegan in 1978 and Avon in 1979. In 1980, she was hired to write the novelization of the movie "Little Darlings," which starred Kristy McNichol and Tatum O'Neal, because "I was considered an expert on adolescent female preoccupations." Ballantine owned the novelization rights; Nancy Coffey, who was then editor-in-chief, offered Pilcer the job.

Pilcer agreed to take time out from her second novel, *Maiden Rites,* for "Little Darlings." "I liked writing on assignment then—it gave me a break from my own creation." The project was scheduled to take three or four months.

Pilcer earned a total of $15,000 and a 6% royalty for writing the book. Paramount sent her the 125-page script, which she rated as "fair," and stills so she could see what the actors looked like.

"I discovered that writing a novelization wasn't nearly as easy as I thought," says Pilcer. "The script was bare bones, from which I had to write 250-300 pages." She found this difficult because her own style is economical. "I had to write inner monologues and landscape descriptions, which I never write. I really had to pad my style." Pilcer's first draft came to only 100 pages. "I had to start all over again and develop an expansive style," she says. "It's a peculiar situation—you have to stick to the script, yet at the same time, you have to expand it."

Halfway through her second draft, Pilcer got a panicked call from Ballantine: could she finish by the end of the month? "I had strong doubts. The three-to-four months had already been cut in half by the time it took to get the script and the stills." But when Ballantine offered a $5,000 bonus (over the $15,000 advance), Pilcer found a way. "Everyone was pleased. The book needed very little editing, and I made more money than from *Teen Angel,* which took a year to write." The movie was shown on cable television, increasing the sales of the book, which sold over 150,000 copies.

Pilcer debated whether to use her name on the book and ultimately did because her by-line reads "by Sonia Pilcer, author of *Teen Angel.*" "If I could boost the sales of *Teen Angel,* I thought it was a good idea," she says. "I wasn't ashamed of what I wrote—I did the best I could within the genre."

Would she do another? "Yes. It's a lot more fun and more challenging than writing articles for women's magazines. I'm interested in film and in finding literary equations for such things as zooms and close-ups." Writing *Little Darlings* also helped Pilcer to write the screenplay of *Teen Angel* for Universal.

Training at Odd Jobs

The catch? Pilcer agrees that novelizations are hard to find. "Only the top five or six movies every year are made into novelizations. It's a dead field for writers." But for those who want to buck the odds, Pilcer suggests research. Find out which publishers produce the most novelizations. "Ballantine does a lot. Call an editor there. It is difficult if you're not in the industry, but you can read *Variety* or *Show Business* to find out what movies are being made that really interest you. Unfortunately, a novelization is not the kind of thing you write on speculation."

Little Darlings made Sonia Pilcer realize she could do new things with her writing. "I had to learn to describe trees and the sky. Because I had only written urban novels, I'd never done that before," she says. "I'm not a purist. My training as a writer has often been at odd jobs like this. All kinds of experience as a writer can only help you, even if you're dipping into popular forms of writing. The novelization gave me another tool—the more genres you can get under your belt, the better."

Novelizations, ghostwriting, pornography, screenwriting, genre fiction—ways to write for a living do exist. They have their drawbacks, but so do waitressing, teaching, and selling life insurance. "Underground writing," in contrast, is an odd job that can train a writer in many aspects of the craft—writing to deadline, learning discipline, sharpening technical skills, keeping many threads going at once, experimenting with plot and dialogue, and writing for a specific audience.

Daryln Brewer

Fiction Writers:
Your Readers Want to Hear You

The centuries-old tradition of poetry recitations—or readings—seems to extend solidly to the sponsors of today's literary events. Wherever there's a reading series, whether it's long or short, full of well-known writers or first-time readers, most of those readings will be by poets, of poetry. Sponsors still seem to feel there's a more natural marriage between short poems and reading aloud. Poetry is considered more of a performance art; poets try to do their best with each short poem. At a prose reading, the audience is presented with just one "package," a full one, and sponsors seem to fear the audience's attention won't last all the way through it.

Yet when short-story writers Tillie Olsen and Grace Paley read from their works in San Francisco, over 600 people came to hear them. In New York, Ann Beattie and Leslie Epstein each drew SRO crowds at the Writers Community.

Lewis MacAdams, a poet who coordinated the San Francisco Poetry Center's reading series for three years, described the center as open to readings by "storytellers," but said that most of the writers who applied to read there were poets. Are fiction writers really shyer? And why?

"A Painful Interruption to My Writing"

Maxine Kumin, a Pulitzer Prize-winning poet and a novelist and short-story writer, probably speaks for many writers when she describes the process of giving readings as a "terrible, painful interruption" to her writing. "I don't travel well," she says, "and a reading tour puts you on stage all the time—you have to be 'up' every minute. It makes me too nervous to be ego-gratifying or any fun." Kumin continues to give several readings a year because she counts on the income and because, for all the trouble they are, readings offer a change from her isolated life in New Hampshire.

Kumin finds that she is generally invited to read her poetry, not fiction. She reads her fiction only if she is in one place long enough to give two readings. Although she is best known as a poet, she also feels that sponsors think of poetry readings rather than fiction readings as the accepted and common practice. "But it's a shame more fiction isn't read aloud—storytelling is a wonderful art too."

Is there any difference between reading fiction and poetry? "Reading fiction makes me slightly less nervous," says Kumin. "Other than that, not much—I try to choose short, self-contained stories or novel chapters. Something that finishes, as a poem would."

"I Give 25 Readings a Year and Enjoy Each One"

Al Young, also a poet and novelist, gives about 25 readings a year and enjoys every one. "I write more for communication than for self-expression," he says. "I delight in reading my work out loud, and audiences seem to enjoy hearing it."

Young does not find that readings disrupt his writing unless he takes two or three weeks off from writing to do a block of readings. "But since it's part

190

of my income, I don't mind taking the time every few months."

Unlike many writers, Young feels it's easier to read fiction than poetry. "With poetry, your time at the podium is a lot more fragmented. It has to be held together with anecdotes, some discussion of the poems, etc. With fiction, you have a narrative the audience can follow. Fiction disarms everyone, and its audiences are always more relaxed." Young usually reads both poetry and fiction to an audience, "but I always begin with poetry. I find it impossible to return to poetry if I start with fiction. The audience just doesn't come along."

Young believes that reading sponsors now prefer fiction readings over poetry. "They've heard so much poetry that fiction seems refreshing."

Al Young worked in radio for years and writes fiction designed to be read aloud. He has developed a presentation, or performance, that gets the work across to an audience. What about the writer who can't act?

"Every Book Has Its Own Voice"

"Not all books should be read aloud in public—some just aren't suited for it," says Virginia writer Mary Lee Settle, who won a National Book Award in fiction. "But every book should have its own voice—what you hear in your head as you read to yourself. By reading aloud, I share this voice of the book, testing and recognizing when it works or when it loses pitch. For this reason, readings are an enormous help to me as a fiction writer. The drawback to reading aloud simply as a performance is that a good reader can often cover up a lot of bad writing. For a shy or average reader, the voice of the book itself will come through and be strengthened."

Public readings can be less of a problem for the

short-story writer than for the novelist. In a number of days, a short-story writer can. have at least one story ready for a reading. By definition a story is self-contained and usually short enough to be heard in one sitting.

During the months or years required for writing a novel, the writer does not necessarily polish one chapter and make it ready for the public before going on to the next. Even if the middle of the book seems perfect to the writer, it may only confuse an audience that has never heard the beginning. As Maxine Kumin points out, a composer does not play a work-in-progress; a painter does not exhibit a half-finished painting.

Mary Lee Settle is one of the few writers *Coda* talked to who enjoys reading works-in-progress out loud at all, "though I prefer to have plenty of other writers in the audience, as a leaven for students and the general public." She likes getting the feedback, "though you have to remember that the listeners are not seeing the whole design of the book, so their comments may be off the mark. Still, I find it valuable to see if the voice of the book is getting across."

Fiction Writers—Don't Wait! Speak Up!

Mary Lee Settle also believes that reading sponsors don't think to invite fiction writers, partly because of the poetry habit and partly because a fiction writer must have a good reputation as a reader in order to get invited anywhere.

Audiences do not come out for any writer—poet or novelist—who is unknown to them. This leaves a sponsor with the choice of blitzing the community with enticingly detailed publicity, or inviting a well-known writer.

The irony is that writers all agree that readings help sell books. But if writers can't get readings because their books don't sell, how can they help sell the books? If there's an answer to this, it's probably for writers to start drumming up readings in their own neighborhoods, then gradually move into the community, region, state, and so on. And to keep writing.

Writers should not be discouraged if there seem to be ten poetry readings for every fiction reading. People love to hear stories, and reading sponsors are becoming more aware of this. But writers should not wait passively for sponsors to change their programs; the best way to break the poetry reading habit is for fiction writers to let sponsors know as soon as possible that they're available for readings.

For writers who would still rather write and write only, who cannot imagine making themselves or their work accessible in thirty minutes to a one-time audience, consider these words from *How to Get Happily Published*,* by Judith Appelbaum and Nancy Evans:

• "Your book is one out of 40,000 published each year.

• The best way to sell a book is face-to-face with a prospective buyer. In public appearances, your knowledge of your book is your most important asset, not your salesmanship or acting ability.

• Writers seem to think that hustling for something they've created is undignified. But dignified people do it every day for a dignified reason: they believe in their work."

Debby Mayer

How to Get Happily Published, by Judith Appelbaum and Nancy Evans. Harper & Row, © 1978. **193**

Four

ON POETRY

Writers and Teaching

Everyone agrees that teaching takes time away from writing—any job does—but what are the other effects of teaching on one's work? Is all that talk about writing exhausting—or stimulating? Does the writer see the flaws in his or her own work more clearly after identifying those in the work of the student? Or is teaching another, more acceptable, excuse for something else: not writing?

Here are the thoughts of seven writers.

Russell Banks (*Continental Drift,* Harper & Row): In at least one way, writing is like a sport: no matter how well you do it, you still have to do the basics. I'm a better writer because of teaching. Teaching makes me deal with the basics of writing and forces me to constantly recapitulate my own history—to try to remember how I became a writer, to recreate my own past and my beginnings as a writer.

The negative aspect of teaching is the lack of time. I don't feel threatened by the likelihood of talking my work out in the classroom, but it takes a long time to teach. And to write.

Rosellen Brown (*Civil Wars,* Knopf): When I'm teaching, it's very difficult to achieve the kind of concentration I'm used to. I have so many distractions because of the engagement with people. The tape keeps running in my head.

I also find it much easier to think about my teaching than to sit at a desk and write. Teaching takes energy and is exhausting, but anything is easier than having to confront the page and not escape into talking about it.

The talk of the classroom comes tantalizingly close to discussing what it is I'm trying to do, but not quite. I spend a lot of time with bad work and I spend a great many words on that, but I'm not really confronting questions about my own work. It's not quite the same at the graduate level where I do ask myself some of the same questions the students do and where some of the work is fine. Sometimes I ask myself, 'What would they say to me if I brought my work into a workshop?'

One thing that's particularly strange and disquieting about teaching and not good for writers is how students relate to you. The teacher becomes a role model; it's nice to feel useful but it's strange to feel that I'm in a position people want to emulate, especially when I'm still battling all the questions. I still feel like a beginner between books. A terrible humility is forced on you as a writer. There's a tremendous temptation to dishonesty if you let yourself be seduced into the authority that comes with the job. Then it's hard to go back to the page as a beginner.

There's also the pressure of knowing that your forthcoming work will be read by your students. It's bad enough to have to deal with critics. Students assume that everything you do is wonderful—what happens if you compromise that by making the mistakes we're all allowed? This gives me pause. I don't want to fail before myself and I also don't want to fail before my students.

Nicholas Delbanco (*Group Portrait*, William Morrow): The occupational hazard of teaching is garrulity. Words get cheapened; teaching increases the risk of automatic writing, running on or off at the mouth . . . I have to be careful not to let that become a habit in my prose.

In my job, however, I have not been relegated to the teaching of writing alone. More writers should teach substantive literature courses. It puts you in the presence of greatness and makes you consider what the masters knew and you and your students don't. From courses I've taught, I've stumbled on the subjects of two of my books—*In the Middle Distance* and *Group Portrait*—and have been very grateful for that. It's also lovely to be in the presence of challenging, serious young writers. Bennington has been generous and given me time off and time away. I work hard on my own work when I'm not teaching. During the semester, I fiddle, dabble and revise . . .

One promise I made to myself was never to write a novel about academia. Writers who teach ought to remember to look elsewhere for subjects—otherwise we'd all write about writing.

Elizabeth Hardwick (*Sleepless Nights*, Random House): I have no negative feelings about being a teacher of writing. Teaching has no effect on my own writing and it is doubtful that I have any effect on the writing of the students. I try to lead them to reading and to thinking about what they put on the page and I hope that may be useful. Some of my students have been remarkable and that has been a gain for me.

Most writers teach a light schedule indeed and I cannot see why this interruption should be peculiarly draining. For myself the classroom is much less burdensome than the mail and other matters attendant upon our profession.

I feel that the employment of writers in our universities is an altogether fine thing. In France, England and other countries the alternative is journalism of various kinds, a very complicated enterprise suitable, without corruption of style and intention, to only a few. And writers are a tremendous insertion in the English departments of the country because they bring, or should bring, great knowledge, enthusiasm, and even ideas to the study of literature.

Cleopatra Mathis (*The Bottom Land,* Sheep Meadow): Going over the students' poems doesn't challenge me, motivate me to write more, or make me work harder. Beginning writers don't make errors that are complex.

But I do get excited when I teach the poems of other writers whom I respect and love. I get charged up to go home and work afterward. This helps my work a great deal, keeps me on my toes and helps me identify what it is I love about good writing. This would happen to a lesser degree if I were reading at home, but the chance of having the time to sit leisurely and read the work of masters is not likely.

When I first came to Dartmouth, I had no time to write. What saved me was teaching the poems and essays of others. I felt fired up for approaching my own work at the end of the school year in June and I didn't feel the gap of not having written for so long. Teaching poetry sustained me.

When I teach good poems I look at them in a much closer way. I can't be as lazy as when I read them myself. And seeing the students respond in their own work makes poetry far more alive for me. The good poems do the teaching for me, and I learned as much reading them again as the students who read them for the first time.

Mark Strand (*Selected Poems,* Atheneum): Teaching takes time and energy, energy that might be better spent working on my own poems and stories. Also, if I have a good day in class, then I don't particularly feel like writing afterward. I don't feel that the teaching of writing helps my work at all—my students' work is in no way related to mine. I'm there to offer suggestions and provide reasonable alternatives, to be involved with what *they* are writing.

Hilma Wolitzer (*In the Palomar Arms,* Farrar, Straus & Giroux): All experience is useful for a writer and teaching is another experience. Teaching writing stimulates my own work, and pointing out students' mistakes makes me more aware of my own. Also, it's as exciting to discover a good manuscript in class as it is to read a good published book.

I believe there's a chain of responsibility—writers should help each other. What better way than in a workshop? Finally, all writers must work in isolation and the community of writers is very supportive. You go back to the isolation fortified—and that works for both student and teacher.

Daryln Brewer

The Poet as Business Person

No wonder poets have to seem
So much more business-like than business men—
Their wares are so much harder to get rid of.

Robert Frost

Somewhere along the line in literary history, poets got a bad reputation. That is, they were found wanting, by their fellow citizens, for mental health, social graces, and civic responsibility. They were found instead to be unstable, if not immoral.

It's true that much of Louis Untermeyer's *Lives of the Poets* reads like a soap opera. At 25, Christopher Smart was so deeply in debt he could not leave his room at Pembroke Hall, Cambridge, for fear of creditors. When Shelley's wife Harriet hesitated at being part of a ménage à trois with Mary Godwin, Shelley left her and their two children and set up a second family with Mary.

In the U.S., Emily Dickinson became a total recluse. She loved music but would not enter a room where it was being played, preferring to listen from outside the door.

Hart Crane and Dylan Thomas drank to excess. In despair, Crane jumped from a steamer in the Gulf of

Mexico; his body was never found. At 39, Thomas collapsed and died during a trip to New York.

As every living poet knows, the stereotype of the unstable, immoral, drugged, and drunken poet is no more true for poets as a group than it is for any other profession. Scientists and business tycoons jump off bridges, too, but the public tends to forget that, because instability doesn't fit in with the image of the methodical or ruthless.

What's forgotten about poets is that for every Dylan Thomas who had to be escorted so he wouldn't be lost, there is a T. S. Eliot, working quietly in a bank while he wrote brilliant poetry. Or a Wallace Stevens, a lawyer on the legal staff of the Hartford Accident and Indemnity Insurance Company, and a vice-president of that firm for twenty years. Or William Carlos Williams, writing poetry in and around the demanding life of a physician.

Poets share their writing lives with law practices, real estate, graphic design, psychology, and dozens of other unrelated fields. Many poets, though, want their jobs and their writing to dovetail as often and as closely as possible; the fields of publishing, teaching, and service to the arts attract them.

Poets Have Orderly Minds

Harvey Shapiro is the author of half-a-dozen poetry collections, including *Lauds and Nightsounds* (Sun Press). He is also an editor at the *New York Times Magazine*, after several years as editor of the *New York Times Book Review*. There he was in charge of a system that selected books for review (from 40,000 submitted annually) and assigned and edited reviews. The only consistent time he's had for writing poetry is late at night. He works in notebooks, writing lines or writing automatically, even if he's not working on a specific poem.

"It's important to keep communication going with your writing self," he says, "not just to produce poems to send out, but to keep the door open." In fact, Shapiro generally finds writing on vacations difficult, because he is so used to writing against the pressures of his job.

Peter Davison, author of *Barn Fever* (Atheneum) and five other poetry collections, has worked in publishing for almost 35 years. Poetry editor of the *Atlantic Monthly* since 1972, he has also worked for Atlantic Monthly Press (a separate division of the Atlantic Monthly Company) since 1956. Robert Giddings, the poet and biographer of Keats and Hardy, once told him, "You must be well-suited for administration—poets have orderly minds."

As editorial director of the press (1964-1979), Davison edited between six and eight new books a year and was also in charge of budget and staff. As senior editor (since 1979), his major responsibility is acquiring new books, ten or twelve of which he edits himself. Editing includes drawing up a financial breakdown for each book—expenses required in publishing it, sales estimate, income expected, etc. "You have to know the numbers," he says.

Stealing Time for Poetry

When does he write poetry? Quoting William Carlos Williams, Davison says he " 'steals time.' At midnight, commuting, walking. I always carry a notebook, because it's essential to get a poem down when it comes." On vacations and weekends he has more time to revise, something he does "a lot" of, and after three or four years, another book collection has evolved.

"Yes, writing poetry this way can be frustrating, but most poets are frustrated by their writing at least part of the time. I do think it's harder to be a poet with a job than it was in Wallace Stevens' day. The workday is more fragmented, because of the telephone. When I started in publishing all the work was still done by letter. Now to get someone's attention, you have to call."

The stakes are also higher in publishing than they used to be. George Orwell's *Down and Out in London and Paris* was originally published by Victor Gollancz in 1933, six weeks after it had been accepted. "Today," says Davison, "there's a 15-month time structure to work with, plus major investments to be made in printing, paper, and overhead. Now even a small publishing house has a staff of fifteen. It used to be simpler."

The Poet as Anti-Romantic

Seeking a job that might be easier to write with, many poets teach, for while the work is intensive, the hours may be fewer and summers can be free. Robert Pack is a teaching poet who doesn't even take summers off. He teaches two courses each in the fall and spring semesters at Middlebury College in Middlebury, Vermont (plus overseeing independent studies), and one course in the winter term. Summers he teaches at the Bread Loaf School of English, a postgraduate program at the nearby Bread Loaf campus that runs from the end of June until mid-August. Then the Bread Loaf Writers' Conference begins. Pack has directed that since 1972, a job that encompasses fundraising for a five-figure budget, hiring a teaching staff of twenty, and reviewing 1,200 applications, each with a manuscript of prose or poetry, to select 230 students.

Pack works on his poetry in the morning, teaching only in the afternoon. He gets up by 5:30 A.M. and although not all of every morning is free, he may write until noon—a full workday in itself, by many standards. His latest collection, *Faces in a Single Tree: A Cycle of Monologues,* was published by David Godine.

"Yes, I wish my schedule weren't so heavy," he says, "but the parts I could give up—the two Bread Loaf sessions—are the parts I most enjoy. My wife and I have three children and big expenses coming with their college educations, so I can't let up."

Robert Pack has what he calls an anti-romantic view of being a poet. "Poets are only more sensitive than other people in respect to language," he says. They don't necessarily feel grief or joy more deeply than anyone else. They don't have special privileges, and they are bound by every citizen's responsibilities to family and society.

"One is a poet only when one is writing. I feel an obligation to be active in the life of Middlebury College as well as the larger community. I do my other activities in harmony with my poetry. The nature of social activity, for me, does not grate against the activity of writing a poem. My only conflict is finding time to do all the things I care about."

Poetry Is Not a Solitary Affair

Judith Johnson Sherwin, a poet (*How the Dead Count*, Norton), playwright, and fiction writer, taught rarely during most of her writing career. She felt that her writing tended to become academic, and she wanted to stay away from the university influence. Sherwin believes in poetry as a performance art, and feels a strong sense of communality in art. "Poetry is not a solitary affair between the eye and the page," she says. "It's made and received in cooperation with other arts. For me, the text is a score; the poem happens in performance."

Although teaching didn't appeal to Judy Sherwin at first, organizing did, and the Poetry Society of America interested her. Founded in 1910 by a group that admired poets such as Robert Frost, Carl Sandburg, and Vachel Lindsay—the populist poets of their day—the PSA wanted to make poetry accessible to all.

"One of the major assets of the Society is that its members are people who love poetry and have devoted their lives to it," says Judy Sherwin. "They are a strong resource for poetry nationwide."

In 1973 Sherwin was elected to the Society's Governing Board, which makes major policy and financial decisions. From there she was elected to two terms as president (1975-1978) and then served on the PSA Executive Committee, which makes day-to-day administrative decisions for the group. In seven years, Sherwin and the Governing Board turned the Society around from a relatively inactive group with dwindling membership to a vital national organization constantly improving its community outreach.

During Sherwin's tenure, the membership doubled (to 1,000). The Society also improved the quality and range of its *Bulletin* and of its programs, which include readings, lectures, discussions, and awards.

Then a couple of years ago, Judy Sherwin tried teaching again, at the college level, and found she enjoyed it tremendously—and that she no longer feared an academic influence on her work. In fact, she says, "As I get older, I have to make more of an effort to remain open to new forms, new subjects. Teaching helps me make that effort."

The Poet as a Whole Personality

Wallace Stevens walked to his office every morning, composing poetry in his head and stopping occasionally to jot down notes. In the office his secretary typed his legal briefs and correspondence—and his poetry. Stevens disliked being known as a split personality. "I prefer to think I'm just a man," he said, "not a poet part-time, businessman the rest."

That's the way most poets think of themselves today—as whole, not split, personalities.

Debby Mayer

207

Poetry Anthologies:
Boon or Bane?

The first English-language poetry anthology was called, simply, *The Poets* and published in Edinburgh in 1777. Safe to say that ever since then poets have regarded poetry anthologies with ambivalence. On the positive side, anthologies do introduce new readers to poetry. And having a poem chosen by an anthology editor gives a poet positive reinforcement and usually some cash. On the other hand, anthologies seem always too confined, too limited, and either too general or too specific. They may also siphon off sales from the individual collections of the very poets they seek to honor, without even representing the best work of those poets. And some poets believe publishers promote and distribute their anthologies at the expense of their own poets' books.

Poetry Smorgasbord = Poetry Starvation

Gregory Orr, who has three poetry collections in print with Harper & Row (*The Red House* is the latest) and who teaches writing workshops and literature courses at the University of Virginia, is not ambivalent. He believes poetry anthologies should not be allowed in the college-level classroom. He believes college teachers rely on them far too heavily, to the detriment of both education and contemporary poetry in the United States. Instead, students should read, and teachers should teach, individual books of poetry only.

"An anthology published for classroom use counts on the cowardice of the teacher," says Greg Orr. "The students get only a smattering of each poet, and this helps the teacher evade issues. If there's confusion or a problem with one poet, the teacher can just go on to the next one. With individual volumes, there's no missing what the poet is about. Teaching a poet's book requires real teaching."

Students in Orr's literature classes read between five and eight poets a semester, each from the poet's own book. His writing students read one collection each week. In all cases, Orr puts the books on reserve in the library, so that a student who can't afford all the books can still do thorough reading. "Reading five or six poets in a course," says Orr, "gives a student a much more realistic idea of what those poets are like and also what contemporary poetry is."

Orr does not believe in the smorgasbord theory—that after sampling poets in an anthology a student will then go back and read favorite poets in depth. Too many students, he finds, consider themselves "done" with a poet once they've read a few poems in an anthology. And the worst part of that is that most poets are not represented well in an anthology format. It's partly economics: a publisher of a book of poems generally sets the reprint fees for those poems. An anthologist may wish to use the seminal poem of a poet's *oeuvre* only to find its reprint fee far beyond the anthology's budget. So the anthologist settles for a "cheaper" poem, one that costs less because it is a less important part of the poet's work.

If money doesn't dictate the student's exposure to

poetry, space may. "For example," says Greg Orr, "Galway Kinnell's *Book of Nightmares* is put together carefully, intentionally, in ten parts that run 75 pages. An anthologist can't reprint the whole thing, but to reprint one section does that book an injustice—and the student, too."

Putting Money Where the Money Is

Greg Orr also objects to anthologies as an "economic deception" that favor the publisher over the poet. An anthology earns more money faster than an individual volume, so a publishing company invests more in it—thereby undercutting its own poetry volumes. A case in point is the Doubleday *Treasury of American Poetry,* an anthology of 838 pages and 109 poets compiled by Nancy Sullivan, a poet and teacher from Rhode Island. Commissioned for the Literary Guild, a book club Doubleday owns, it sold 100,000 copies through that club and others at $8.99 each. A trade edition sold almost 9,000 copies at $14.50 each.

Doubleday also publishes individual volumes by contemporary poets such as James Dickey, Norman Dubie, Robert Graves, and Carolyn Rodgers; by no stretch of the imagination will their poetry books sell 100,000 copies. Nancy Sullivan was impressed with Doubleday's distribution and promotion of her anthology. "It was terrific. If only they would put the same effort into individual collections. They don't, of course—no publisher does."

Still, the Doubleday anthology proves that poetry can sell, particularly when aided by thorough promotion and distribution. Although she agrees with Greg Orr that an anthology can be a safety zone for a teacher, Sullivan says, "What charms me is that a lot of people who wouldn't have poetry in the house now do, with my anthology. I do believe anthologies introduce people to poetry."

William Cole, an editor who has compiled 35 poetry anthologies, agrees. "As a young man, I discovered poetry through Louis Untermeyer's *Modern British and American Poets.*" Cole takes the discovery aspect a further step, pointing out that through anthologies readers discover not just "poetry" but many different poets. "The greatest thing about being an anthologist is the opportunity it affords to call attention to poets and individual poems that might otherwise remain hidden away. I get very excited about the English poets Frances Cornford, Charlotte Mew, and Anna Wickham. I rejoice in the work of my favorite young American poet, Ted Kooser, and if I'm not careful will soon have used, in one book or another, the complete works of Hilaire Belloc in various collections."

Sales to Students—A Poetry Lifeline

On the other hand, some of the most-often anthologized contemporary poets—such as Adrienne Rich and Stanley Kunitz—now have editions of their collected poems available. For survey courses, which cover a longer time span, Greg Orr suggests the editions of "selected poems" for the writers usually taught. *"The Selected Poems of Yeats* is beautiful," he says. "You see him grow, get the feeling of a life— what persists along with what changes. You don't get that just from reading 'Sailing to Byzantium.'

"Students pay $25 for one biology text," Greg Orr points out. "They come to college knowing they'll need books, prepared to spend a certain amount on them. We're under no obligation to make poetry cheaper than other courses."

While such sales put no extra strain on students, they can mean a lifeline for poetry publishing— alternative presses, university presses, and commercial presses. Even in university towns few bookstores—if any—stock a wide selection of contemporary poetry.

Gregory Orr has found a way to use his professor's leverage with local bookstores. In Charlottesville he works with two stores, giving each a list of between forty and fifty different books. Each store buys two copies of each book with the understanding that Orr's students will buy them during the semester. At the end of the term, Orr checks with the stores to be sure the books have sold as he expected. If they haven't, the stores can return them for full credit, but so far this hasn't been necessary.

"The bookstores found what I was asking them to do very sensible, once they understood that my students and I were guaranteeing them steady, modest sales," he says. "And if a class buys twenty copies of a small press book, it's a great help to that press. Multiply that by just two dozen colleges in the country, and the impact for a small press would be tremendous."

The Case of the Missing Poets

Those purchases might also be the only way those students discover some good contemporary writers. Orr is concerned because "more and more high-quality contemporary poetry is being published by small presses and university presses—and that work is not getting into anthologies. You can read some anthologies and not know that certain schools of poetry or groups of poets even exist—much less individual poets." He cites Stan Rice of Berkeley as one example. Winner of the Edgar Allan Poe Award from the Academy of American Poets, Rice has published three books with small presses. Yet, along with many other contemporary poets, Rice is not included in the *Norton Anthology of Modern Poetry*, the book most students see.

As an editor at W.W. Norton, John Francis' primary job was working on some of its many literature anthologies. He agrees that each anthology is a compromise—"a compromise any teacher—even a teacher who is a writer—understands. First, anthologies are an economical solution to the book problem. The *Norton Anthology of Modern Poetry* includes over 150 poets, which allows the teacher and student some choice. A student couldn't possibly afford that many individual volumes. Every college offers survey courses in literature, and anthologies make those survey courses possible."

Francis also points out that few individual collections have the kind of notes the Norton anthologies have. "Teachers cannot afford to spend class time going through *The Waste Land* line by line, explaining Eliot's allusions and even his own notes," he says. "They want to talk about the meaning and art of the poem as a whole. In Norton anthologies, the notes help students get through a first reading on their own and prepare to discuss the whole poem."

Dean Johnson, editor at Houghton Mifflin in Boston, makes another point: "If teachers have well-prepared students in small classes—as they get in colleges such as Oberlin or Kenyon—they can be more freewheeling. But if they're at the University of Kansas with 4,000 students of varying abilities taking the same introductory literature course, they don't have that kind of flexibility."

Johnson is the sponsoring editor of *Contemporary American Poetry,* a text anthology compiled by poet A. Poulin, Jr. who teaches at the State University of New York in Brockport and is the publisher of BOA Editions, a small press. Poulin's anthology includes forty poets in 600 pages, from Ashbery and Ammons through Levertov and Logan to Wilbur and James Wright. Its third edition was published in 1980, five years after the second edition was published, and

Poulin says, "trying to keep track of forty poets for five years is extremely difficult even for me, who reads out of pleasure and interest and because it's part of my profession. Not to mention the expense of all those books and magazines. And trying to understand forty different poets?"

The majority of college English teachers, says Poulin, are not poets or specialists in contemporary poetry. "They probably teach several different courses each week: two sections of English composition, a course in the Victorian novel, and a survey of British and American poetry since 1945. They can't devote the time and money necessary to keep up with one poetry course. An anthologist does that, and an anthology helps teachers."

Poulin fears that the alternative to such massive study—other than using anthologies—is that individual teachers would latch onto groups of poets and teach only their favorite groups. "Then students wouldn't even come into contact with other poets, as they can with an anthology in hand."

Poetry—Not TV Commercials

Gregory Orr's response? "Teachers 'do' too many poets anyway, in too short a time," he says. "Students would not be hurt by studying fewer poets. This is poetry we're talking about, not TV commercials."

But is he not also talking about graduate students, or undergraduate juniors and seniors at the very least? What about huge introductory courses in state universities? "Even in a course with many sections, teachers have some leeway," says Orr. "Standardization of material is a form of tyranny, and I want to spark some rebelliousness. Teachers have more liberty than they realize."

Orr objects to what he describes as a mental set. "Half-a-dozen book salesmen will come to an English teacher in a semester. They barely know the poets their companies publish—only their anthologies. That's where their loyalty is. My loyalty and the loyalty of every poet who teaches, is to poetry."

Debby Mayer

Special Collections: Poetry in the Hothouse

The past thirty years have seen the growth of a curious new market for poetry known as special collections. These collections, scattered across the United States in libraries of large universities, will buy a poet's work even if no one reads it or studies it. They don't care about changing tastes, bestsellers, and literary fads. They are a kind of poetry bank, patiently saving everything just in case some scholar may need it. Looked at another way, they are time capsules, collecting poetry which may be unknown now but might become famous in the future.

They collect chapbooks, little magazines, broadsides, signed editions, poetry postcards, and posters; plays, novels, and journalism by poets; anthologies and variant editions; manuscripts, letters, photos, personal possessions, records, tapes, and films. They collect, in the words of the late Cyril Connolly, "not only . . . what an author has written but what he has tried to throw away; his notebooks, correspondence, false starts; they will sort it all out for him and accept material which is never to be shown. . . . It is probably the best thing that has happened to writers for many years."

Many of the collections began with passionately committed individuals: a psychiatrist in Minneapolis who saved every little magazine he could find, back in the 1920's; a poetry lover who wrote to all the poets he knew, asking for the papers they threw away; a couple editing a little magazine who decided that someone, somewhere, had to save the "thin volumes of poems by housewives in Iowa;" the librarian of a great university known for science who purchased an entire storeful of avant-garde poetry to change the university's image.

The collections owe their growth to devoted librarians who look at every catalogue and announcement and ferret out every publication by a chosen poet or press. They gain recognition when some of their holdings become unexpectedly important, suddenly talked about and studied in English classes.

Coda wrote to librarians at 38 special collections to find out more about their unsung services. Twelve of the biggest collections are listed below. To show how thorough they are, they are listed here with a random sampling of their holdings, including some less-famous poets or presses whose books or papers they collect. (The samples do not necessarily represent complete or typical holdings.)

Twelve of the biggest collections

Address	*Range*	*Sample holdings*
S.U.N.Y. at Buffalo Poetry Collection 420 Capen Hall Buffalo, New York 14260 (716) 636-2917 Att: Robert J. Bertholf, Curator	20th century poetry in English and in translation (probably the largest collection in the world)	Kayak Archive Sonya Dorman Siv Cedering Anselm Hollo Richmond Lattimore Stanley Plumly Louis Simpson John Tagliabue Byron Vazakas Paul Zweig

University of Texas Humanities Research Center P.O. Box 7219 Austin, Texas 78712 (512) 471-9119 Att: Dechard Turner, Director	20th century English and American literature	Gregory Corso Charles Henri Ford Gerard Malanga James Tate Louis Zukofsky Archive
Indiana University Lilly Library Bloomington, Indiana 47405 (812) 335-2452 Att: Acquisitions Department	20th century American poetry, including manuscripts. Papers of poetry anthologists Louis Untermeyer and Oscar Williams	A.R. Ammons James Broughton Stanley Kunitz David Meltzer Howard Moss Muriel Rukeyser David Shapiro Robin Skelton Mary Ellen Solt
Brown University The Harris Collection John Hay Library Providence, Rhode Island 02912 (401) 863-1514 Att: Rosemary Cullen, Curator	20th century American and Canadian poetry and plays	*Aphra* *Ark River Review* *Beloit Poetry Journal* *Northern Journey* *Poesie* *Wormwood Review*
Northwestern University Library Special Collections Evanston, Illinois 60201 (312) 492-3635 Att: Russell Maylone, Curator	Underground and young writers of the U.S., Canada, and England, from the late 1950's to the present	Carol Berge Douglas Blazek Edward Dorn Sandra Hochman Don Lee D.A. Levy Diane Wakoski

Washington University Rare Books and Special Collections Olin Library St. Louis, Missouri 63130 (314)889-5495 Att: Holly Hall, Acting Chief	20th century American and British poetry	Donald Finkel James Merrill John N. Morris Howard Nemerov Robert Sward May Swenson Constance Urdang Mona Van Duyn
University of Wisconsin Department of Rare Books and Special Collections Memorial Library Madison, Wisconsin 53706 (608) 262-3243 Att: Deborah Reilly, Assistant Curator	20th century little magazines in English (probably the largest collection there is)	*Assembling* *Circus Maximus* *Experiment* *Moving Out* *Room of One's Own* *Woman Poems*
University of California at Berkeley The Poetry Archive, Bancroft Library Berkeley, California 94720 (415) 642-6481 Att: Anthony Bliss, Rare Books Librarian	Postwar Bay Area and California poetry	Robert Duncan Thom Gunn Josephine Miles Jack Spicer City Lights Archive Auerhahn Press Archive

University of California at San Diego	Poetry in English	Paul Blackburn

University of California at San Diego
Archive for New Poetry
The University Library
La Jolla, California 92093
(619) 452-6766
Att: Michael Davidson, Director

Poetry in English published since 1945

Paul Blackburn Archive
Clayton Eshleman
Ken Friedman and the Fluxus poets
Marianne Moore
Lew Welch Archive

Boston University Libraries
Special Collections
771 Commonwealth Avenue
Boston, Massachusetts 02215
(617) 353-3696
Att: Dr. Howard Gotlieb, Director

Contemporary American poetry

Ben Bellitt
Richard Frost
Nikki Giovanni
William Heyen
Maxine Kumin
Loreen Niedecker
Lucien Stryk
Andrew J. Young

The Library of Congress
Washington, D.C. 20540
(202) 426-5521
Att: David Kresh, Recommending Officer for Poetry in English

Poetry in English including most work sent for copyright registration

Sam Cornish
Eloise Loftin
Thomas Lux
Tony Towle
John Stevens Wade

Yale University
Sterling Memorial Library
1603A Yale Station
New Haven, Connecticut 06520
(203) 436-8335
Att: Susan Steinberg, American Studies Bibliographer

American literature

Grilled Flowers
Hot Water Review
Sun and Moon
Michael Davidson
Rochelle Ratner
Martin J. Rosenblum
Primus St. John

Taste Not an Issue

Special collections, unlike other libraries, are non-discriminating. "Our holdings are meant to out-live changes of taste," states Rosemary Cullen, curator of the little magazines collection at Brown University. "They represent the history of our culture, and for that, the bad is as important as the good."

Special collections are the only libraries which try to preserve work in its original condition. They keep dustjackets on the books. Rubber stamps or bookplates are placed carefully so as not to conceal a book's design. Weak bindings and flimsy paper covers are left untouched, not reinforced with plastic or new boards. A book kept by a special collection is often in better shape than the author's own copy.

These books are treasures, easy to damage and difficult to replace. You may read them only on the premises, after checking your coat, briefcase, and notebooks at the door. You must show your reader's card or explain your purpose to a librarian. You may be asked to leave if you are seen using a pen or indelible pencil while reading. Often the chairs are hard, the lights dim. The poetry around you seems to have been buried in a catacomb. Casual curiosity, the curiosity that builds new audiences for poetry, quickly withers. But, if the work you heard about is published by a small press or is unpublished, you may not find it anywhere else.

Hide the Books or Rebind Them?

Since the main purpose of special collections is preservation, use of current poetry is rare. The Black Mountain collection of the State University of New York at Stony Brook and the Bay Area collection of California State University at Hayward are used "very slightly." The Rare Books Division at U.C.L.A. at Westwood, which emphasizes New York School poets, is used "about five or six times a week."

Heavy use is exemplified by the Lockwood Library of the State University of New York at Buffalo. This collection is perhaps the biggest and oldest of contemporary poetry and poetry criticism in the English-speaking world, according to staff member Beverly Ruth Vander Kooy. In 1975 Lockwood received about twelve visitors a day.

Most librarians would like to see the books and papers used much more, but there are problems. "With books," states Rita Bottoms, head of Special Collections at the University of California at Santa Cruz, "the dilemma is whether to hide them in special collections or to rebind them for circulation—which ruins them.

"We're different. We encourage use of books by putting them in the stacks (lending section) whenever possible. With manuscripts, we find out the copyright status and author's wishes as soon as we obtain them. Authors who want their papers kept private must tell us this. We never sequester anything except by specific request. With fragile and rare material, we're very lenient. You don't need a note from God to see our holdings."

Another special collection which lends books is the Harriet Monroe Modern Poetry Collection at the University of Chicago. Only broadsides and the most fragile publications are withheld. Says librarian Charles Helzer, "Harriet Monroe was quite explicit that this collection be constantly used." Harriet Monroe was founding editor of *Poetry* magazine of Chicago and bequeathed to the collection all her files up to 1936. (Files since 1936 have gone to Indiana University's Lilly Library.)

The usual caution is also thrown to the winds at Harvard's Woodberry Poetry Room. "Many little magazines are in shreds from too much use," boasts curator Stratis Haviaras. "We display the latest issues of about 200 little magazines and 4,000 to 5,000 current poetry books." The books are borrowed from Harvard's main research library, which houses the room's overflow. Manuscripts, worksheets, broadsides, posters, and about 4,000 recordings—including several made expressly for the room by T.S. Eliot, Donald Hall, and W.D. Snodgrass—are kept in use constantly. Readings and workshops are held frequently in the room.

Money for the Woodberry Room comes from an endowment set up at its inception in 1931, when its main attraction was the personal library of Amy Lowell. In 1949, Finnish architect Alvar Aalto redesigned the room and all its furniture, including the record cabinets. Aino Aalto, his wife, designed the fabrics for the upholstery. The emphasis is on comfort, light, and warm textures.

In Tucson, the University of Arizona has remodeled a small white house for its Poetry Center, which preserves about 4,000 poetry books and over 125 tapes of campus readings of poetry and fiction. Tapes include Marvin Bell, Edward Field, Leslie Silko, and Ruth Stone, to name a few.

The Elliston Poetry Room in the main library at the University of Cincinnati houses 12,000 publications, about 300 hours of taped readings, and 400 records. The Room sponsors readings, workshops, and a radio program on station WAIF. Like the Harvard and Arizona Poetry Center collections, it has its own card catalogue and listening equipment.

Most special collections do not lend books, but all are eager for more visitors. The opportunity for reading is there, and a few words with a librarian will usually get you in. But how many readers know about the collections?

Limelight Is for Libraries, Too

"We need a lot more publicity," says Beverly Vander Kooy. "One of our methods is to tie in with local readings by displaying all of the visiting poet's works. For this, we depend on the sponsors to inform us of readings in advance. We also want poets to know that they can come here to find work they've lost and that we're a good source for anthologies." For young poets, she points out that little magazines in special collections are the best source for work by their contemporaries who don't yet have a book.

California State University's Floyd Erickson recommends that collections be promoted by the English Department. Professors can use the local special collection to bring their poetry courses up to date, getting the jump on textbooks and anthologies, or to shop for books for their classes. Young writers can be taught how to select outlets for their own work from the collection's little magazines.

Who Buys Poetry?

Besides special collections, the only libraries that can be counted on to buy poetry are academic research libraries, suggesting that poetry is more often studied than read for pleasure. These libraries buy only hardcovers, however. Small press books, which represent the majority of poets now writing, are almost exclusively the province of the special collection.

If you're interested in selling poetry books to special collections, remember that each has its own purchasing guidelines. To get in touch with them, start by using the lists here.

For other special collections, you must rely on getting your work reviewed in magazines which librarians read, like *Choice, Kirkus Reviews, Library Journal, Small Press Review,* and *San Francisco Review of Books.* Next, make sure your work is listed in standard bibliographies, such as *Subject Guide to Forthcoming Books, Books in Print,* and *The Small Press Record of*

Books. These tactics may result in sales to many regular academic libraries and even to public libraries. But if the binding is paper and the edition is small—500 copies or fewer—special collections may be your only library market.

Many special collections librarians like to meet poets and publishers personally. Donald Kunitz of the University of California at Davis and Stratis Haviaras of the Harvard Lamont Poetry Room participate in local book fairs in order to keep in touch with editors. Some collections rely on poets as advisors. Perhaps a collection near you would like your recommendations for purchase.

Readers Wanted

The collections listed here are only a sampling. Special collections are quietly performing an important task by buying poetry and preserving it for scholars and future readers. They are probably supporting poetry more than anyone has yet realized.

But what good is a market without readers? For a new or unknown poet, purchase by a special collection is not the key to publicity and new audiences. The special collections themselves need publicity. Their need for readers is just as acute as it is for poets. Without readers, the collections are mausoleums; with readers, they can be centers of continual discovery.

Nelson Richardson

Additional Special Collections in the U.S.

Address	*Representative poets or presses in collection*
U.C.S.B. Library Special Collections Santa Barbara, California 93106 (805) 961-2311 Att: Christian Brun, Head of Special Collections	Charles Bukowski Archive Bob Brown David Kherdian *Cafe Solo* Painted Cave Books Water Table Press
California State University Library Special Collections Hayward, California 94542 (415) 881-3612 Att: Elsa Glines, Acquisitions Librarian	Oyez Press Mary Norbert Kate Philip Lamantia Michael McBride Michael McClure
New American Poetry Collection **Kenneth Spencer Research Library** University of Kansas Lawrence, Kansas 66045 (913) 864-2700 Att: Alexandra Mason, Spencer Librarian	Jack Kerouac Kirby Congdon Larry Eigner Kenneth Koch
Harriet Monroe Modern Poetry Collection Joseph Regenstein Library University of Chicago Chicago, Illinois 60637 (312) 753-2904 Att: Jacqueline Coats, Head of Acquisitions	Archives of *Poetry* of Chicago Allen Ginsberg Rochelle Owens Mark Strand Toothpaste Press

University of California at Los Angeles
Special Collections and Rare Books
University Research Library
Rm. A1713
Los Angeles, California 90024
(213) 825-4988
Att: James Davis, Curator

Imamu Amiri Baraka
Tom Clark
Clark Coolidge
Kenneth Rexroth
Aram Saroyan

University of Arizona Library
Special Collections
Tucson, Arizona 85721
(602) 621-6423
Att: Louis Hieb, Acquisitions

W.H. Auden
W.S. Merwin
Gary Snyder
Philip Whalen

University of California at Davis
Special Collections
Shields Library
Davis, California 95616
(916) 752-1621
Att: Donald Kunitz, Head of Special Collections

Helen Adam
Daisy Aldan
Ron Bayes
James Bertolino
John Brandi
Joanne Kyger

University of California at Santa Cruz
Special Collections
Santa Cruz, California 95064
(408) 429-2547
Att: Rita Bottoms, Head of Special Collections

Kenneth Patchen Archive
William Everson
George Hitchcock
Perishable Press
IO
Caterpillar

S.U.N.Y. at Stony Brook
Special Collections
Stony Brook, New York 11794
(516) 246-5650
Att: Evert Volkersz, Head of Special Collections

Conrad Aiken
Jack Hirschman
Robert Kelly
Toby Olson
Joel Oppenheimer
Rosemary Waldrop

227

University of Connecticut Library
Special Collections
Storrs, Connecticut 06268
(203) 486-2524
Att: R.H. Schimmelpfeng, Curator

Black Mountain Poets
Charles Olson Archive

University of Florida
Rare Books Division
Library West
Gainesville, Florida 32611
(904) 392-0321
Att: Sidney Ives, Chairman

Duane Locke
Peter Meinke
William E. Taylor

New Mexico State University Library
P.O. Box 3475
Las Cruces, New Mexico 88003
(505) 646-1508
Att: Dr. James Dyke, Director

All books stocked by Gotham
Book Mart in New York City

Trinity College Library
Watkinson Library
Hartford, Connecticut 06106
(203) 527-3151, ext. 307

Small press examples of fine printing
David R. Godine publications

Beloit College Library
Beloit, Wisconsin 53511
(608) 365-3391
Att: Dennis W. Dickinson, Director

Vanity presses

Temple University Library
Contemporary Culture Collection
Philadelphia, Pennsylvania 19122
(215) 787-8667
Att: Pat Case

Insect Trust Gazette
Yarrow Stalks
Small presses of the late 1960's

University of Washington Library Special Collections Seattle, Washington 98195 (206) 543-0742 Att: Gary Menges	Theodore Roethke Archive William Stafford David Wagoner
University of Hawaii Library Special Collections 2550 The Mall Honolulu, Hawaii 96822 (808) 948-8230 Att: Eleanor Au, Head of Special Collections	Black Sparrow Press Hawaiian poets and presses Phyllis Thompson
University of Southern Illinois Morris Library Carbondale, Illinois 62901 (618) 536-3391 Att: Alan Cohn, Humanities Librarian	Denise Levertov Diane DiPrima Robert Bly Midwestern and Illinois poets Kulchur Foundation Publications

Large Public Libraries with Special Collections

San Francisco Public Library Civic Center San Francisco, California 94102 (415) 558-3511 Att: Mrs. Nancy Nee, Head of Literature, Philosophy, and Religion	Bay Area small presses
Brooklyn Public Library Grand Army Plaza Brooklyn, New York 11238 (212) 780-7700 Att: Monte Olenick, Chief of Language and Literature Division	Brooklyn small presses Marianne Moore

Milwaukee Public Library
814 West Wisconsin Avenue
Milwaukee, Wisconsin 53203
(telephone omitted by
request)
Att: Acquisitions
Department

Milwaukee poets and presses
California poets
Women poets

Detroit Public Library
5201 Woodward Avenue
Detroit, Michigan 48202
(313) 321-1000
Att: Ann Rabjohns, Head of
Language and Literature
Department

Michigan poets and presses
Broadside Press
Bardic Echoes Press
Ghost Dance Press
Red Hanrahan Press
El Soplon Press
Zeitgeist

New York Public Library
Fifth Avenue and 42 Street
New York, New York 10018
(212) 790-6315
Att: Stephen Green, Room
108, Current Periodicals
Section

Big Deal
Glassware
Not Guilty
Stroker
Sun
Sunbury

Suggested Reference

Subject Collections, 2 vols. (A
guide to book collections by
Library of Congress subject
headings in academic,
public, and special libraries
and museums in the U.S.,
Canada, and Puerto Rico.)
R. R. Bowker

Note: See Appendix for addresses of publishers.

Poetry Readings: Why Go to Them, Why Give Them?

One of my latest sensations was going to Lady Airlie's to hear Browning read his own poems—with the comfort of finding that, at least, if you don't understand them, he himself apparently understands them even less. He read them as if he hated them and would like to bite them to pieces.

Henry James

"Poetry readings are now an established part of the cultural life in this country," says poet Galway Kinnell. "On any given night, there are probably more people listening to poetry in the United States than in the rest of the world combined." Poets now read everywhere, not just in colleges, bookstores, and poetry centers, but in lofts, cafes, prisons, on the Staten Island Ferry—even on the Showboat Becky Thatcher on the Muskingum River in Marietta, Ohio. They may come dressed in masks, or chant and wear costumes. Younger poets read in pairs, or with a well-established poet. They may read their own work, the work of other poets, or poetry in translation. Well-known poets attract so many listeners that in some

231

places reservations have to be made in advance; young poets have been known to read to an audience of one—someone who showed up just to get out of the rain.

"Readings Force Me to Exchange"

"Readings have helped my identity, my confidence, and given me exposure," says Mark Nepo, whose book, *Angels on Horseback,* was a finalist in the 1982 National Poetry Series. He has given over forty readings in community colleges and universities in upstate New York, where he lives, and in a few art galleries in New York City. He read first in an open reading in a local coffee house.

Nepo believes the poetry reading is a two-way experience. "Readings are not just for people to come and hear me," he says. "They let me see people. I learn more about human nature, which helps me write more. Creation happens in solitude; readings force me to exchange.

"Reading a poem to myself is the last phase of creation; reading to an audience launches a poem out into the world," says Nepo. "Poetry is essentially oral, and I like to think that reading aloud is the natural process by which poetry first came about."

Nepo has made almost no money through readings; two-thirds of the readings he's given have been for free. When he does get paid, he usually makes $200. Regardless of payments, Nepo believes the poet should be available to the audience both before and after the reading. "One shouldn't just get on and off stage," he says.

Giving a strong performance is important, "but the work comes first," says Nepo. "If the performance gets in the way of the work, then the meaning of what's being said is lost. The voice needs to support the words, not overpower them." He also believes in memorizing. "When I only have to look down once at the poem I'm reading, I spend a lot more time looking at the audience. That gives me more freedom to be with the audience, and I feel a better connection to them."

Nepo finds West Coast audiences different from those in the East. "In the East, I sense whether an audience has connected to my poetry through its silence. Only at the end of the reading is there applause, or lack of it. In the West, audience reaction is spontaneous," he says. "When I read in San Francisco, if someone in the audience particularly liked a line, they'd say 'yea' or 'wow' or I'd hear one brief hand clap or laugh of recognition."

The People's Art

"Readings are part of the political work of poetry," says poet Audre Lorde. "They are a very important way of making public contact, the way nothing else really does." Lorde didn't always feel that way, however. "At the beginning, my readings were more of a showcase—I read work I had completed and was comfortable with. I lost interest in that rapidly." Lorde admits she would have stopped reading altogether if she had not risked a change. "Now I use the intensity of the reading to find out how the audience feels," she says. "A poem is not finished until I feel the flavor of the audience reaction rising up to me. Reading is part of the creative process."

Poets are often members of an audience as well, and Lorde feels that "listening to poetry is like the high you get from going to the symphony versus listening to an excellent stereo. The contact has a liquid quality to it. A particular life and a breath illuminate a poem at a reading," she says. "People often make contact with a poet at a reading the way they don't on the page, and that makes a poetry reading a circular thing: not just a performance for the poet, but a dynamic that goes back and forth.

"Readings bring you closer to the people you want to reach," says Lorde. "Thirty years ago, the average person in the street wouldn't have anything to do with a poet. Now I teach poetry to policemen," she says. "The disenfranchised peoples of this country—from the beats through black poets to the feminist and lesbian poets writing today—have reclaimed poetry as a living art. The rise in the number of readings has brought back poetry as the people's art."

Lorde has made more money by reading than from selling her books. "That's not to be construed as a measure of the importance of either books or readings, but poets also have to eat and pay rent," she says. "Readings have increased the sales of my books, too. It's easier for the public to buy a book after a reading. Once they have made the connection, people hunger for the touch of the book."

Because reading to an audience is such an emotional experience, Lorde is usually exhausted afterward and doesn't like receptions. She tries to include a "Question and Answer" session into the reading itself. "It's important not to end a reading by dropping through a trap door, but a writer shouldn't be fingered afterward."

Lorde encourages young poets to read. "The reading keeps the word alive and keeps our creative and political courage going."

"Poets Are Exhilarated After a Reading"

One of the nation's most active sponsors of poetry readings is the Loft in Minneapolis, run by Susan Broadhead. "Some poets are wonderful raconteurs," she says. "They explain what events led up to the poem, what was happening during the time the poem was being written, and how the poem got written. A poet who does that really has the audience in the

234

palm of his or her hand." Others, she says, talk about their political beliefs, for instance, Carolyn Forché, who spoke at the Loft about her experience in El Salvador. Others aren't anecdotal at all. "June Jordan has said that she writes personal poetry, but she won't read it," says Broadhead. "She feels that would be self-indulgent. She wants to speak as a representative of the community. She gives only a brief introduction and then reads the poetry in an expressive, impassioned voice.

"Finally, some poets are just bad readers," says Broadhead. "Some aren't good at sharing themselves. But that's just like everything else—there are bad movies and plays, too."

The Loft chooses its readers in a variety of ways. For its "Mentor Series," established poets who give both readings and workshops are selected by a committee. Mentors are paired with younger or less-established poets who must apply by submitting anonymous manuscripts. Because the mentor naturally draws a bigger crowd, the young poet has a larger audience too. "The series is good for the career and development of new writers," says Broadhead.

Another type of reading at the Loft is the Lottery Reading. To make sure the selection committee doesn't have a blind spot, the names of poets who have applied for and been denied the opportunity to read at the Loft are put in a lottery and chosen at random. Poets in Performance is a new series at the Loft, in which poets are trained to bring out the theatrical quality of the work. Payment for readings varies as much as the programs themselves: $45-$2,000.

"Books aren't often sold on the spot at the Loft, but eventually they sell in the local bookstores," says Broadhead. "A poet who reads at the Loft becomes known in Minneapolis and St. Paul. The audience for poetry has rapidly increased in the Twin Cities: about fifteen other organizations or bookstores now schedule readings here.

"One of the frustrating things about literature is the distance between the audience and the poet in the printed form," she says. "One of the gratifications of the poetry reading is the direct communication with the audience. The poetry reading is a communal experience that one doesn't get from reading the poem on the page." Through these readings, Broadhead says that poets are finding another persona, a healthier identity. "Many are exhilarated and keyed up after a reading—as if they have gotten a kind of regeneration."

Poetry readings have negative aspects too, although most poets are reluctant to talk about them. Yet poets do complain about the conditions of the reading: huge spaces without proper acoustics, readings which are not publicized, no payment, and of sponsors who schedule too much exhausting activity for them. Sponsors, on the other hand, complain of poets who are not reliable, of not being able to get books from publishers, and of poets whose voices don't project.

Poetry readings may have affected our language as well. It is possible that the proliferation of readings has given a lightness to poetry and made poets write more humorously. The syntax of contemporary poetry is quite simplified—perhaps poetry has become less complex so an audience will understand it at first hearing? One poet mentioned the pressure to be amusing between poems, as if the poetry itself isn't sufficient.

"Like Studying Literature—Without the Homework"

Poets who read at the Poetry Center of the 92nd Street Y in New York City are in great company. T. S.

Eliot, Robert Frost, W. H. Auden, Wallace Stevens and Elizabeth Bishop are among the many poets who have read at the Y since 1939. "We are able to attract the world's leading writers to the Y partly because they feel it's an honor to become a part of this grand literary tradition," says Shelley Mason, director of the Poetry Center. "In programming the series, we consider the season as a whole, instead of a series of individual readers," she says. "We ask ourselves: Who are the established voices in the world that our audience should hear? Who are the foreign writers who may be celebrated in their own countries, but who are relatively unknown here? And finally, who are the newly emerging writers we'd like to introduce at the Poetry Center?"

Members of the Poetry Center can get an overview of contemporary world literature: poets, novelists, and playwrights. "Being a member of the Poetry Center is like studying literature—without the homework," says Mason.

The Poetry Center attracts members for several reasons. "Of course people are curious about the so-called 'famous writers' on our program. More than 1,200 people fought their way in to hear Czeslaw Milosz shortly after he won the Nobel Prize, in part to see what a Nobel Prize winner looks like," she says. "But on a deeper level, many people come to readings hoping to find a human point of entrance into books that may be difficult to read. Poetry can be hard to approach unguided. After a reading, many listeners return to the poetry on the page with fewer inhibitions. The extraordinary number of books we sell after a writer's appearance seems to confirm this.

"Of the thirty readings each season, only three or four are truly memorable," says Mason. "That's probably the law of averages in any art form." Yet even the less-inspiring readings don't seem to keep people away. "Our audience is very faithful, and the particularly wonderful thing about them is their willingness to attend readings by poets they've never heard of."

"Readings Are Not a Luxury, but a Staple"

Writers such as Robert Bly and Gary Snyder usually draw the biggest audiences at the College of Marin in Kentfield, California. May Sarton's readings sell out, too. "Because this is an environmentally conscious community, ecological poets draw the biggest crowds—as well as feminist and lesbian poets," says Steven Barclay, who runs the series there. Barclay claims that the College of Marin presents more readings and events than any other college or university in the country—120 programs a year.

Barclay chooses the poets who will read at Marin by his own intuition, knowing what sells, and knowing who people would like to hear. He follows no formula, but has one restriction. "We're in bad financial straits, so we can't afford to have readings that will draw only fifty people," says Barclay. They pay the poet $500-$2,000 to read; the public is charged from $6-$8.

"There's a bigger poetry community now than ever before," he says. "People have come to accept the reading not as a luxury, but as a staple. Readings are the equivalent of going to the opera or to hear music—the audience becomes very involved. The reading clarifies what the writer is trying to say in his work. When a poem means more to you on a personal level, it can change your whole impression of poetry from something boring and remote to something deeply emotional."

A Higher and Purer Life

One of the best and busiest readers in the country by far is Galway Kinnell. In one month, his schedule has been known to include San Jose, Chicago and Burlington, Vermont. He often gives as many as five readings a month, and on occasion has given up to thirty .

"I don't write any differently due to readings, nor do I get any sense of the quality of my poetry through the reaction of the audience," says Kinnell. "Occasionally I've become aware of flaws in my work at a reading—not because of the reaction of the audience, but simply because I'm reading to an audience. I may feel poetry more in that situation.

"People used to go to readings to see what a poet looked like," he says. "Twenty years ago a poet was an unusual item. At that time, I was occasionally introduced as 'A Living American Poet.'" Now Kinnell thinks most people go to readings because they like poetry. "The audiences are knowledgeable and attentive," he says. "They want to see the person whose work they've already come to like. Frequently a rapport and warmth develops between poet and audience.

"A reading should give an audience a sense of a higher and purer life than the one they're living day to day," he says. "It should give clarification and illumination, through language, of human experience.

"Maybe it's not such a bad thing that financial support has dried up for poetry readings in some places, and that people have been forced to pay for readings," says Kinnell. "These audiences seem to value readings more. They're not there because it's good for them, but because they like it. Perhaps there's a more natural feeling in the room as a consequence."

Kinnell makes a good part of his income from readings, as do many better-known poets. "It might be possible for a poet with small needs to live by readings alone," he says. "There are few other countries where that's possible.

"By their nature, not all readings are first-rate," says Kinnell. "In music, one has to get to a certain level before one can give a concert in New York. But anyone can give a poetry reading. The poetry reading is a completely democratic institution."

Daryln Brewer

Five

ADVENTURES IN PUBLISHING

Orphans' Tales: What to Do When Your Editor Leaves

David Nemec is a writer of fiction and nonfiction whose most recent novel is *Mad Blood* (Dial). His editor, Rick Kot, was fired one month before *Mad Blood* was published. (Dial was absorbed by Doubleday and only four out of eighteen staff members were retained.) "I was left without an editor—no one to follow up on publicity, no one to talk up my book," says Nemec. *Mad Blood* was handed over to one of the editors who remained, but his new editor was "swamped with books he'd inherited and found it impossible to devote much individual attention to any one book," he says.

Nemec has had six editors, one for each book he's published. He has never published two books with the same editor. One of his editors did buy a second book of his, but then moved to another house. "Writers and editors seem to have great difficulty establishing a continuing relationship," says Nemec, who thought he'd finally found the perfect editor in Kot. "It's an unfortunate outgrowth of the transiency that now exists throughout the publishing industry."

Both Rick Kot and Nemec's agent saw *Mad Blood* as a breakthrough book for the author, but the whole ordeal has turned out to be a major disappointment. "An editor keeps the ball rolling—he's the key person between publicity, subsidiary rights, and all the other departments. No one in publicity even read my novel," he says. "It's frustrating to feel you're alone in supporting and promoting your book."

Nemec has had a particularly difficult time because he tends to relate best to younger editors who are the first to get fired when cuts are made. He thinks the frequent movement of editors also makes it tough to establish a career as a fiction writer. "Not long ago, a first novelist would get a contract on his second book even if he'd only finished an outline," he says. "Now editors want to see the finished product."

Nemec has been writing on and off for eighteen years, full-time for the past seven. He has had the same problem with magazine editors. "I've sold stories to magazines, the acquiring editor has left before the piece has come out, and then it's a struggle to get it published at all," says Nemec. "In terms of book publishing, when a writer has no track record at a particular house, he has to start over each time from square one. Even writers who have published six or seven books find themselves continually on square one."

Learn the Publishing Process

"An editor leaving a house—especially with a novelist's first or second book—is the worst thing that can happen to a writer," says Rick Kot, who now works at Harper & Row. "An editor's departure is particularly hard for a first novelist because an acquiring editor usually does much more promotional work on a first novel," he says. "After all, you're starting with a blank slate.

"All books, and especially fiction, need personal attention," says Kot. "An editor gets quotes for books and sees that copies are sent out for review and to notables in the industry. The editor is both advocate and spokesperson; he wants to get people both inside and outside of the publishing house to talk up a book."

Kot was dismissed from Dial with one week's notice, one month's severance pay, and a free copy of "How to Write a Perfect Resume." "A lot of editors have been fired or are leaving the business," he says. He doesn't know the reason for the many defections, but feels it's the rare house that can hold on to younger editors.

You Can't Take It with You

An editor may take a writer with him to a new house, depending on what stage a book is in and if the original publisher wants to release it. "This is open to negotiation between the agent, editor and both publishers," says Kot. If the first publisher thinks a book will make a lot of money, however, it's very unlikely they'll let it go.

Many agents now request an "editor's clause" in book publishing contracts, which states that if the editor leaves, he or she may take that writer along to the next house. "Maybe if you're a superstar writer or have a very powerful agent, you'll get an editor's clause," says Kot, "but in my experience most publishers refuse to accept it." Even if the original publisher does relinquish the rights to a book, a writer may still run into trouble: the second publisher may not want the book.

Kot advises writers to "learn as much about publishing as you can. I don't believe in mystifying the publishing process. I have always tried to explain it to a writer each step along the way. I believe in introducing authors to the key people in the house—they need to feel free to speak with others in the house besides the editor. It's hard to make such connections in bigger houses, but if it works, a writer feels part of the whole system, instead of having only a tenuous line to one editor," he says. "Be prepared to go in fighting. Be informed. And have a good agent who will work for you."

An Uphill Battle

But, even the top agents in the business can't avoid trouble when an editor leaves. "Having an editor change jobs is devastating," says literary agent Jean Naggar, "and it's particularly difficult for new writers because they bond strongly with the first editor. Outside of the agent, an editor is the first strong validation of a writer's work. No matter how good the author/agent relationship is, the editor is one more impartial person on the writer's side," says Naggar. "When an editor leaves, a writer feels lost. I try to fill that gap; I try to see the new editor and the publicity people, but rarely does an editor feel quite the same commitment to an inherited project. It's uphill all the way."

Naggar told of a battle with an imprint publisher (an autonomous publishing division within a larger company that is editorially independent, yet has the use of the support systems—such as publicity, subsidiary rights, sales, and production—of the larger organization), one she fought for a year. Two people were involved in the imprint—the publisher, and below him, a senior editor. The book in this case was a 2,000-page science fiction trilogy written by an author with five hardcover books to her credit. The house wanted the book, but author and editor couldn't reach an agreement. Just as Naggar was about to take the book back, she ran into the publisher at a party. She told him his offer wasn't a fair one; he doubled it. The next day, the editor called and said both she and the publisher were excited about buying the book. They did and a publication date was set for eighteen months later.

After working on the book for over a year, the editor announced that she was leaving to go to another house. By this time, the author had received the final check and a letter of acceptance. The date for a paperback auction had been announced. Then the publisher called Naggar and said he didn't want to do the book. He said the editor who left was the one excited about it. "You wouldn't want me to publish the book if I didn't think I could do a good job with it, would you?" he asked. All 2,000 pages had been fully retyped and copy-edited, what Naggar considered to be the initial stage of production. Up until that point, no indication had come from the publisher that the manuscript was anything less than hoped for, but Naggar soon received a letter claiming nonacceptance. The publisher also wanted the five-figure advance back—money which the writer had lived on for almost two years while she made revisions and awaited publication.

What makes this story even more amazing is that "imprints differentiate themselves from larger houses by claiming that the publisher is personally committed to books they buy," says Naggar. The writer hired a lawyer, and the case was eventually settled—she would repay one quarter of the original advance in three installments keyed in with payments from a new publishing house.

But reselling the book wasn't easy. In the two years since it had originally made the rounds, hardcover houses had decided science fiction wasn't profitable. For that reason, Naggar couldn't find a hardcover publisher for the book. Eventually a paperback house bought it, but they couldn't sign the papers until a settlement had been reached with the original publisher. The original publisher, of course, wouldn't release the rights until he settled with the author. A regular "Catch-22." "The book has done well, but the spectacular publishing effort we had hoped would herald the book did not come off," says Naggar.

Kicking Up a Fuss

"I like to think that with an agent, a writer at least has a partner in misery if his editor leaves," she says. "Although that's no protection against an editor's departure, at least an agent can kick up a fuss." One thing Naggar advises authors to do is to get a book done as soon as possible. "An author may think he has a long time to finish a book, but prompt completion is essential. If an editor lasts one year at a publishing house, I'm happy—honestly."

After numerous bad experiences with editors who change jobs, Naggar insists on two things in contracts she negotiates. "Where it states that the publisher will advise an author on acceptability, I insist that the publisher notify the author of acceptance or non-acceptance of a manuscript, in writing, within thirty days," she says. Secondly, when an editor buys a book on the basis of a proposal and a chapter or two, and when material is handed in periodically, she asks the editor to evaluate that material, in writing, stating whether it is acceptable so far, and confirming that the book adheres to the pattern initially proposed. "Each editor sees a book differently," says Naggar. "One editor has a certain vision of a book—author and editor discuss that and are on the same track—and then a new editor comes in and says, 'That's not what I had in mind.' There's nothing objective about editing, no right or wrong way to edit a book."

Naggar also insists that authors (even those who say they don't want to bother their agent) never send a letter to their editor, even a cover letter, without a carbon copy to her. "Keeping good files is absolutely essential," she says. "You never know when you might need them. You hope you won't, but you don't know." Letters from editors with delivery dates or revisions, or letters of philosophy which discuss how a book should be shaped, should also be kept. With these, a writer can prove that indeed the book handed in is the book signed up, or that changes to the original outline have been discussed with and approved by the editor. When an editor leaves, Naggar says, publishers will often take advantage of the opportunity to turn down a book. "Between the time a book is signed up and ready to be published, five books may have already been published on the same subject, which makes a title less attractive to that publisher or any other," she says. And by then, the author has invested a lot of time in writing the book.

"The industry is in a state of tremendous turmoil. A lot of editors aren't sure where they're going, but more money and continued growth help lure them away," says Naggar. "Publishers have caught on too; they balk at the editor's clause because they've cottoned to the fact that editors are leaving more often and want to take their books with them."

Less Dour for Poets

An editor's departure can be less dour for poets. When C.K. Williams' editor, Jonathan Galassi, left Houghton Mifflin for Random House, Williams didn't have too much trouble going with him. "The situation is different for poets because so little money is at stake," says Williams. "Galassi was my third editor at Houghton Mifflin. He and I became friends and he was my favorite editor. After he left, Houghton Mifflin seemed to lose interest in me. I don't know if it was inter-office confusion or what, but they let one of my books go out of print without even notifying me."

Galassi couldn't legally or technically offer Williams a chance to go with him to Random House, but he did express an interest in looking at his next book. Houghton Mifflin didn't argue. "It might have been trouble for me, but it wasn't," says Williams. Galassi subsequently bought and published Williams' next book, *Tar*.

Interest Charges Alone Can Cost Over $25,000

"In the old days, a decade or more ago, it was almost axiomatic that if a close relationship existed between an author and an editor, and the normal contractual terms could be agreed upon, the editor would take a writer with him to the new house," says Jack Macrae, an editor who moved from E.P. Dutton to Holt, Rinehart & Winston. But once the stakes got higher and interest rates went up, the original publisher wanted the advance paid back—with interest. "The whole business has been under tremendous pressure in the last few years, and publishers now make it clear that when a writer signs a contract, it is with the publisher, not with the editor—the point being that if the editor leaves, the publisher and his associates are still there," he says.

Occasionally a publisher will let an author leave, even today, and the interest costs are frequently waived if the book in question is a "smallish book," but on bigger books, the interest is sometimes compounded. "Buying such books becomes impossible for any publisher no matter how much the author or his original editor at the new publisher wants them," says Macrae. "In some cases, the interest alone can cost over $25,000—money the second publisher cannot apply against the author's advance, and therefore has little chance of earning back."

Macrae does not think the editor's clause should be standard in publishing contracts. "The writer is signing with the publisher, not only with the editor," he says. "If the editor put up the money, it'd be one thing, but the fact is, the publisher puts up the money." And some publishers, says Macrae, are paying 12% or more in interest for money these days.

Why are so many editors changing houses? Is it that they're not secure where they are, or that better opportunity exists elsewhere? "It's probably a combination of both," says Macrae, "but mostly the former." He thinks the root of the problem is an inability on the part of publishers to make good editors feel secure. "If an editor is on the make, simply out for him-or herself, then a writer is justified in becoming angry at the roving editor. But if conditions have changed in the house, then the writer should be more sympathetic to the editor's dilemma," he says. "I never would have thought I'd leave Dutton [Macrae was there for fourteen years], but when you get a new owner or boss, either you can or you can't work together.

"Another reason author/editor relationships are changing is because certain literary agents don't seem to value that relationship enough. Some agents look for top dollar alone and only consider short-term prospects, with little thought of a writer's career," says Macrae. Agents, of course, get a percentage of the author's advance and some, he says, can't see beyond that figure. "Nobody wants to talk about this fact, and certainly most agents don't act in this manner, but the few who do don't want to be inhibited by anything, including the relationship between author and editor," he says.

"The money side of the business got exaggerated and overblown some years ago when enormous advances were paid, primarily as a result of large subsidiary rights sales. Publishers lost sight of what sort of business we're in, forgetting that, in the best of circumstances, the book-buying public is relatively small. Trade book publishing is not a big-money business.

"As every year passes, the financial constraints seem to grow, and my guess is that we'll see fewer, not more, publishers," says Macrae. "There'll be more mergers and consolidations—a reflection of the financial reality of this capital-intensive and speculative business."

Can writers or their editors do anything to improve the situation? "If more editors worked harder and produced better and more successful books in the houses that employ them, the business would be a good deal more stable," he says. "And if authors rewarded editors they profess to admire by not shopping around for higher advances for each new title, the careers of both author and editor would be a good deal more fruitful than they are today."

Daryln Brewer

The Rapid Evolution of the Paperback: All to the Writer's Good?

In France, the paperback edition of a book is almost always published before the hardcover. Only after a book has earned a certain reputation will a publisher decide to put the pages in a more lasting form. Most books are published the other way around in this country: first the hardcover edition is published and, with luck, a year or so later, the book comes out in paperback. But the situation is changing so rapidly in the paperback industry that anything is possible these days. "Reprinting was the rule until recently; now that may be the exception," says Jack Romanos, publisher of Bantam.

Paperback publishers have traditionally reprinted hardcover fiction—with the exception of genre fiction, which has been published for years only in paperback. But paperback houses are now publishing more original fiction, in both hardcover and softcover. This came about partly because paperback publishers could seldom afford the extraordinarily high prices of most reprint rights; paper costs and inflation also made it difficult for paperback houses to earn back their investment.

Hardcover publishers are responding by establishing paperback lines of their own. Although very little original fiction has been published in these lines, many quality, out-of-print titles have been reissued in trade paperback.

Hardcover and paperback houses have also invented the "hard/soft deal," where a book is sold to both a hardcover and softcover house. Although hard/soft deals are generally made with more commercial writers, houses will often join together if that helps the book, the author, and the house. The advantage of such a deal to a writer is that he or she keeps 100% of the royalties, except of course, monies paid to an agent. (The writer and the hardcover house customarily split the money from a book's sale to paperback.) Sometimes such deals are made on the signing of the contract; at other times, they are struck later in the publishing process. However, a paperback editor who has bought all rights to a book, will still have a hard time selling hardcover rights to a hardcover editor. "It's a labor of Hercules," says Patrick O'Connor of Washington Square Press. [O'Connor has since left Washington Square Press.]

When hard/soft deals are struck with paperback and hardcover lines in the same house, another advantage for the writer may be the consolidation of all publishing ventures under one roof. "Writers may feel a sense of continuity and permanence when publishing both editions of a book with one house," says Parker Ladd, paperback expert at the Association of American Publishers. "With one father image looming in the background for the whole writing experience, publishing will become a healthier business."

The all-night auction, standard practice when blockbuster hardcovers were being sold to paperback, is more or less a thing of the past, although smaller, more tame auctions will continue to take place. The bottom line is still money: Ballantine, for example, still has to outbid Pocket Books for a title, even if the book was published originally by Ballantine's parent, Random House.

Mass-Market vs. Trade

There are two basic kinds of paperbacks: mass-market, the small "rack-size" book—approximately $7'' \times 4\frac{1}{2}''$, that which "easily fits in the back pocket of a pair of jeans," as Walter Meade describes them, and the trade paperback, usually a larger or "oversized" softcover book. A few other publishers, such as North Point Press in Berkeley, California publish a third kind of paperback—one not yet popular in this country, but very much like the sort published in France: a paperback with a dust jacket.

The method of distribution has always distinguished the two major kinds of paperbacks. About half of all mass-market books are distributed by "wholesalers." For instance, a salesman from Warner Books calls on a wholesaler who, in turn, distributes books to airports, drugstores and grocery stores. Trade paperbacks, like their hardcover cousins and some mass-market books, are distributed through "direct distribution" in which salesmen personally call on and sell directly to bookstores and colleges. But now this distinction is starting to blur because trade paperbacks are being distributed through wholesalers as well.

A good example is Washington Square Press, an imprint at Simon & Schuster which publishes rack-size as well as trade paperbacks and which reprinted *The Color Purple,* by Alice Walker, in trade paperback. Books published by Washington Square have the benefit of both wholesale and direct distribution. One might see, then, *The Color Purple* in both the airport and the local literary bookstore. Many paperback editors feel that wholesale distribution is essential to the future of all types of paperback publishing. Having this vast network already set up is seen as a great advantage to mass-market paperback publishers as they branch out and publish hardcover books, trade paperbacks, and original fiction.

"We've seen enormous growth in the trade paperback in particular," says Walter Meade, president, publisher and editor-in-chief of Avon. "Some books published in trade paperback are the finest available—from *One Hundred Years of Solitude* to self-improvement books." According to the Association of American Publishers, trade paperback sales increased by 30% in the first nine months of 1983.

We Try Harder

The size of paperback printings is also changing. An average mass-market printing used to be between 100,000 and 250,000 copies. Now a rack-size book might have a printing of only 15,000-20,000 copies. This scaling down may help literary titles, because while they probably would not sell 200,000 copies, they might sell 10,000. Literary imprints such as Avon's Bard, or Windstone at Bantam, keep literary titles in print and give recognition to less commercial, more serious writers such as Laurie Colwin, Margaret Atwood, and Thomas Pynchon. Eventually, first novelists may have the opportunity to publish books under these imprints, too. "Most of Windstone's books are reprints now," says Jack Romanos, "but we hope to do more originals soon."

Paperback houses have had a hard time attracting original manuscripts from serious writers, however. "There's nothing like having to prove yourself, which we've had to do to the community of agents and writers," says Walter Meade. Romanos agrees: "We've had a tough time breaking into the literary mafia. We have less access to books because the literary community still thinks of us last."

Although agents have traditionally sent manuscripts to paperback houses "in desperation," says Patrick O'Connor, he thinks "clever, entrepreneurial agents should start to orchestrate entire deals. Agents should send a manuscript to an editor in a hardcover house with a note saying the book would also appeal to so-and-so in a paperback house."

Because paperback houses have long been regarded as #2, paperback editors often have to try harder with books they publish. "If a hardcover house publishes a book and sells the reprint rights to a paperback house, they often make a profit before the book ever goes to press," says Romanos. "The incentive to perform is not the same, and when hardcover editors question whether or not a book should go back to press, the answer is no. They play it safe. We can't afford to have that attitude at Bantam. We buy books with the expectation of making a profit, not just laying off enough rights to cover our investment."

The Biggest Problem for Paperbacks

The pioneers who started the 44-year-old paperback industry are now retiring and a new generation—people who grew up reading paperbacks—is taking the reins. "The editors are younger, the retailers are younger, the agents are younger, and many of the writers are younger," says Romanos.

Readers are younger too. "College students and those in the 25-30-year-old group are much more comfortable with paperback editions," says Parker Ladd. "A whole new reading group naturally gravitates toward the paperback. Paperbacks mean convenience—they don't mean the classics or remind the reader of a textbook. The hardback book intimidates the young reader today."

"The only group not getting younger is book reviewers," says Romanos. Reviewers are undisputably the biggest problem for paperback houses publishing original fiction. But Judith Appelbaum, who used to write the "Paperback Talk" column in the *New York Times Book Review,* says paperbacks do get reviewed. "One thing I looked for when I worked at the *Times* was a prejudice against reviewing paperback originals, and I found none," she says. "Reviewers read galleys, which all look alike, whether finally published in hardcover or trade paperback."

A paperback novel was reviewed on the front page of the *New York Times Book Review: Waiting for the Barbarians,* by J.M. Coetzee, a novel about South Africa published by Penguin. While this breakthrough gave the industry much hope, Jack Romanos says it's virtually impossible to get a mass-market paperback reviewed. Ken Davis, author of *Two Bit Culture: The Paperbacking of America* (Houghton Mifflin), says the same is true of trade paperbacks. "Hardcover books still get preference—there's a built-in resistance against paperbacks," says Davis. One problem, says Appelbaum, is that paperback houses often don't get galleys to reviewers on time.

"Publishers need to initiate and indoctrinate reviewers to the paperback," says Parker Ladd. He says the stigma seems to be going away, but it takes time. "In due course, the word 'paperback' will lose its taint of unpleasantness," says Oscar Dystel, former chairman of Bantam, now a publishing consultant. Walter Meade took a slightly different tack: "Sometimes when you get a paperback book reviewed, you wish you hadn't."

Ann Patty of Poseidon Press, a hardcover imprint under the auspices of Pocket Books (the paperback sister of Simon & Schuster), says the only thing that really helps writers is editors—paperback or hardcover. "We have a strong commitment to talented young writers here because they are an investment in the future. But it's always a fight. New writers don't pay back the company immediately, and a house must have commercial books to balance the list."

Are paperback editors as good as their hardcover counterparts? "They may be better," says Jack Romanos. "Paperback editors learned their craft on paperback originals and they are more in tune with the wants and needs of the marketplace. They are more open-minded and have more room to experiment than a rigid and traditional editor. Paperback editors are willing to gamble on something new, different, or untested."

Will These Changes Help Writers?

Judith Appelbaum thinks the changes in paperback publishing will be good for writers because more houses are publishing original work. "It makes no sense to talk about paperback publishers anymore," says Appelbaum. "Just about every house publishes in both formats." She also believes that writers will be able to maneuver more and structure many different kinds of deals. Oscar Dystel agrees that the paperback industry is becoming more integrated. "We no longer have paperback publishing—just publishing in general," he says.

"The changes have got to make it better for younger writers," says Romanos. "Paperback publishers have grown up to be real publishers. Now the book dictates the format rather than the publishing program or the need to fill a slot on a list. We're not married to any size or format. A book that would normally have been published in mass-market might demand to be a trade paperback or a hardcover. We now have the flexibility and the rights to do that."

Romanos stresses the importance of building an

audience through paperbacks. "Writers make a big mistake insisting on publishing in hardcover," he says. "If we don't think a book will be successful in hardcover, we skip that step totally. Why print 7,000 copies of a first novel in hardcover when a writer might better reach his audience if we publish 75,000 as a paperback?"

Are Paperback Prices Too High?

"The difference is price, not format," says Appelbaum. "One important way to get a writer a bigger audience is by making books cheap—$3.95 instead of $17.00."

John Dessauer at the Center for Book Research in Scranton, Pennsylvania agrees, saying that a book doesn't sell better just because it's published in paperback. "That's one of the great traps of paperback publishing," he says. "What sells better is cheaper, and in the last two years, the average price of a trade paperback has risen 50%. That affects the popular notion of the paperback as a reasonable commodity."

Dessauer says the trade paperback is suffering because of skyrocketing prices. Although publishers may still be making money, Dessauer says fewer copies of trade paperbacks have been sold; the number of units (individual books) is down. "I keep hearing that the paperback is the panacea now—that trade paperbacks are the wave of the future. But all I see is a decline in unit sales and increases in price. The problem is that publishers and retailers look at dollar figures, not unit figures." And this, he feels, is bad for writers.

"If the public buys fewer books, new writers aren't helped," says Dessauer. "Only the established or well-reputed author benefits." Even if more novelists are being published in trade paperback, "the boost is temporary—a short-term solution, not a long-term one," he says. "We're only better off if people buy more books."

The bigger problem, Dessauer says, is that the public simply doesn't support literature. "Novelists have the impression that if their books are available in bookstores, then the problem is solved. But the average American bookstore is catering to the average American's taste. It's difficult to sell literature in our society and I often feel that poets and fiction writers don't face up to this reality."

How Do So Many People Live Without Poetry?

No one in the paperback industry sees much improvement in the publishing of poetry. "Poetry is neither an outgrowth nor a consideration of paperback houses," says Ken Davis. "They just don't see it as their business." "We can't even pay for the printing of a book with poetry," says Ann Patty. "Poetry is so difficult to publish, and I can't foresee publishing it unless it sells a lot."

Most poetry sells very little. "In the quiet times when my mind retreats into poetry—that which is committed to memory—I wonder how so many people live without it," says Walter Meade, "but they do. It takes a capacity for feeling to get to poetry and most people are busy desensitizing themselves." Jack Romanos says Bantam hasn't been successful with the poetry it has published. "We've never been able to capture the market. I don't see us experimenting with poetry in the near future. It would get lost on our list."

Patrick O'Connor, a poet himself, thinks paperback publishers should pay more attention to poetry in general. "It's time to see our modern giants in mass-market paperback," he says. And younger poets too. "Out of chapbooks and our literary magazines is coming a whole new generation of good poets."

The Avon Novel

"Writers today are awesomely accomplished," says Walter Meade, who published *Our Deal,* a first novel by Norman Levy. Levy's book is a trade paperback, the first in a series called "The Avon Novel."

Norman Levy was delighted to be published by Avon. His father used to run a bookstore on 42nd Street in New York City, where Levy was introduced to the first generation of trade paperbacks published by Anchor, Vintage, and Meridian. That was in 1953, when *A Farewell to Arms* sold for 35¢. Levy later managed one of the first all-paperback bookstores, Grand Central Paperbacks, also in New York. He had no qualms about publishing in paperback. His only complaint has been that familiar echo: getting reviewed.

"I was consulted on the cover of the book, which is embossed," he says. (Levy managed to get cover consultation in his contract.) "Avon created a whole style with my book—they used a special type, and the quality of the paper is exceptional." Most important, he says, "my book will last—both physically and because Avon is committed to it as part of their backlist.

"Avon continues to impress me," says Levy. His advance was about the same he would have received from a hardcover house publishing a first novel; the difference was in the print run: Avon published 20,000 copies of *Our Deal.* "1,500–3,000 copies are usually printed of a first novel," he says, "and they're priced at $15.95. Then just the author's immediate family reads the book. I like the idea of a big audience." *Our Deal* costs $5.95. It was advertised in the *New York Times Book Review,* the *New York Review of Books,* the *Washington Post* and the *Village Voice.* "Avon spent infinitely more money on the book than a hardcover house would have," says Levy. Avon gave him a publication party at the Ritz-Carlton in New York and sent him on tour to Houston and St. Louis.

Avon is also sponsoring a contest for first novels by writers under eighteen. Walter Meade says these are not new efforts to help first fiction, but "the same thing all publishers are engaged in—to flush talent out of the woodwork."

"Writers should decide which publisher they want, and a publisher ought to be able to put a book in any format," says Meade. "If a book appeals to readers still in college, for instance, it doesn't make sense to publish it in hardcover. The price is too high, and a writer would lose two years time when the audience could be approached directly. The rapid evolution of the paperback is all to the writer's good."

"Walter Meade is a very good editor, and he believes that publishers have to take risks and publish books that will shake up a house," says Levy. "He is right. *Our Deal* shook up the house. The copy editor, the art director, the publicity department—all the people at Avon were excited about working with an original manuscript." And as anyone in publishing knows, enthusiasm makes all the difference—no matter in what form a book is published.

Daryln Brewer

On Literary Fiction in Paperback

"The appeal of many excellent books is extremely limited in our society. To pretend otherwise is to ignore reality. If publishers persist in featuring paperback books of too limited appeal, then the whole industry will suffer in the long run and the attractiveness of the paperback as a commodity will lessen. I'm not saying not to publish literary fiction or scholarly books, but we must realize that a limited audience will buy them."

John Dessauer

"I believe there's a movement toward literary lines in paperback houses, especially mass-market, but a publisher has to make a good book sell. If a publisher can find the market for such books, print enough copies but not overprint, and use wholesale distribution, then selling literary books might work. For all our interest in the bottom line and in making money, the real thrill is to publish a good book, the kind you want to give a friend."

Patrick O'Connor

"One of the most difficult aspects of the publishing process is to search for, discover, evaluate and then to actually publish first novels on an economically sound basis. It's a self-defeating policy for publishers to discourage first novels; they are the essence of book publishing."

Oscar Dystel

"If authors present well-formed manuscripts which represent a lot of hard work and which aren't drafts promising better quality in the future, there's opportunity for publication. A writer must ask, 'Have I done the best I can?' If a book has not been published, perhaps the manuscript isn't up to the quality it should be. We live in such stressful times that writers aren't spending as much time as their forerunners did in writing good manuscripts."

Parker Ladd

"Most paperback books of original fiction are still category books: romances, science fiction, westerns and thrillers. Not much literary fiction is originated in paperback houses."

Ken Davis

The Blossoming of the Trade Paperback

As defined in the previous chapter, a trade paperback is a larger or oversized softcover book, usually more expensive than the mass-market paperback. Most hardcover publishers have established trade paperback lines of their own which reprint quality fiction and publish some original work.

"I yearn for the respectability of publishing in hardcover, but I know if I had done that to begin with, my books would be extinct now," says Armistead Maupin, whose fourth novel, *Baby Cakes*, was published by Colophon, Harper & Row's trade paperback line. Instead, Maupin has sold almost 100,000 copies of the first three books in his quartet.

Maupin was one of the first writers whose work was published originally in trade paperback instead of hardcover. His editor thought the book would reach its market more effectively in the trade paperback format. "At first I was puzzled and felt downgraded by the publisher," he says. "But later I realized I'd rather be selling more copies and get my books to the public than worry about image. A writer has to make himself visible in any way he can." And visible he is—a

Harper & Row salesperson said she received an order for *Baby Cakes* from a Chicago bookstore which was the largest single order she had filled for a trade paperback.

Maupin's biggest audience is in San Francisco where he lives and where his novels are first published in serial form in the *San Francisco Chronicle*. Because of their popularity, his books are published simultaneously in hardcover, but in small numbers, about 1,500 copies. "Only my most serious fans will buy the hardcover," he says, "but publishers have to print some in hardcover for the critics and for the libraries."

Maupin finds the psychology of paperback publishing fascinating. "The hardcover still suggests serious, solid literature," he says. "It's as if books have more to do with format and presentation than with content." The lower price on his books ($8.95) also encourages people to buy them, but actually "readers haven't stopped to notice that a trade paperback costs almost as much as a hardcover," he says.

Maupin's books have also been published in England by Corgi Books and this year he'll go on a national tour for the first time. "The whole story is survival," he says. "With all the books published today, writers are lucky if they sell 4,000 copies of a book. I keep reading that only 400 writers live exclusively off their writing in this country. I guess I'm lucky because I must be one of them."

Editors Must Have Flexibility

Maupin's editor at Harper & Row, who otherwise edits only nonfiction, is Hugh Van Dusen, editorial manager of Colophon. "I have a hunch that a lot more original literary fiction will be published in trade paperback in the next two to five years," says Van Dusen. He also sees an upsurge in the reprinting of literary fiction, especially "mid-list" fiction (mid-list fiction does not make the bestseller list, but does get critical acclaim). "Mass-market publishers are no longer reprinting mid-list books," he says. "They say they are, but they are retreating from all sorts of publishing. We used to sell mid-list titles to all the mass-market houses. Now only lines such as Penguin, Harcourt Brace or Vintage (Random House) will buy them." Trade paperback lines, he says, are more likely to buy mid-list titles.

As an example of how well a trade paperback of quality literature can sell, Van Dusen cited *Shiloh and Other Stories,* by Bobbie Ann Mason (published by Harper & Row), which sold 18,000 copies in trade paperback in three months. "We can't do that every time, but publishing an unlikely book in the larger format and selling a lot of copies at the trade price should give hardcover publishers courage to do their own edition of a trade paperback."

Reprinting novels in trade paperbacks wasn't common practice until recently, because "the public wasn't used to paying $6.95 or $7.95 for fiction in paperback," says Van Dusen. "But now, when we sign up certain new novels, we plan at the outset to publish them in trade paperback as well as hardcover."

Some publishers have just begun publishing trade paperbacks, while others have been doing so for years. But whether these trade paperback imprints are established or new, "fiction is being reprinted that was never reprinted before," says Van Dusen. "Publishing which might have been called experimental ten years ago is now being initiated by various houses," he says. Some good examples are the Penguin Contemporary American Fiction and Eastern European lines, and Vintage, which publishes translated Latin American fiction.

The proliferation of the trade paperback has also affected the inner workings of the hardcover publish-

267

ing house. "We used to have separate groups of paperback and hardcover editors," says Van Dusen. "Now we have trade editors who can do either or both editions of a book. We look for books which we can publish in both formats. Whether to publish a book in hardcover or paperback is now a marketing distinction, not an editorial distinction." Van Dusen thinks that editors must have flexibility. "It's the only thing that makes sense. Trade paperbacks are not taking over, but we must give editors the opportunity to publish books in both paper and cloth."

Van Dusen feels the *New York Times'* policy to combine the mass-market and trade paperback bestseller lists is unfortunate for trade paperbacks. "Now only mass-market books will be on the list," he says. However, he thinks the *New York Times* is becoming more flexible about reviewing trade paperbacks. "I want to give them credit. The *New York Times Book Review* has reviewed at least two original trade paperbacks on its front page. If they see an important book, they are not prejudiced just because a publisher decided to publish it in paperback. As more and more original paperbacks are published, the review media in general are going to have to treat books equally."

Trade Paperbacks: Good for Poetry

Poetry books have been published simultaneously in hardcover and trade paperback for years. (The paperback and hardcover sheets of a book are printed at the same time, which results in one printing and lower costs.) The emphasis, however, is on the trade paperback edition; the hardcover printing of a poetry book can be as low as 750 copies. "Trade paperback publishing has helped poets for a long time and that situation won't change a great deal," says Van Dusen. Trade paperbacks are particularly important to poets because they are used as textbooks in high schools and colleges.

Patricia Hampl, a Minnesota poet whose most recent book of poems is *Resort and Other Poems,* published last year by Houghton Mifflin, agrees: "Poetry books are usually published that way as a matter of course and so it was with my book," she says. At the same time *Resort and other Poems* was published, Houghton Mifflin reissued in trade paperback a 1981 title of hers, *A Romantic Education.* "That pleased me because it gave the book a second life," she says.

"More people are reading poetry now than five or ten years ago," says Hugh Van Dusen. "There seems to be an upturn in the interest in poetry. We publish as much poetry as we ever have." That's only three or four titles a year, however Van Dusen says, "I hear a lot of moaning and groaning but there's no less chance now for a poet to be published than before. In fact, it's probably greater, taking into account the university and small presses."

Can We Do Away with Hardcover Editions?

"Holt, Rinehart & Winston has an ongoing commitment to poetry," says Ward Mohrfeld, editor of Owl Books, their trade paperback line. Although they have always published poetry simultaneously in hardcover and paperback, no hardcover poetry books will be published on their next list. "The hardcover is too expensive and the paperback lasts just as long—something publishers have been telling librarians for years," he says.

Publishing poetry poses a particular problem for Holt—they lose money on it. "We publish newer, younger poets—sometimes their first book—and we assume these books will never show a profit," he says. Poetry is published under what he calls a "special exception status." Editors usually have to show a financial projection of a book to justify publication; not so with poetry. "The whole economic poetry structure is different. We publish poetry in spite of the fact that we lose money," he says.

The economics of publishing fiction in trade paperback are slightly different than for publishing poetry. Under the Owl imprint, Holt publishes original fiction, reprints fiction from their own backlist, and buys fiction from other houses. Reprinted fiction is less expensive to publish than original fiction, but a publisher cannot earn back its advance on either if they print fewer than 10,000 copies. "Even that's tight," says Mohrfeld. "Printing 12,000–15,000 copies is more comfortable." A publisher must also sell a minimum of 1,000 copies a year of an original trade paperback to make a profit—and more copies the first year the book is published. "We have a houseful of editors who would love to publish good original fiction in trade paperback, but we run into financial barriers," he says.

Sometimes, even a hardcover is cheaper. "A small printing of a hardcover can earn more money than a trade paperback because we can sell the hardcover at a higher price," says Mohrfeld. "It's often easier to launch a hardcover in the marketplace too, because the review media unfortunately still don't give equal attention to paperbacks."

Mohrfeld is not convinced that trade paperback publishing is going to have a dramatic effect on the publishing of literary fiction. "The audience isn't there," he says. "I'm pessimistic about public taste. Trade paperback publishing is not a magical solution. Publishing fiction is difficult and I still think about it in cautious terms. There are so few serious readers of fiction—regardless of the price of a book or what format it's published in," he says.

Wanted: "A Clearer Image"

Rhoda Weyr, a New York literary agent, says that the trade paperback is not nearly as important as is touted. "The trade paperback may be the herald of things to come, but it hasn't come yet," she says. "Publishers haven't figured out yet what they should publish in trade paperback versus hardcover."

She believes trade paperbacks have not been published in an intelligent or logical way. "No one has focused in on what trade paperback publishing can or can't be," she says. Weyr thinks the new wave of publishing books in trade paperback started in 1976 with *Even Cowgirls Get the Blues,* by Tom Robbins (Houghton Mifflin). "They took a book without a hardcover market and put it in trade paperback and it worked," she says. "But it doesn't always. Publishers are notoriously bad in figuring out their markets."

"My real concern is when I get a knee-jerk reaction from publishers who say, 'Let's try it in trade paperback.' Publishers would be more successful if they really thought it through. Publishers have to learn to pinpoint markets and promote books," she says. "They don't do that. They shouldn't say, 'Let's get the book out there and see what happens.' The garment industry doesn't do that. They don't put out ballgowns in the Midwest in the middle of July."

The manufacturing costs of publishing a trade paperback are very similar to those of publishing a hardcover book. For this reason, Weyr doesn't understand the logic when a publisher says a novel should be published in trade paperback and gives price as the explanation. "I ask the publisher, 'How can you price the book lower?' They answer, 'Because we can print more copies.' I ask, 'Why can you print more copies?' And they say, 'Because we'll price it lower and it will find more buyers.' This is circular reasoning and no publisher will explain why they aren't just as arbitrary with hardcover prices."

Weyr also thinks publishers can be short-sighted when putting a hardcover title in trade paperback and it's an agent's responsibility to make sure that the author is consulted before doing so. "If a publisher tries to sell a title to mass-market and finds they can only get $5,000–$10,000, they'll keep the rights themselves and do a trade paperback edition. That's not necessarily bad for the writer who may benefit by staying with one house, but on the other hand, the writer may be better off taking only $7,000 and getting more copies out in mass-market. Publishers often base these decisions on an immediate monetary concern rather than a long-term one," she says.

Weyr doesn't think the trade paperback will help the first novel. "It's not difficult to sell the first novel," she says. "It's the second one that's hard if the first book didn't sell well. I don't think a first novel that no one wants to publish in hardcover should be published in trade paperback. Instead, why not take an author who already has a following and put the book in a trade paperback line that has an identifiable image?"

She disapproves strongly of publishers who don't make their trade paperback lines easily recognizable on the bookstore shelf. "If I like a certain kind of novel, I should be able to identify a book visually as one I want to read," she says. "Penguin and Modern Library have done this for years." Publishers must also be patient. "Keeping mid-list titles in print could make a lot of money because there are a lot of mid-list readers, if the books are given time," she says.

Trade paperback lines which aren't instantly successful have also caused problems for paperback editors. "The turnover of paperback editors is rampant," she says. "This is not because the people are inadequate, but because results haven't been magical. When a publisher's paperback line hasn't blossomed, the management says, 'Let's try someone else.' "

Still, Weyr thinks that trade paperbacks are the wave of the future. "People who live in small houses have space considerations and paperbacks are not as intimidating to kids," she says.

"They Kept My Books Alive"

Publishing books in trade paperback may not be a solution for every author, but it certainly has been beneficial for Paule Marshall. Her book, *Praisesong for the Widow,* was published by Putnam in 1983 and was reprinted in trade paperback by Obelisk (Dutton). "Trade paperback lines have been a great boon to writers like myself who only publish a book every five or ten years," says Marshall. "The big publishing houses are setting up paperback lines that have brought books of mine long out of print back to life. Normally, my books wouldn't have seen the light of day," she says.

Paule Marshall's books have been revived in trade paperback by both commercial houses and by the small press. The Feminist Press reissued Marshall's book, *Brown Girl, Brownstones,* originally published by Random House in 1959. "The book has been selling well and is now considered a modern classic," she says. The Feminist Press also reissued *Reena and Other Stories,* written between 1954 and 1969. Random House is planning to reissue her major novel, *The Chosen Place, The Timeless People,* in their Vintage Library of Contemporary World Literature. "I hope this helps to sustain interest in my work," says Marshall. *"Brown Girl, Brownstones* did so well that *Praisesong for the Widow* was able to benefit from that interest."

Marshall calls the trade lines in the major houses

"an important new breakthrough for quality fiction. Perhaps this indicates a return to what publishing used to be when I first started out, when there was a commitment to nurture the serious writer."

Putnam held a trade paperback auction for *Praise-song for the Widow* in much the same way books are sold to mass-market houses. "But there are several different approaches," says Marshall. Her agent submitted one of her books to Random House and in another case, a publisher approached her directly. Two of her books have also been chosen by the Quality Paperback Book Club.

Does a writer make any money from books reprinted in trade paperback? "I suppose you can, but I haven't, not big money," says Marshall. "I still have to teach and give readings and lectures to manage a reasonably decent income. I might make some money in the future, but right now the exposure afforded me by the trade paperback is proving helpful."

Daryln Brewer

Major Paperback Publishers

Trade Paperback Imprints at Hardcover Houses

This list includes those hardcover publishers which publish literary fiction and/or poetry in trade paperback—original work, books from their own backlist, or that which they buy from other houses. Except where otherwise indicated, the name of the trade paperback line is the same as the hardcover publisher.

Arbor House Publishing Company. Reprints fiction from their own backlist and buys fiction previously published by other houses. No original fiction; no poetry. 235 East 45 Street, New York, New York 10017.

Atheneum Publishers. Reprints fiction from their own backlist and buys fiction from other houses. Original poetry is published simultaneously with the hardcover in a dual edition. No original fiction. 597 Fifth Avenue, New York, New York 10017.

Congdon & Weed. Reprints their own fiction and buys fiction from other houses. No original fiction; no poetry. 298 Fifth Avenue, New York, New York 10001.

Crown Publishers. Reprints their own fiction and buys fiction from other houses. No original fiction; no poetry. 1 Park Avenue, New York, New York 10016.

Delacorte Press. Under the *Delta* imprint, reprints their own fiction and buys fiction from other houses; emphasis on contemporary writers. No original fiction; no poetry. 1 Dag Hammarskjold Plaza, New York, New York 10017.

Dodd, Mead & Company. Reprints their own fiction and poetry and buys both from other houses. No original fiction or poetry. 79 Madison Avenue, New York, New York 10016.

Doubleday Publishing Company. Under the *Dial* imprint, publishes original fiction, reprints their own fiction, and buys fiction from other houses. No poetry. 245 Park Avenue, New York, New York 10167.

E. P. Dutton. Under the *Obelisk* imprint, reprints their own recent fiction and buys fiction from other houses; emphasis on contemporary writers. Reprints their own fiction and buys fiction from other houses for their *Dutton Trade Paperback* line. No original fiction. Dutton publishes one of the five winners of the National Poetry Series, in a dual edition, but no other poetry. 2 Park Avenue, New York, New York 10016.

Farrar, Straus & Giroux. Under the *FS&G* and *Hill & Wang* imprints, reprints their own fiction and poetry, and buys both from other houses. Some original poetry in dual editions; no original fiction. 19 Union Square West, New York, New York 10003.

Harcourt Brace Jovanovich. Under the *Harvest/HBJ* imprint, reprints their own fiction and buys fiction from other houses; emphasis on contemporary writers. No original fiction; no poetry. 757 Third Avenue, New York, New York 10017.

Harper & Row, Publishers. Under the *Colophon* imprint, publishes original fiction, reprints their own fiction, and buys fiction from other houses; emphasis on contemporary writers. No poetry. 10 East 53 Street, New York, New York 10022.

Holt, Rinehart & Winston. Under the *Owl* imprint, publishes original fiction and poetry, including one of the winners of the National Poetry Series. Reprints their own fiction and buys fiction from other houses; emphasis on contemporary writers. 521 Fifth Avenue, New York, New York 10175.

Houghton Mifflin Company. Publishes original fiction and poetry in dual editions; reprints their own fiction and buys fiction from other houses. 1 Beacon Street, Boston, Massachusetts 02108.

Little, Brown & Company. Under the *Little, Brown* and *Atlantic/Little, Brown* imprints, reprints their own fiction and buys fiction from other houses. No original fiction; no poetry. 34 Beacon Street, Boston, Massachusetts 02106.

Macmillan Publishing Company. Under the *Macmillan* and *Collier* imprints, reprints their own fiction and poetry, and buys both from other houses. No original fiction or poetry. 866 Third Avenue, New York, New York 10022.

McGraw-Hill. Reprints their own fiction and buys fiction from other houses. No original fiction; no poetry. 1221 Avenue of the Americas, New York, New York 10020.

William Morrow & Company. Under the *Quill* imprint, reprints their own fiction and poetry and buys both from other houses; emphasis on contemporary writers. No original fiction or poetry. 105 Madison Avenue, New York, New York 10016.

W.W. Norton & Company. Publishes original fiction and poetry in dual editions. Reprints their own fiction and poetry and buys both from other houses. 500 Fifth Avenue, New York, New York 10110.

The Putnam Publishing Group. Under the *Perigee* imprint, reprints their own fiction and buys fiction from other houses. No original fiction; no poetry. 200 Madison Avenue, New York, New York 10016.

Random House. Under the *Vintage* imprint, reprints their own fiction and poetry and buys both from other houses. No original fiction or poetry. (See also *Vintage* in the mass-market list.) 201 East 50 Street, New York, New York 10022.

St. Martin's Press. Reprints their own fiction and buys fiction from other houses. Publishes some original fiction; no poetry. 175 Fifth Avenue, New York, New York 10010.

Charles Scribner's Sons. Reprints some recent fiction and poetry, but the emphasis is on the Scribner Library of Contemporary Classics, which reprints Fitzgerald, Hemingway, etc. No original fiction or poetry. 115 Fifth Avenue, New York, New York 10003.

Simon & Schuster. Under the *Touchstone* imprint, reprints their own fiction and buys fiction from other houses. No original fiction; no poetry. 1230 Avenue of the Americas, New York, New York 10020.

Mass-Market Paperback Houses

Mass-market paperback publishers (houses which have traditionally reprinted books in the small, "rack-size" format, approximately 7″ × 4½″) are now branching out and publishing hardcover books, trade paperbacks and original fiction. The following list includes those mass-market paperback houses which publish literary fiction (in either mass-market or trade paperback) and indicates whether or not they publish original fiction.

Avon Books. The *Bard* mass-market imprint publishes literary fiction originals and reprints, including a

Latin American series in English translation. Quality fiction is also published under the *Avon* mass-market imprint. A new trade paperback line for original fiction, *The Avon Novel,* has recently been established. 1790 Broadway, New York, New York 10019.

Ballantine/Fawcett Books. Ballantine and *Fawcett* are mass-market imprints; *Ballantine Trade* and *Fawcett Columbine* are trade imprints. All publish literary fiction originals and reprints. 201 East 50 Street, New York, New York 10022.

Bantam Books. Bantam Classics and the *Windstone* imprint publish literary fiction; about half of *Windstone's* titles are original. Quality fiction is also published under the *Bantam* imprint. Each imprint publishes both mass-market and trade paperbacks. 666 Fifth Avenue, New York, New York 10103.

Berkley Publishing Group. Berkley reprints some literary fiction in mass-market. No original fiction. 200 Madison Avenue, New York, New York 10016.

Dell Publishing Company. The *Laurel* imprint reprints literary fiction in mass-market. Quality fiction is also published under the *Dell* mass-market imprint. No original fiction. 1 Dag Hammarskjold Plaza, New York, New York 10017.

The New American Library. Quality imprints in mass-market are *Signet, Mentor, Signet Classics* and *Meridian Classics.* The *Plume* imprint publishes literary fiction originals and reprints in trade paperback. 1633 Broadway, New York, New York 10019.

Penguin Books. The *Penguin American Library, English Library* and *Modern Classics* are their mass-market lines. The *Contemporary American Fiction* series publishes literary fiction originals and reprints in trade paperback. *Writers from the Other Europe* (East European contemporary fiction in English translation) is another literary trade series. 40 West 23 Street, New York, New York 10010.

Pinnacle Books. Pinnacle reprints some literary fiction in mass-market and trade paperback. No original fiction. 1430 Broadway, New York, New York 10018.

Pocket Books. Pocket and the *Washington Square Press* imprint reprint literary fiction in mass-market and trade paperback. *Washington Square Press* also publishes original fiction. 1230 Avenue of the Americas, New York, New York 10020.

Vintage Books. Vintage publishes literary fiction originals and reprints in mass-market and trade paperback. *Aventura: The Vintage Library of Contemporary World Literature* is a series of works of fiction in English translation. (See also *Random House* in the trade paperback list.) 201 East 50 Street, New York, New York 10022.

Warner Books. Warner reprints some literary fiction in mass-market and trade. No original fiction. 666 Fifth Avenue, New York, New York 10103.

John Fox

Behind the Blurb

Blurbs: quotes of praise from writers, critics, experts, and movie stars are found on the majority of books published today. Most publishers consider blurbs an important tool in the selling of a book. But just how important are they? How do you get one? Are blurbs just friends helping friends, or do they come from someone who really believes in a book? Are they edited honestly? Do they help get a book reviewed? Do they affect a bookstore browser's decision, do they increase sales? These are questions *Coda* posed to a variety of bibliophiles: writers, editors, reviewers, and booksellers.

Getting blurbs is usually the job of a book's editor, who sends advance galleys to people the editor and the writer think will help the book. The goal is to get the book reviewed, to get people to talk it up. Good blurbs are also sent to sales representatives, who convey that enthusiasm to bookstore buyers.

Jane Rosenman, an editor at Delacorte, says, "You want to make a statement about the book by the blurb you choose. For example, a quote from Geoffrey Wolff or Michael Arlen, both of whom have written powerfully about their fathers and families, would immediately identify a certain type of biography. If you don't do that, the blurb loses its effectiveness."

Ineffective blurbs, according to Rosenman, are "back-scratching. That's how a blurb can backlash—most people can tell when a publisher is just propping up a book. A book with a blurb by a well-connected author's friend is the kind that gives blurbs a bad name.

"Well-chosen blurbs—especially on a first novel—can be crucial in drawing the attention of reviewers. After all, no one wants to publish a book and send it into a vacuum. Just like everything else in life, blurbs are only effective when used with discrimination and forethought."

Independent or alternative presses count less on blurbs than the commercial houses do. "We don't solicit blurbs for any of our books—they clutter them up," says Bill Zavatsky, editor of SUN in New York City. "A blurb is useless unless it says something meaningful about the book. I've known writers who give blurbs just to get their name on a book. The motive is selfish—it promotes their own career."

"I try to read or look at all books that come to me by young or unknown writers to see if I should plug them, but generally I avoid writing blurbs for established writers, where it might become a matter of currying or trading favors," says Edward Hoagland (*African Calliope*, Random House). In a letter to the *New York Times Book Review,* Hoagland complained of being offered a "$250 honorarium" to write a blurb for a book published by Readers Digest Press. "I understand the need for blurbs," says Hoagland, "but let's nip that practice in the bud."

Blatantly purchased blurbs are a relatively new phenomenon; old traditions in the blurb world are hacked-up and misappropriated quotes. Again in the *New York Times Book Reivew,* Rollo May complained of being misquoted, in the form of a blurb, by a publishing house. When a friend asked May to read his book and write a blurb, May responded that he hadn't the time to read the book, but that he thought his friend was "a person of integrity and profound thought." When May received a copy of the book, he saw his quotation on the front of the jacket, implying that May thought the book had such qualities. "This is not the first time that a publishing house has misquoted statements of mine in order to make them mean something I did not at all intend," says May. "I think there is an important point of ethics here."

Alice Quinn, an editor at Knopf, defends trade publishing and its use of blurbs. "We never pull a blurb from a bad review or a letter that's not complimentary. You can't just blot out the bad parts."

Do blurbs sell books? Yes, says Janet Bailey, who runs Barbara's Books, a small bookstore in Chicago. "Buyers for bookstores have a radar to blurbs," she says. "I am much more likely to buy a book with a blurb on it from a writer I admire. Of course some writer's names are seen so frequently you begin to discount them. Much blurb-giving seems to be based on friendship, but that doesn't necessarily mean it's dishonest. Writers want to spot talent, to give encouragement, and to see other writers make a living from their writing—they have a sense of commitment to other writers. Even blurbs you don't trust—you put them in context and they still have an impact."

Kay Sexton, vice president and director of merchandise communications at B. Dalton headquarters in Minneapolis, disagrees. Blurbs—even from writers she admires—do not affect her decision to buy a book for the chain. "I've worked in the bookstores and have done a lot of selling and I've never seen anyone read blurbs," she says. "The customers don't care. They dip into a book. I also think it's just friends helping friends. Quite often the blurb writer and the author publish with the same house. Perhaps it helps a little for first fiction and poetry and for bookaholics, but those names don't mean anything to your average reader. Jacket design is more important."

Bill Harahan of the Madison Avenue Bookshop in Manhattan thinks the negative opinion about blurbs stems from literary snobbery. "I like blurbs," he says. "A book has to have something that will catch someone's eye. The book business is becoming more self-service. As labor becomes more expensive and all costs go up, the big chains like Barnes & Noble, Walden, Brentano's, and B. Dalton have fewer trained personnel. For that reason, it's good to have information on a book so that customers can help themselves."

Michael Arlen (*Thirty Seconds,* Farrar, Straus & Giroux) thinks blurbs once had a use, but are now degraded. "Publishers have made it difficult to be communicative," Arlen says. "All they want are adjectives. I try to say something individual and concrete, something besides, 'one of the most important books of our time,' which you'll see on 55 books at the same time, something that conveys a message about a book. Otherwise I feel I'm just writing advertising copy.

"Often I try to say no as gracefully as possible. If I'm going to give a blurb, I'm going to do it right. It's like recommending a friend's child for college."

Galway Kinnell doesn't give blurbs at all. "They're ads that remain on your book forever, defacing it. So many poetry books have extravagant blurbs that one without a blurb is a relief. Such a book has a fitting modesty for its physical presence."

Kinnell doesn't have a solicited blurb on any of his books. "Blurbs may help a first novel, but their effect on a first book of poems is small," he says. "A book of poetry continues to sell over the long term because people like it—poetry doesn't have a first surge, as some novels do."

But what if someone really does believe in a book? Kinnell thinks they should write an introduction or a preface instead, or help write the jacket flap copy, which should give all the necessary description of a book. Kinnell isn't the only one who refuses to write blurbs: writers as diverse as I. B. Singer and Laurie Colwin won't either. And this can cause problems for a writer. "A lot of people get mad at me when I refuse to give them a blurb," says Kinnell.

Alice Quinn thinks that poets are more shy than novelists about asking friends for blurbs, but shyness didn't stop Ross Talarico from asking actress Candace Bergen for a blurb for his book *Almost Happy* (Release Press). "Love Poem to Candace Bergen," first published in *December* magazine, is part of that book. When Talarico sent her the magazine and an earlier book of his poems, she responded with a letter of great praise, not just for that poem, but for his poetry in general.

Talarico is grateful for blurbs he's received from poets he respects, but he says, "anytime you can get a blurb from someone outside the literary clique, that's good. People who do other things and who are interested in other things and who like my poetry—that's wonderful."

Whether you write them or edit them, love them or hate them, read them or not, blurbs are here to stay. Writers should insist their editors choose blurbs wisely, if at all. For better or worse, blurbs do seem to help many readers—as well as reviewers and buyers for bookstores—judge a book by its cover.

Daryln Brewer

Six

NUTS AND BOLTS

On Cloud Nine: 21 Heavens for Writers

Since the original publication in *Coda* in 1980 of "15 Heavens for Writers," new writers' colonies have started, established ones have grown, and some have closed. The demand for places to work without intrusion from the outside world has also led to the opening of writing spaces in the city. The Writers Room and the Writers' Studio are examples of those operating in New York City.

Retreats away from the city provide work and living space for periods of 1 week to 7 months for writers, artists, and composers. A colony may be ideal for a writer who can take a short leave from daily responsibilities to work on a specific project. Writers may remain as solitary as they like or exchange ideas and draw inspiration from one another. Some retreats offer total quiet and seclusion, while others are brimming with activity: readings, workshops, and concerts. Each colony possesses its particular atmosphere; all share the scarce resources of peace and natural beauty.

The following list of 21 retreats brings *Coda*'s previous information up-to-date. Weeks of uninterrupted work are the closest a writer may get to heaven, so colonies are often booked far in advance. Write to individual colonies to find out what each offers and how to apply. Be sure to include a self-addressed stamped envelope with all inquiries. Don't be discouraged by a long waiting list—it's worth the effort to work in an atmosphere where respect for quiet prevails.

Bellagio Study and Conference Center

The Rockefeller Foundation, 1133 Avenue of the Americas, New York, New York 10036. (212) 869-8500. Susan E. Garfield, Coordinator.

Established 1959. 1-month residencies from January 20-December 20 for up to 7 artists and scholars. In the Italian Alps, near Lake Como. 5 accommodations with space for spouses of residents; 2 single rooms. All rooms have bathroom and study. Meals provided. No children. Writer must pay own travel costs. Preference given to new applicants and those who "expect their work at the Center to result in publication." Application required. Apply 1 year before preferred month of residency.

Blue Mountain Center

Blue Mountain Lake, New York 12812. (518) 352-7391. Harriet Barlow, Director.

Established 1981. Fifteen 6-week residencies 3 times a year between June 15 and October 30. Open to all writers, including writers of nonfiction, and artists who do not require extraordinary studio space or facilities. Interested in writers and artists whose work addresses social problems—civil liberties, environmental health and safety, peace, economic justice, etc. Located on private land in the center of Adirondack State Park, with a lake and recreation facilities. Individual rooms, including private bathroom, in 1 central lodge and a smaller building; all meals provided. Spouses must apply individually; no children or pets. Housing and meals free of charge; no other financial aid. Resume, work samples, reviews, 3 references, and project description required. Specify preferred time of residency. Deadline: March 1.

Centrum

P.O. Box 1158, Port Townsend, Washington 98368. (206) 385-3102. Carol Jane Bangs, Director, Literature Program.

Established 1979. Three 2- to 3-month residencies given between January 1 and October 1 to poets, fiction writers, or writers of creative nonfiction. Selected writers deliver 2 lectures or readings during the residency period. Residency includes housing in Fort Worden State Park, a restored Victorian military base on Puget Sound, a $600 per month stipend, and travel expenses. Families welcome. Funding for the program is on a yearly basis. Funds for 1984 residencies were provided in part by the NEA. Details for next year have not been confirmed. Write to the program director for more information.

Cummington Community of the Arts

Cummington, Massachusetts 01026. (413) 634-2172. Carol Morgan, Executive Director.

Established 1923. Open all year for artists of all disciplines. July and August: 1-month residencies for 25 artists ($500/month, financial assistance available); full-time children's program (ages 5-14) in summer ($300/month per child). September-June: 1- to 6-month residencies for up to 15 artists ($300/month). April and October: work-month residencies, during which 15 artists work 3 days per week for the community and 4 days on their own projects ($125/month). November-March: applications for residencies of shorter duration (2-week minimum) are accepted, but priority is given to applications for monthly residencies ($200/2 weeks; $250/3 weeks). 10 hours community work per week required of all residents. 150 acres in the Berkshires; workshops, concerts, readings, and community meetings. All fees include room and board. Spouses must apply individually. Application, work sample, and project proposal required. Deadlines: 1st day of the month, 2 months in advance of residency. Deadline for July and/or August is April 1.

The Dobie-Paisano Fellowship

The University of Texas at Austin, Main Building 101, Austin, Texas 78712. (512) 471-7213. Audrey Slate, Director.

Established 1967. Two 6-month residencies, February 1-July 1 and August 1-January 31, on a 265-acre ranch. Open only to writers who are native Texans, living in Texas, or whose lives or work have been substantially identified with the state. 1984-85 stipend: $7,200 and free rent for each residency; families welcome. Write for an application form after January 1, 1985.

Dorland Mountain Colony

Box 6, Temecula, California 92390. (714) 676-5039. J. Patrick Liteky, Director.

Established 1979. 2-week to 2-month residencies for writers, visual artists and composers from June to November. 300-acre nature sanctuary. Cottage facilities—working studio, kitchen, and bath—available without charge; established artists may make tax-deductible contributions. Residents provide own meals. Gas for cooking, hot water, and refrigeration available: no electricity, but gas lamps provided. Some small living stipends when possible. Request application: allow 3 months for the committee to respond. Deadlines: September 1 for January 15-June 1 residencies; March 1 for June 1-November 15.

Dorset Colony House for Writers

Box 519, Dorset, Vermont 05251. (802) 867-2223. John Nassivera, Director.

Established 1979. Open from September 10-May 28 for residencies of up to 1 month, with possible renewal. Facilities for 10 writers and playwrights, and visual artists with limited space needs. Located on 3 acres of land in a small New England village; near hiking and cross-country ski trails and a swimming area. Individual rooms in renovated farmhouse dating from the late 1800's, two common rooms, and a kitchen available. Residents work in their rooms and prepare their own meals. $30/week voluntary contribution. Spouses welcome for weekend visits; no families. Resume, work sample, and project proposal required. No deadline.

The Fine Arts Work Center in Provincetown

24 Pearl Street, Box 565, Provincetown, Massachusetts 02657. (617) 487-9960. Susan Slocum, Director.

Established 1968. Open October 1-May 1 for twenty 7-month residencies—10 writers, 10 visual artists. Permanent and visiting writing staff, readings, concerts; writing fellows publish *Shankpainter,* a magazine of prose and poetry. Living/working space and monthly stipend provided. Families welcome. The Center aims to aid "young candidates of outstanding promise" as well as established artists. Work sample required. Deadline: February 1.

The William Flanagan Memorial Creative Persons Center

The Edward Albee Foundation, Inc., 14 Harrison Street, New York, New York 10013.

Established 1968. 1-month residencies from June

1-September 30 in Montauk, Long Island for up to 6 writers and painters. Housing provided; shared kitchen. The only expense is food. No financial assistance. No families. Applications considered from January 1-April 1. Work sample, biography, project proposal and 1 or 2 recommendations required.

Hambidge Center

P.O. Box 33, Rabun Gap, Georgia 30568. (404) 746-5718 or 746-2491. Mary C. Nikas, Executive Director.

Established 1944. Open April-October for three 2-week to 2-month residencies. All creative artists except performing artists. 600 acres. Nature seminars, art-and-craft workshops, concerts, lectures. $60-75/week, according to accommodation, studio, and meals; no financial aid. No families. Work sample and resume required for admission. Apply at least 2 months prior to preferred period of residency.

Lacawac Sanctuary

R.D. #1, Box 518, Lake Ariel, Pennsylvania 18436. (717) 689-9494. Dr. Wallace Bell, Curator.

Two 10- to 12-week internships, from June-August, for artists and scientists. Writers are chosen occasionally. 467-acre nature preserve near Lake Wallenpaupack, wilderness and a glacial lake. Room and workspace; $600 stipend for food. Interns provide 20 hours/week of service to the Sanctuary. No families. Besides internships, other informal use by writers may be possible; further information available from the curator. No set deadline.

The D.H. Lawrence Summer Fellowship

D.H. Lawrence Fellowship Committee, English Department, Humanities Building, University of New Mexico, Albuquerque, New Mexico 87131. (505) 277-6347. Lee Bartlett, Director.

Established 1958. One fellowship to a poet, fiction writer, and/or dramatist who works in English. Fellowship includes June-August residency at the D.H. Lawrence Ranch in the Sangre de Cristo Mountains near Taos, a 4-room house, and a $700 stipend. Families welcome. Work sample, resume, and project description required. Deadline: January 31.

The MacDowell Colony

100 High Street, Peterborough, New Hampshire 03458. (603) 924-3886; from New York City, (212) 966-4860. Christopher Barnes, General Director.

Established 1907. Open all year for twenty-thirty 1- to 2-month residencies. All creative artists except performing artists. 450 acres of farm and woodland, graphics workshop, library. Suggested fee is $10-15/day; fellowships are available. Fees and fellowships cover room and board. Couples must apply separately; no children. Work sample required for admission. Deadlines: January 15 for summer (June, July, August); April 15 for fall (September, October, November); July 15 for winter (December, January, February); October 15 for spring (March, April, May).

The Millay Colony for the Arts

Steepletop, Austerlitz, New York 12017. (518) 392-3103. Ann-Ellen Lesser, Executive Director.

Established 1974. Five 1-month residencies available year-round to all creative artists except performing artists on the 600-acre estate of Edna St. Vincent Millay. No fee. Room and board provided, but no other financial aid. No families. Resume and work sample required. Deadlines: February 1 for June, July, August, and September residencies; May 1 for October, November, December and January; September 1 for February, March, April and May.

Montalvo Artists-in-Residence

Montalvo Center for the Arts, P.O. Box 158, Saratoga, California 95071. (408) 867-3421. Gardiner R. McCauley, Executive Director.

Established 1940. Open all year for writers, visual artists, architects, composers and musicians. Five 3-month residencies, with possible extension to 6 months, if space available. 19-room Mediterranean-style villa on 175 acres of gardens and wooded trails. Library, concerts, theatre, arboretum. 3 apartments are in the villa and 2 are in a cottage. Residents work in their apartments and provide their own meals. Spouses welcome; no children. $100/month for single person, $115 for a couple, includes utilities. Limited financial aid. Application form, resume, project description, and recommendation required. Apply 6 months before desired residency period.

Northwood Creativity Fellowships

Alden B. Dow Creativity Center, Northwood Institute, Midland, Michigan 48640. (517) 631-1600, ext. 403. Carol Coppage, Executive Director.

Established 1979. Open June-August. Up to four 10-week fellowships given to individuals in any discipline with an innovative project that has "the potential of making an impact in its field and improving the quality of life." On the campus of Northwood Institute, 125 miles north of Detroit, Michigan. Room, board, private study, $25/week stipend. No families. Resume, project proposal, work sample, budget for materials required.

Ragdale

1260 North Green Bay Road, Lake Forest, Illinois 60045. (312) 234-0366. Alice Ryerson, Director.

Established 1976. Open all year except last 2 weeks in June and last 2 weeks in December. Eight-ten 1-

week to 2-month residencies for writers and artists. Secluded 19th-century landmark houses on the Illinois prairie, near Chicago. Concerts and poetry readings. $70/week for room and board; some financial aid available; no families. Project proposal required. Inquire about deadlines.

The Ucross Foundation

Ucross Route, Box 19, Clearmont, Wyoming 82835. (307) 737-2312. Heather Burgess, Director.

Established 1983. Residencies of 2 weeks to 4 months for up to 4 creative artists. Residency periods are January-May and August-December. 200 acres at Big Red, homestead of the Powder River Ranchers, in Ucross. Individual rooms in a renovated schoolhouse; studio space for all residents in a reconstructed barn; all meals provided. Housing and meals free of charge; no other financial aid. Spouses must apply individually. Request application form; work sample and project description required. Deadline: October 1 for January-May residency period, March 1 for August-December.

Virginia Center for the Creative Arts

Sweet Briar, Virginia 24595. (804) 946-7236. William Smart, Director.

Established 1971. Open all year. Residencies of 1-3 months for 13 writers, 8 visual artists, and 3 composers at Mount San Angelo, an estate on 450 acres, 1½ miles from Sweet Briar College. Suggested fee is $15/day for room, board, and separate studio space; financial assistance available. No families. Apply at least 3 months in advance.

The Helene Wurlitzer Foundation of New Mexico

Box 545, Taos, New Mexico 87571. (505) 758-2413. Henry A. Sauerwein, Jr., Executive Director.

Established 1954. Open April 1-September 30 for writers, visual artists, composers, choreographers, and other creative artists. Residency period flexible; usually 3 to 6 months. 12 separate studios/apartments; free rent and utilities. Residents buy and prepare their own food. No financial aid. No families. Resume, work sample, and project description required. No deadline.

Yaddo

Box 395, Saratoga Springs, New York 12866. (518) 584-0746. Curtis Harnack, Executive Director.

Established 1926. Open all year (except December 22-January 4) for writers, visual artists, photographers, and composers. 2-week to 2-month residencies. Up to 32 residents from April 15 through Labor Day; up to 12 residents from September to April 15. 19th-century estate on 400 acres. Full fellowships provide room, board, and studio space. Spouses must apply individually; no families. Application and work sample required. No application fee. Deadlines: August 1 and January 15.

A Desk of One's Own

The Writers Room, Inc.
1466 Broadway, Room 505, New York, New York 10036. (212) 944-0252. Dey Gosse, Executive Director.

Established 1978. Open all year, 24 hours a day. One large room with 20 desks, separated by low partitions; space for 45 writers. Open to writers with a specific project for periods of 3 months, with renewal possible. Kitchen and bathroom, storage area for files and typewriters, small reference library. Costs for 3-month period range from $80-125. Some funded residencies are avaliable. Application and references required.

The Writers' Studio
The Mercantile Library Association, 17 East 47 Street, New York, New York 10017. (212) 755-6710. Claire J. Roth, Library Director.

Established 1982. Carrel space for 14 writers (3 spots reserved for writers of children's literature) for periods of 3 months; renewable up to 1 year. Open to authors and scholars currently engaged in a specific project. Unpublished writers must submit evidence of serious intent. Founded in 1820, the Mercantile Library is a nonprofit, private lending library of 185,000 volumes. Writers receive lockers to store typewriters and manuscripts, a library membership, and access to a special reference collection. $150 for 3 months. Formal application required. No deadline.

Stacy Pies

Helping Writers Help Themselves: 10 Groups That Offer Information and Services to Writers

When a writer needs practical information—such as grant deadlines, emergency loans, or advice on where to send one's work—the best place to start is with a writers' organization. The following 10 groups provide helpful services to poets and fiction writers.

The Academy of American Poets
177 East 87 Street, New York, New York 10028
(212) 427-5665
Henri Cole, Executive Director
Founded 1934
Services: Two $1,000 fellowships, 3 book awards which include publication, and 124 $100 college prizes annually; literary programs such as readings, workshops in the New York area and regionally.
Publications: *Poetry Pilot*, a monthly bulletin available to contributors of $15/year or more, includes notices of literary events and prizes. *Poetry Pilot* supplement, 2 issues/year, contains a comprehensive list of newly published books of poetry. *Envoy*, a newsletter, to 14,000 members of regional affiliated societies.

Associated Writing Programs

Old Dominion University, Norfolk, Virginia 23508
(804) 440-3839
Eric Staley, Director
Founded 1967; 6,122 members

Membership: Open without charge to faculty and students of member institutions—100 creative writing programs across the U.S. Others must file an application and pay according to the rates below.

Dues: Institutions, $200/year; Individuals, $25/year; Students or unemployed writers, $15/year.

Services: Annual awards, which include publication, for the novel, short fiction, poetry and creative nonfiction in conjunction with university presses.

Publications: *AWP Newsletter*, 6 issues/year, $10. Articles of interest to writers and teachers; also lists conferences, contests, etc. *Intro* is an annual anthology of student work. A *Catalogue of Writing Programs* ($10) describes 256 such programs, as well as writers' colonies, in the U.S. and Canada. Periodic surveys of English departments, arts councils, and the private sector determine the availability of jobs for creative writers; a *Job List* ($5) based on these surveys is available to subscribers who pay dues (1,700 people are currently using this service).

The Authors Guild*

234 West 44 Street, New York, New York 10036
(212) 398-0838
Peter Heggie, Executive Director
Founded 1921; 6,000 members

Full Membership: By invitation of the Membership Committee, and by application from writers with 1 or

---

*The Authors Guild and the Dramatists Guild, Inc. are corporate members of the Authors League of America, which focuses on matters of interest to all authors, such as copyright protection, equitable taxation of royalties, and freedom of expression.

more books published by an established American publisher within 7 years prior to application; or 3 works, fiction or nonfiction, published by a magazine of general circulation within 18 months prior to application.

Associate Membership: Available at the discretion of the Membership Committee. Includes all membership rights except voting.

Dues: $60/year

Services: Provides a collective voice for U.S. freelance writers in matters of joint professional concern such as contract terms and subsidiary rights; keeps members informed on market tendencies and practices, with an emphasis on new markets; offers advice and assistance to members with individual professional and business problems.

Publications: The *Authors Guild Bulletin* contains news articles and columns on the publishing business, by staff writers, members, lawyers and publishing experts; includes transcripts of Guild symposiums. 4 issues/year, for members.

Coordinating Council of Literary Magazines (CCLM)

2 Park Avenue, New York, New York 10016
(212)481-5245
Jennifer Moyer, Executive Director
Founded 1967, 358 members

Membership: Open to any non-commercial literary magazine that has been in existence for at least 1 year and has published 2 issues.

Membership fee: $10

Services: Yearly grants, from $100 to $5,000, include awards to short-story writers (and the literary magazines that publish them), editors, and college literary magazines. The CCLM library—16,000 issues of 1,600 different literary magazines—is open to the public.

Publications: *CCLM News*, 4 issues/year, $5, features a center pull-out section on technical resources for small press publishers. Also includes a listing of grants, book fairs, news of all CCLM activities and important news that affects publishers of literary magazines. *Directory of Literary Magazines*, $5; *Catalog of College Literary Magazines*, $3.

The International Women's Writing Guild

P.O. Box 810, Gracie Station, New York, New York 10028
(212) 737-7536
Hannelore Hahn, Executive Director
Founded 1976; 2,000 members, 5,000 associates

Membership: Open to all aspiring or accomplished writers; workshops and conferences open to members and non-members.

Dues: $20/year, foreign $26/year

Services: Manuscript referrals to New York agents; Talent Bank/Work Market Placement Service; regional writing workshops. Annual conference and retreat at Skidmore College, Saratoga Springs, New York in July/August; annual mid-year conference in Sonoma, California; health and life insurance at group rates; round robin manuscript exchange.

Publications: *Network*, 6 issues/year, includes articles of interest to members and discusses Guild activities.

National Endowment for the Arts

1100 Pennsylvania Avenue, N.W., Washington, D.C. 20506
(202) 682-5451

Frank Conroy, Literature Program Director
Founded 1965

Services: Literature Program Categories of Support, 1985-86: $20,000 individual fellowships for published fiction writers, poets and translators; grants for nonprofit, tax-exempt organizations that publish, distribute or promote volumes of poetry, fiction, plays and other creative prose by contemporary writers; sponsor residencies for writers.

Publications: *Arts Review*, a monthly newsletter, focuses on all the art forms under the Endowment; it discusses the various NEA grants and lists application deadlines. Regular columns include Legislative Notes, Money and Management, and Spotlight on Grants.

PEN American Center

(Poets, Playwrights, Essayists, Editors, Novelists, Translators and Agents)
568 Broadway, 4th floor, New York, New York 10012
(212) 255-1977
Karen Kennerly, Executive Director
Founded 1922; 2,000 members

Membership: By invitation, to writers who have published 2 or more books of literary merit in the U.S.; in some cases, 1 book of outstanding merit; and to editors and agents who have rendered distinguished service to literature. Branches in Boston, Washington, D.C., Houston and San Francisco; 80 branches worldwide.

Dues: $45/year

Services: Literary events*; the PEN Writers Fund and the NYSCA-PEN Fund give grants and loans up to $500 for professional, published writers facing acute financial emergencies; group medical insur-

---

*Nearly all PEN events are open to the public; non-members are welcome to purchase publications and apply for PEN-sponsored grants and awards.

ance; 12 annual literary awards totalling about $28,000.

Publications: The *PEN Newsletter* reports on issues vital to the literary community, covers PEN's activities in the U.S. and abroad, and features interviews and reminiscences by international literary figures. 4 issues/year, free to members, $5/year for non-members. *Grants and Awards Available to American Writers*, $6 to individuals, $9.50 to libraries and institutions.

Poetry Society of America

15 Gramercy Park, New York, New York 10003
(212) 254-9628
Dennis Stone, Administrative Director
Founded 1910; 1,200 members

Membership: Determined by the Governing Board. Send an SASE for application. Poets should return the application with 3 copies of 5 poems. Poets of "recognized standing" should submit a resume and list of publications with their application.

Associate Membership: Open to writers, educators, critics, editors and scholars. Granted by the Governing Board on the basis of resume.

Dues: $20/year.

Services: Sponsors ongoing readings series nationwide; in New York at the National Arts Club, and in cooperation with the Poetics Institute of New York University; honoraria awarded; published poets may apply with a letter and resume to the Program Committee. Seminars and educational programs in 6 regional centers around the U.S. Van Voorhis Poetry Library contains 5,000 books of poetry, biography and commentary. Poetry workshops. Annual poetry awards program; $5,000 to members, $5,000 to non-members. All programs are open to the public.

Publications: The *Poetry Review*, a magazine, publishes poetry and essays on poetic theories and principles (submissions with an SASE are welcome); contains a letter from a poet abroad, translations, and "Notes and Comments;" 2 issues/year, free to members, $5/year to non-members. The *Newsletter* includes contest-winning poems, notices of members' publications, honors and awards; 3 issues/year, free to members, $8/year to non-members.

Poets & Writers, Inc.

201 West 54 Street, New York, New York 10019
(212) 757-1766
Galen Williams, Founder and Chairman of the Board
Elliot Figman, Executive Director
Founded 1970

Services: Information Center keeps up-to-date files on more than 5,700 poets and fiction writers: their addresses, teaching and reading preferences, etc.; answers questions related to the needs of writers and makes referrals; keeps addresses for each state arts council and over 640 sponsors of readings and workshops nationwide. Write, or telephone between 11 a.m. and 3 p.m. (EST) weekdays.

Eligibility for listing with the Information Center is based on publication. You may apply in poetry, fiction, or a combination of both. Write for specific guidelines. Performance or multi-media writers should request the special guidelines for that category. For U.S. citizens and permanent residents only. There is a 1-time processing fee of $5 with application.

Readings/Workshops Program provides fees for writers giving readings or workshops in New York and other states. Applications are submitted by organizations (libraries, colleges, community centers, etc.) wanting to engage a writer. Call or write for guidelines and required application.

Publications: *Coda: Poets & Writers Newsletter*, 5 issues/year $12/1 year, $22/2 years, $2.50/single issue. Writers listed with Poets & Writers: $10/1 year, $18/2 years. Libraries, $18/year. News and comment on publishing, jobs, grants, taxes, legislation, and other practical topics. Books include *A Writer's Guide to Copyright* ($4.95), *A Directory of American Poets and Fiction Writers, 1983-84 Edition* ($14.95), *Literary Agents: A Writer's Guide* ($5.95), *Sponsors List* ($3.95), *Literary Bookstores* ($3.50).

Teachers & Writers Collaborative

5 Union Square West, New York, New York 10003
(212) 691-6590
Nancy Larson Shapiro, Director
Founded 1966

Services: Hires writers to teach workshops in the community. Information source for those interested in teaching writing and literary arts to adults and children; distributes language arts books by various publishers.

Publications: *Teachers & Writers* magazine, 5 issues/ year, $12.50. Books by Teachers & Writers staff and other writers who relate their experience in the classroom and offer writing exercises. Publications of student work.

John Fox

Guide to Writers' Resources

Poets & Writers' Information Center receives over 8,000 queries each year from authors, publishers, editors, sponsors of readings and workshops, and others interested in writing. Authors call with questions ranging from "Is there an organization for science fiction writers?" to "Where can I find a book contract that will protect me?" Answers to these questions often involve referrals to organizations and reference materials for more information, detailed discussions of procedures, and advice. Writers are often surprised, and relieved, to find that groups exist to represent their interests or serve their needs, and many have asked for a list of these resources to keep on hand.

The following alphabetical list, compiled by the Information Center staff for its daily use, is a convenient guide to resources of interest to writers and readers. If you need a resource which is not listed here, be sure to call the Information Center at (212) 757-1766 between 11 a.m. and 3 p.m. Monday-Friday.

Academic and Professional Journals
Directory of Publishing Opportunities in Journals and

Periodicals, Marquis Who's Who, Inc., 200 East Ohio Street, Chicago, IL 60611 (lists addresses and submission information)

Arts Organizations

Center for Arts Information, 625 Broadway, New York, NY 10012, (212) 677-7548

Awards and Grants

Gadney's Guide to 1800 International Contests, Festivals and Grants, Festival Publications, P.O. Box 10180, Glendale, CA 91209

Grants and Awards Available to American Writers, PEN, 568 Broadway, 4th floor, New York, NY 10012, (212) 255-1977

Money Business: Grants and Awards for Creative Artists, The Artists Foundation, Inc., 110 Broad Street, Boston, MA 02110

Note: There are also announcements of awards and deadlines in each issue of *Coda: Poets & Writers Newsletter.*

Co-operative Publishing

Co-op Publishing Handbook, by Michael Scott Cain, Dustbooks, P.O. Box 100, Paradise, CA 95969

Copyright Information

Reference Guides:

Copyright Handbook, by Donald F. Johnston, R. R. Bowker, P.O. Box 1807, Ann Arbor, MI 48106

Writers' and Artists' Rights, by Don Glassman, Writers Press, Box 805, 2000 Connecticut Avenue, Washington, DC 20008

A Writer's Guide to Copyright, Poets & Writers, Inc., 201 West 54 Street, New York, NY 10019

For Forms:

The Copyright Office, Library of Congress, Washington, DC 20559

For Telephone Information:

The Copyright Office, Washington, DC, (202) 287-8700

Emergency Money

Authors League Fund, 234 West 44 Street, New York, NY 10036, (212) 391-3966

Carnegie Fund for Authors, W. L. Rothenberg, Chairman, 330 Sunrise Highway, Rockville Center, NY 11570

PEN Writers Fund, PEN, 568 Broadway, 4th floor, New York, NY 10012, (212) 255-1977

Health Insurance

Support Services Alliance, Inc., Crossroads Building, 2 Times Square, New York, NY 10036, (212) 398-7800

ISBN (International Standard Book Number)

International Standard Book Numbering Agency, R. R. Bowker Company, 1180 Avenue of the Americas, New York, NY 10036, (212) 764-3384 or (212) 764-5100 (ask for Mr. Emery Koltay's office)

Jobs for Writers

College and University Positions:

Associated Writing Programs, Old Dominion University, Norfolk VA 23508, (804) 440-3000

Modern Language Association, 62 Fifth Avenue, New York, NY 10011, (212) 741-5588

Readings and Workshops:

Sponsors List, Poets & Writers, Inc., 201 West 54 Street, New York, NY 10019 (includes state-by-state listings of Poets-in-the-Schools programs)

Legal Aid Information

Assistance Organizations:

Authors League of America, Inc., (Members only), 234 West 44 Street, New York, NY 10036, (212) 391-9198

Volunteer Lawyers for the Arts, (Low income only), 1560 Broadway, New York, NY 10036 (212) 575-1150

Reference Guides:

Law and the Writer, ed. by Kirk Polking and Leonard S. Meranus, Writer's Digest Books, 9933 Alliance Road, Cincinnati, OH 45242

Making It Legal, by Marion Davidson and Martha Blue, McGraw-Hill, 1221 Avenue of the Americas, New York, NY 10020

The Writer's Legal Guide, by Tad Crawford, Hawthorn Books, 260 Madison Avenue, New York, NY 10016.

Library of Congress Catalog Numbers

Library of Congress, Cataloging in Publication Program, Washington, DC 20540, (202) 287-6372 (not for self-published books)

Literary Agents

Associations:

Independent Literary Agents Association, c/o Elaine Markson Literary Agency, 44 Greenwich Street, New

York, NY 10011 (list available only by writing to them; enclose SASE)

Society of Authors' Representatives, Inc., P.O. Box 650, Old Chelsea Station, New York, NY 10113, (212) 741-1356 (does not recommend agents or agencies)

Reference Guides:

Literary Agents: A Writer's Guide, Poets & Writers, Inc., 201 West 54 Street, New York, NY 10019

Literary Agents of North America, Author Aid Associates, 340 East 52 Street, New York, NY 10022

Literary Market Place, R. R. Bowker, Box 1807, Ann Arbor, MI 48106

Writer's Market, Writer's Digest Books, 9933 Alliance Road, Cincinnati, OH 45242

Manuscript Submissions

Publications running "Manuscripts Wanted" columns (for magazines and small presses);

AWP Newsletter, Associated Writing Programs, Old Dominion University, Norfolk, VA 23508

CCLM Newsletter, Coordinating Council of Literary Magazines, 2 Park Avenue, New York, NY 10016, (212) 481-5245

Coda: Poets & Writers Newsletter, Poets & Writers, Inc., 201 West 54 Street, New York, NY 10019

Small Press Review, P.O. Box 100, Paradise, CA 95969

Note: Most regional literary newsletters also list manuscripts wanted.

Poetry Libraries

The Academy of American Poets, 177 East 87 Street, New York, NY 10028, (212) 427-5665

Beyond Baroque Library of Small Press Publications, 681 Venice Boulevard, Venice, CA 90291, (213) 822-3006

The Community Writers' Library, McKinley Foundation, 809 South 5th Street, Champaign, IL 61820, (217) 344-0297

Coordinating Council of Literary Magazines, 2 Park Avenue, New York, NY 10016, (212) 481-5245

The Poetry Society of America, 15 Gramercy Park, New York, NY 10003, (212) 254-9628

Note: For further information and listings, see "Poetry in the Hothouse," Part Four.

Print Shops

Open Studio, 187 East Market Street, Rhinebeck, NY 12572

The Print Center, P.O. Box 1050, Brooklyn, NY 11202, (212) 875-4482; street address: 200 Tillary Street, Brooklyn, NY 11201

The West Coast Print Center, 1915 Essex Street, Berkeley, CA 94703, (415) 849-2746

The Writer's Center, Glen Echo Park, Glen Echo, MD 20812, (301) 229-0930

Prison Programs

Art Without Walls, 72 Fifth Avenue, New York, NY 10010, (212) 924-6780

COSMEP Prison Project, c/o Joseph Bruchac, *Greenfield Review*, R.D. 1, Box 80, Greenfield Center, NY 12833, (518) 584-1728

PEN Prison Program, 568 Broadway, 4th floor, New York, NY 10012, (212) 255-1977

Readings

Regional literary newsletters usually list readings. Some examples are—

Chicago:

Two Hands News, Stone Circle, 2050 North Halstead, Chicago, IL 60614, (312) 248-4484

Michigan:

The Poetry Resource Center of Michigan Newsletter and Calendar, 621 S. Washington, Royal Oak, MI 48067

New York City:

New York City Poetry Calendar, 397 1st Street, Brooklyn, NY 11215, (212) 475-7110 (to submit listing). Subscriptions: 13 East 3 Street, New York, NY 10003

New York, Upstate:

NEWSletter, Niagara-Erie Writers, P.O. Box 186, Central Park Station, Buffalo, NY 14215

San Francisco:

Poetryflash, P.O. Box 4172, Berkeley, CA 94704

Seattle:

Poetry Exchange, c/o Horizon Books, 425 15th Avenue East, Seattle, WA 98112

Southern California:

Poetry Newsletter, Beyond Baroque, P.O. Box 806, Venice, CA 90291, (213) 822-3006

Washington D.C.

The Poetry Clearinghouse, Folger Library, 102 East Capitol Street, S.E., Washington, D.C. 20003, (202) 546-2461

Small Presses

Associations:

COSMEP (Committee of Small Magazine Editors and Publishers), P.O. Box 703, San Francisco, CA 94101

The Maine Writers & Publishers Alliance, P.O. Box 143, South Harpswell, Maine 04079

New England Small Press Association, 45 Hillcrest Place, Amherst, MA 01002

Books:

Small Press Record of Books in Print, Dustbooks, P.O. Box 100, Paradise, CA 95969

International Directory of Little Magazines and Small Presses, Dustbooks, P.O. Box 100, Paradise, CA 95969

Directory of Small Press & Magazine Editors and Publishers, Dustbooks, P.O. Box 100, Paradise, CA 95969

Book Clubs:

Small Press Book Club, c/o *The Small Press Review,* P.O. Box 1056, Paradise, CA 95969

Book Review Journals for Small Presses:

Many literary magazines and regional literary newsletters review small press publications; for annotated listings, consult *The International Directory of Little Magazines and Small Presses,* Dustbooks, P.O. Box 100, Paradise, CA 95969

Distribution:

An Intelligent Guide to Book Distribution, by Michael Scott Cain, Dustbooks, P.O. Box 100, Paradise, CA 95969

For addresses of distributors, consult listing in the *International Directory of Little Magazines and Small Presses.*

Special Interest Writers' Associations

Association of Hispanic Arts, 200 East 87 Street, New York, NY 10028, (212) 369-7054

Feminist Writers' Guild, P.O. Box 9396, Berkeley, CA 94709

National Association of Third World Writers, 373 Fifth Avenue, Suite 1007, New York, NY 10016

Mystery Writers of America, Inc., 150 Fifth Avenue, New York, NY 10011, (212) 255-7005

National Association of Science Writers, Inc., Box 294, Greenlawn, NY 11740, (516) 757-5664

Science Fiction Writers of America, 68 Countryside Apts., Hacketstown, NJ 07840

Society of Children's Book Writers, Mar Vista Station, P.O. Box 1052, Los Angeles, CA 90066, (213) 347-2849

Western Writers of America, Inc., Meridian Road, Victor, MT 59875, (406) 961-3612

Screenwriting:

The Writers Guild of America—East, Inc., 555 West 57 Street, New York, NY 10019, (212) 245-6180

The Writers Guild of America—West, Inc., 8955 Beverly Boulevard, Los Angeles, CA 90048, (213) 550-1000

State Arts Councils

For addresses, see *Sponsors List,* Poets & Writers, Inc., 201 West 54 Street, New York, NY 10019

Translators

Organizations:

American Literary Translators Association, c/o Dr. Stasys Gostautas, Executive Secretary, University of Texas, Box 688, Mail Station 1102, Richardson, TX 75080, (214) 690-2093

International Writing Program, University of Iowa, School of Letters, Iowa City, IA 52242, (319) 353-5920

National Translation Center, John Crerar Library, 35 West 33rd Street, Chicago, IL 60616, (312) 255-2526

PEN Translation Committee, 568 Broadway, 4th floor, New York, NY 10012, (212) 255-1977

The Translation Center, Columbia University, 307A Mathematics Hall, New York, NY 10027, (212) 280-2305

Directory:

Translation & Translators, R.R. Bowker, Box 1807, Ann Arbor, MI 48107

Publishers' Associations

Association of American University Presses, 1 Park Avenue, New York, NY 10016, (212) 889-6040

Association of American Publishers, 1 Park Avenue, New York, NY 10016, (212) 689-8920

Writing Programs and Conferences

Summer Conference Lists:

AWP Newsletter, April issue of each year, Associated Writing Programs, Old Dominion University, Norfolk, VA 23508

The Writer, May issue of each year, 120 Boylston Street, Boston, MA 02116

Writer's Digest, May issue of each year, Writer's Digest Books, 9933 Alliance Road, Cincinnati, OH 45242

Program Lists:

Associated Writing Programs, Old Dominion University, Norfolk, VA 23508, (804) 440-3000

Sponsors List, Poets & Writers, Inc., 201 West 54 Street, New York, NY 10019, (212) 757-1766

Stacy Pies

14 Major Magazines: What They Want and What They Pay

The Atlantic Monthly

8 Arlington Street, Boston, Massachusetts 02116

Pay: $2,000 and up. The *Atlantic* receives 1,500 to 2,000 submissions a month. They publish an average of 2 stories a month and want stories with a "sense of story, well-developed characters, distinctive language and attention to form." They are "keenly interested" in new writers and often buy from the unsolicited pile.

Cosmopolitan

224 West 57 Street, New York, New York 10019

Pay: $1,000 for an unsolicited manuscript; $2,500 for established writers. They publish 2 short stories an issue, with the exception of the August issue, in which they publish 4. *Cosmopolitan* wants submissions which deal with "male/female relationships, those which are upbeat and have a contemporary plot." They usually want work "from a female point of view or a sensitive approach with which female readers can identify. Most stories have a female protagonist with a sophisticated flare."

Esquire

2 Park Avenue, New York, New York 10016

Pay: $1,500 and up. *Esquire* publishes 1 to 2 stories a month. They are interested in stories "with a masculine element but not necessarily from a man's point of view. In a story written from a woman's point of view, there is usually a strong male character." They are particularly interested in "contemporary pieces and in story content and action rather than stylistic or intellectual exploration."

Family Circle
488 Madison Avenue, New York, New York 10022

Pay: varies, $300-$2,000. A writer whose manuscript is bought from the unsolicited pile will not get paid the same amount as an established writer. Although they don't publish much short fiction, they are "desperately looking for it." They like a "contemporary story with a strong central female character."

Good Housekeeping
959 Eighth Avenue, New York, New York 10019

Pay: $1,000 for a "short short" (1,000 words), with an immediate raise to $1,250 for a writer's 2nd story. $1,250 for a longer story (2,000 to 3,000 words), with a raise to $1,500 for the 2nd story. They read unsolicited manuscripts, but don't often publish them. *Good Housekeeping* publishes 2 pieces of short fiction a month: 1 short short and 1 longer story. They look for "fiction of emotional identification to women." They like "a strong heroine who encounters an emotionally identifiable problem and solves it."

Grand Street
50 Riverside Drive, New York, New York 10024

Pay: $750-$2,000. *Grand Street* receives 50-60 submissions a week and accepts only 8-12 a year, to be published in 4 issues. They tend to "pay professional writers—as distinct from academics and housewives—better than nonprofessionals."

Mademoiselle

350 Madison Avenue, New York, New York 10017

Pay: $1,500. They receive about 10,000 submissions a year and an extra 2,000-3,000 for their annual Young Writers Contest. *Mademoiselle* publishes 1 story an issue. They look for "original, high-quality fiction with some appeal to young women ages 18-25."

McCall's

230 Park Avenue, New York, New York 10169

Pay: $1,250 for a "short short" (up to 2,000 words), and $1,500 for longer stories (not exceeding 5,000 words). *McCall's* receives about 150 manuscripts a week. They often buy from the unsolicited pile. They want "well-written, family-oriented stories with strong characters and good plots."

The New Yorker

25 West 43 Street, New York, New York 10036

Pay: a word rate, with a minimum of $1,000. The *New Yorker* receives between 200 and 500 stories a week and publishes 2 a week. The vast majority of stories they do publish are by writers either known to them or who they have published before. But they do publish 10 or 12 new writers a year. Out of those, 1 or 2 come out of the unsolicited pile. If they have any bias, "it's in favor of the brand new or young writer." (For an interview with Charles McGrath, fiction editor of the *New Yorker,* see "A Renaissance for Short Fiction?", Part Three.)

Playboy

747 Third Avenue, New York, New York 10017

Pay: $1,000 for a "short short" (under 1,500 words) and $2,000 for longer stories. Pay scale escalates for regular contributors. An average of 2 stories are published an issue, and they do buy from the unsolicited pile. They want stories "with a regular structure, not vignettes or loose stories." They do not want pornography. *Playboy* likes "fairly conventional, slightly old-fashioned material." Stories are geared toward a young, male audience which makes it difficult to publish women writers, though they do occasionally.

Redbook
224 West 57 Street, New York, New York 10019

Pay: $850 for a "short short" (9 pages or less), $1,000-$1,500 for a longer story (10 pages and preferably under 20, although they do buy longer stories). *Redbook* receives 36,000 unsolicited manuscripts a year and more for their annual fiction contest. They publish 2-3 stories in each issue and as many as 5 in their special August fiction issue. They also publish a condensed novel occasionally. *Redbook* aims for a "traditional, well-made classic American short story." They are not "pioneers of stylistic innovation or radical experimentalism." They do not want gothic or sweet-savage fiction. They publish "serious fiction writers, not formula women's magazine fiction." *Redbook* was the first publisher for writers such as John Irving, Mary Gordon, and Tim O'Brien. They want to "stay open to young or beginning writers, to give them a break at a time when it's increasingly hard to get one, and to continue with them."

Seventeen
850 Third Avenue, New York, New York 10022

Pay: rates vary, but "upwards of $600." *Seventeen* receives 200-300 manuscripts a month and they do buy from the unsolicited pile. 1 story is published per issue. They look for "fiction of about 3,000 words, for young adult girls. Submissions should be sophisticated, not aimed at children."

Vanity Fair

350 Madison Avenue, New York, New York 10017

Pay: would not disclose amount. They do buy from the unsolicited pile. 1 piece of fiction is published per issue—a short story or an excerpt from a novel.

Woman's Day

1515 Broadway, New York, New York 10036

Pay: "top rates." *Woman's Day* publishes an average of 1 story an issue—sometimes none at all and occasionally a few in the August and Christmas issues. They receive several hundred submissions each month. They do accept unsolicited manuscripts and are eager for short fiction by new writers. *Woman's Day* claims to have difficulty finding good fiction that appeals to a large audience (7 million plus). They don't want stories which appeal only to the New York regional edition.

Daryln Brewer

A Writer's Guide to Reference Books

Writers seeking to publish their poetry and fiction might well be confused by the many directories and reference books available. Which list the most book and magazine publishers? What are the strengths and weaknesses of each? How should the books be used?

This chapter evaluates 10 of the better guides to the literary marketplace. Most of these books are costly, but many can be found in the reference sections of well-stocked libraries.

Literary Market Place

R.R. Bowker Co.

Literary Market Place, commonly known as *LMP*, covers all aspects of trade book and university press publishing in the United States. Writers submitting fiction without an agent will find *LMP* very helpful, but it is designed primarily for use by publishers, bookstores and libraries. It does not, therefore, give such information as whether a publisher is looking for a new work, whether multiple or photocopied submissions are accepted, or what editors' personal tastes are. That information can be found in other handbooks. Following is what *LMP* does offer.

Book Publishers: About 1,700 are listed, 350 of which publish fiction and/or poetry. Entries provide editors' names and what kind of work the house publishes (fiction, business, travel, etc.). The list is cross-referenced by Geographic Location, Fields of Activity (such as Fine Editions and General Trade Books) and Subject Matter (including Fiction and Poetry). Also listed are 180 Canadian and 35 foreign book publishers with U.S. offices.

Magazines: In the past few years Bowker has shifted the emphasis away from *LMP*'s magazine section because of their new *Magazine Industry Market Place* (see below). Only commercial and the better-known literary magazines (about 300 of them) are listed in *LMP*; 60 publish fiction and/or poetry. The Subject Interest cross-reference—including Fiction, Poetry, and Alternative—is helpful, but the sampling is too selective to be of much use to the writer seeking a magazine market.

LMP "yellow pages" give the addresses and telephone numbers of most publishers, editors and agents.

For the self-published author or literary magazine editor, the Book Manufacturing section gives addresses, phone numbers and services offered by typesetters, printers and binders. *LMP* is the only book discussed here that provides this information.

LMP includes useful miscellaneous information such as TV and film outlets, literary organizations, writing conferences, awards and book clubs.

Magazine Industry Market Place
R.R. Bowker Co.

MIMP is to U.S. magazines what *LMP* is to books. About 2,500 magazines are listed alphabetically, a quarter of which publish fiction and/or poetry. *MIMP* is annotated similarly to *LMP*—it is cross-referenced by subject and includes various other comparable sections.

Magazines for Libraries
R.R. Bowker Co.

Although *Magazines for Libraries* is designed primarily to help librarians decide which magazines to purchase, writers will nevertheless find this volume valuable. 6,500 magazines in 117 subject areas are listed. Specialists in certain fields have written critical descriptions of many of the magazines. Only about 1,000 publish fiction or poetry, but they're worth searching out for the excellent critical annotations. Editorial purpose, scope and audience are identified for each entry, and there is a good balance between commercial and literary publishers.

Special features include a bibliography and a list of other directories.

Because it is not published annually, *Magazines for Libraries* should be used in conjunction with *MIMP* for commercial markets and the *International Directory of Little Magazines and Small Presses*.

Writer's Market
Writer's Digest Books

Although its choices for listing are arbitrary, the entries in *Writer's Market* do give a good idea of an editor's tastes and manuscript policies: desired length, how to submit, and the type of work sought. *Writer's Market* is stronger on magazines than on book publishers.

Book Publishers: About 750 are listed; 200 publish fiction and/or poetry. The choice is too selective to be of use except in conjunction with *LMP*. If a publisher is listed in both places, *Writer's Market* annotations provide good additional information, such as the average advance and royalty rates paid by a publisher, whether unsolicited manuscripts are considered, and detailed descriptions of the type of work sought. Indexed by subject.

Magazines: Of the 1,800 that are listed, about 450 publish fiction and/or poetry. Entries are alphabetical under subject matter.

Editors, publishers and agents offer insiders' advice to writers in sections called "Close-ups" which are scattered throughout the book.

Some markets for fiction and poetry in England, Australia, Scotland, New Zealand and West Germany are also included.

Fiction Writer's Market

Writer's Digest Books

Instructional and inspirational selections on the art of fiction writing comprise the first half of *Fiction Writer's Market*. In the second half, the market listings are divided into four groups: Literary Magazines (600), Commercial Periodicals (300), Small Press (200) and Commercial Publishers (180). Since they all publish fiction, there's no need to read through a huge general alphabetical list; that's already been done and very well at that. The annotations are excellent and include editors' names, the kind of fiction they publish, some advice and comment, and payment policies. *Fiction Writer's Market* is indexed both alphabetically and by category (adventure, ethnic, etc.).

Special features include an annotated list of literary agents who handle fiction and a section on contests and awards.

International Directory of Little Magazines and Small Presses

Dustbooks

Here is the most comprehensive, reliable and up-to-date source for poets and fiction writers seeking to publish in literary magazines and small presses.

About 3,000 entries are listed alphabetically, with book and magazine publishers interspersed. About half are magazines, one quarter are book publishers and another quarter publish both. Most of them are in the U.S., but some are in the U.K., Canada and elsewhere.

Included are descriptions of the kind of material each press or magazine publishes; the names of writers recently published by certain presses are also included. Average payment, copyright policy, and editors' names are supplied; entries are cross-referenced by subject as well as by region (states and countries).

Small Press Record of Books in Print

Dustbooks

This companion volume to the *International Directory* lists 18,000 books, pamphlets, broadsides, posters and poem cards published in the preceding year by 2,000 presses listed in the *Directory*. It includes material published earlier than the preceding year if it has not been previously cited in *Small Press Record*. There are four indexes: Author, Title, Publisher (with addresses) and Subject.

Small Press Record can be valuable for determining which press is most appropriate for a writer's work, but it should be used in conjunction with the *International Directory*.

Directory of Small Press & Magazine Editors & Publishers

Dustbooks

Another companion to the *International Directory*, this is an alphabetical list of editors and publishers of literary magazines and small presses, with addresses and telephone numbers. It is particularly helpful if you have the name of an editor but not the name of the press or publication he or she is affiliated with.

CCLM Literary Magazine Directory

Coordinating Council of Literary Magazines

The *CCLM Directory*, which lists 340 fiction and/or poetry markets, is the best value in guides to literary magazines. The well-annotated entries include detailed descriptions of the type of material sought—in the editor's own words—and the names of writers recently published by that press or magazine. Average payment and copyright policy are also included. To be listed in this directory, a magazine must be supported by CCLM, so the list is selective. Use it in conjunction with Dustbooks' *International Directory*. Indexed by state.

CCLM Catalog of College Literary Magazines

Coordinating Council of Literary Magazines

Similar in format to CCLM's *Directory*, and another great buy, the *Catalog* is a good resource for student writers. It lists the 250 undergraduate literary magazines that participated in CCLM's college literary award contest this year. Annotations include a magazine's submission policies—some are forums for the college's own students, but many accept manuscripts from students enrolled elsewhere and non-student writers as well.

John Fox

A Checklist for Giving Readings

Giving a reading can nurture your writing, gratify your ego, take you someplace new, and bring you face-to-face with your readers. Giving a reading is also a job for which you earn money, and it should be treated in a businesslike, professional manner.

Start Locally

Begin with your own neighborhood libraries, Y's, churches, senior citizens' centers—any kind of community center. When you've read in the neighborhood, cast your net wider within your home town. Don't forget junior and community colleges or the local hospital. Always send the prospective sponsor a sample of your work and, if you have them, copies of reviews.

Once the town knows you, move around in your home state, then the region. To find new sponsors, consult the *Sponsors List* (published by and available from Poets & Writers, Inc., $2.95 for writers listed with Poets & Writers, $3.95 for all others), which includes 641 reading/workshop sponsors nationwide. Also get in touch with your state arts council for information on other active literary groups in the state. Only when you have published nationally and/

or established a reputation as a good performer/reader will a sponsor be willing to import you from one region—or one end of the country—to another.

Start Early

The better-paying series, such as those at colleges and universities, book writers a year in advance, making occasional exceptions only for established writers. Even local series at bars and community centers are often booked six months in advance. If you want to go on a reading tour around the publication date of your book, start applying to sponsors as soon as your publisher tells you the date; if it's a year off, so much the better.

Let your editor and/or publisher's publicity department know about scheduled readings at least six weeks in advance, asking them to get books to local bookstores in time for the reading. They cannot do this on short notice.

Ask for the Room You Want

Be sure the sponsor knows what kind of room you want to read in. Be specific: mention lighting, audience seating arrangement, what you will need in the way of table, chair, podium, something hot or cold to drink. If the sponsor cannot give you exactly what you want, ask what kind of room you'll get. Don't let a last-minute surprise throw off the whole evening.

Ask About the Audience

Make clear what kind of an audience is expected and how many people are planned for. Will you be reading to two dozen graduate students in creative writing or does the sponsor hope to attract 200 people of all ages from the community? This will help you plan what to read and avoid an unexpected situation that leaves you wishing you had brought the other book.

Help Promote the Reading

This is easier to do, of course, if the reading is on your home ground. You can check on how the sponsor plans to use free newspaper listings, paid ads, mailings, and posters. You can have your own flyer printed and mail it to friends, relatives, and co-workers. It can also be posted in likely places: libraries, bookstores, restaurants, your office—any-place with a community bulletin board.

If you're reading out of town, check with the sponsor and suggest the above ideas, if they apply. Other than that, think of friends and professional associates in the area who would be interested in the reading and might tell others about it.

Read Short Pieces

Time estimates range from 3-4 to 15-20 minutes per piece. The point is that even with a narrative to follow, an audience cannot concentrate on a first-time hearing for too long. It needs periodic breaks made up of comments or anecdotes about the work. Here is your chance to explain briefly the section from your novel that you are about to read, so that the audience understands it in context.

Four or five 10-minute pieces with brief discussion between them can leave an audience excited and refreshed; an hour-long reading by one writer can leave the audience nothing but exhausted. Read pieces out loud beforehand, to time them. The total time for a reading program will vary according to audience, milieu, and how many writers are reading, and it should be decided on definitely by the writer and sponsor. In general, entire readings should not last much more than an hour, so two writers would not read for more than half an hour each, comments included.

Read Dramatic Pieces

Read some dramatic passages. Also read a balance of light and serious pieces. Making an audience laugh is okay, but know when it has laughed enough. Plan what to begin with, what to end with.

Feel the Audience Out

Always be prepared for a reading, but if for some reason you're not (you caught a cold, your plane was late), tell the audience, although perhaps wait until mid-reading. Be honest. Don't try to be anything you're not. Talk to the audience. Smile a little. Bring alternate pieces, in case you find the audience is not responding to what you originally planned to read.

Sell Your Books

You can do this both by making sure that books are available in local bookstores (both college and community) and by bringing books with you to the reading. Check with local bookstores beforehand to see that they're well-stocked. Make sure to read some pieces from already published work.

Most writers do find that readings sell books and most try to bring along books—or literary magazines, if that's where they've been published. They buy them directly from the publisher, where they usually get an author's discount. If they find that making change while they autograph books and answer questions is too difficult, they ask a friend to come along and take charge of book sales.

Get Paid

Few sponsors outside the academic community can pay the reading fee a writer may deserve and even then, only to nationally known writers. Fees usually range from $100-$500, or $800-$1,000 for the best-known writers.

A low reading fee (less than $100) may be offset by the prestige of the reading series, the chance to sell and promote your work, or the chance to visit old friends or a new part of the country. Or, if a college is paying $200 plus travel expenses, you may be glad to read at a nearby community center or museum for $50—if it doesn't make your schedule too hectic.

A reading fee of whatever size should always be offset by travel and living expenses as necessary, whether it's a round-trip fare for a Greyhound or a 747. You may have to negotiate more firmly in this area than for a fee; every year Poets & Writers, Inc. hears from writers who spent more money getting to and from a reading than they were ultimately paid for it. If your travel costs will leave you an unaccept-able $20 profit on a $50 reading fee, you must stand firm for additional travel money. Be sure the sponsor knows about the fee money for readings and residen-cies offered by the National Endowment for the Arts and about any fee supplements the state arts council may offer.

Get It All in Writing

The importance of getting all the details about a reading in a letter or written contract cannot be emphasized too often or too firmly. Every aspect of the reading engagement should be confirmed by you or the sponsor in writing: date, time, fee, travel money, living expenses and arrangements, what kind of room you'll read in, type and size of audience, time of your arrival and departure, other activities during your visit. If you want to be met at the train station, say so; if you'd rather take a cab by yourself so you can have five more minutes to think, say so. You are the guest, and the sponsor owes it to you to arrange everything carefully beforehand.

If the sponsoring organization works without a written contract for the reading, a clearly written letter confirming the details will serve. From time to time, Poets & Writers, Inc. hears from writers who were paid less than the fee they were verbally promised. Without something in writing, there is no way to argue with a sponsor who says he cannot pay you, for whatever reason. Written confirmation helps both sides stick to their word and can quickly point out any misunderstandings that could spoil a reading for you and your audience.

Debby Mayer

Appendix

Poets & Writers, Inc.

Writing is a solitary occupation, and those who practice it often feel alone. To break their isolation, writers need professional information, they need to know the news of the literary world, they need support. In short, they need to feel connected to a concerned literary community. At Poets & Writers, our Information Center, Publications Program, and Readings/ Workshops program work to meet those needs.

The Information Center at Poets & Writers keeps track of addresses and publication records for over 5,800 poets and fiction writers publishing in the U.S. today. We also answer questions relating to writers' needs and provide information about literary activities. Our telephone lines are open from 11 a.m. to 3 p.m. (EST) Monday through Friday. The Information Center also maintains lists of more than 26,000 people nationwide who have a serious interest in contemporary literature. These lists are available for rental on mailing labels and in specialized print-out form. The lists are computerized and updated daily. The Information Center's services are a valuable resource not only for writers, but also for publishers, agents, schools, and organizations that need to keep in touch with the literary world.

Publications from Poets & Writers include references, source books, guides, and a newsletter. *Coda: Poets & Writers Newsletter* is published five times a year. It is the original source for the articles in this book. In addition to such articles, each issue includes information on grants and awards and publishing opportunities. The 1983-84 edition of *A Directory of American Poets and Fiction Writers* lists 5,533 poets and fiction writers publishing in the U.S. today; the 1985-86 edition, which will be available in the fall of 1985, will list approximately 6,000.

Literary Agents, A Writer's Guide gives advice on how to find and work with an agent. *A Writer's Guide to Copyright* summarizes the 1979 copyright law for writers, editors, and teachers. And *Literary Bookstores, A List in Progress* gives the names, addresses, and specialties of 333 bookstores in the U.S.

The Readings/Workshops Program at Poets & Writers sponsors public readings and writing workshops given by fiction writers and poets. These activities develop perceptive, diverse audiences for literature and help writers survive financially. The program, working with funds provided by the New York State Council on the Arts, provides supplemental fees for readings and workshops presented by organizations in New York State. Libraries, Y's, community centers, colleges and universities, museums, neighborhood houses, prisons, bookstores, religious organizations—all may apply for fee assistance. The Readings/Workshops program has recently received grants to sponsor programs outside of New York State as well.

Poets & Writers, Inc. is a nonprofit organization whose services are supported by both public and private funding. The New York State Council on the Arts has helped Poets & Writers since its inception; their understanding of the needs of writers has made it possible to build, through the Readings/Workshops Program, a solid support system for writers in New York State. Our Information Center and the Publications Program could not exist without the support and encouragement we receive from the Literature Program of the National Endowment for the Arts. We especially thank them for their support of *Coda*, which is the source of this book. Over the years, the NEA's funding has underwritten P&W's services and their Challenge Grant Program enabled us to begin private fund raising. Now, in addition to public funding, Poets & Writers, Inc. receives private support from many foundations, corporations, and publishers. Private individuals contribute generously through the Friends of Poets & Writers. We—and the writers we serve— are deeply indebted and grateful to them all.

For more information, or to order, please call or write Poets & Writers, Inc., 201 West 54 Street, New York, New York 10019. (212) 757-1766.

Contributors

Richard Balkin has his own literary agency in Manhattan and represents more than fifty writers. He has worked in publishing for Bobbs-Merrill, has taught courses in book publishing, and has published articles in many magazines. He is the author of *A Writer's Guide to Book Publishing* (Hawthorn/Dutton, 1977).

Allen Barnett is a freelance writer and editor living in New York City. At the time he wrote the article in this collection, he was coordinator of the Readings/Workshops Program at Poets & Writers.

Daryln Brewer is the current editor of *Coda* and a freelance writer. She has worked at Poets & Writers since 1979 and lives in New York City.

John Fox worked at Poets & Writers while getting his MFA in fiction at Columbia University. His first novel, *The Boys on the Rock,* was published by St. Martin's Press in 1984. He lives in New York.

Richard Grayson has published five books of fiction, the most recent of which is *I Brake for Delmore Schwartz* (1983). He teaches English at Broward Community College in Davie, Florida, where he lives.

Caroline Rand Herron is National Affairs Editor of "The Week in Review" of the *New York Times* and Executive Consultant to Poets & Writers, Inc. She lives in New York City.

Martha King was a staff writer for *Coda* for three years, during which time she also taught creative writing workshops at Mercy College, New York. A collection of her poetry, *Weather,* was published in 1978 by New Rivers Press. Since 1981, she has been at Memorial Sloan-Kettering Cancer Center as a staff writer/editor for the institution's publications.

Debby Mayer is the former editor of *Coda.* Her first novel, *Sisters* (G. P. Putnam), was published in 1983. Since leaving P&W to devote full-time to her writing she has won a CAPS Award and has spent six months as Writer-in-Residence for the Upper Hudson Library Federation. She lives in New York City and Hollowville, New York.

Lisa Merrill is the Director of Publications at Poets & Writers and is the managing editor of *Coda.* She has worked at P&W since 1972 and lives in Rockland County, New York.

Stacy Pies is a poet, freelance writer, and editor who has worked for Poets & Writers since 1979. She is currently completing a PhD. in Comparative Literature at the Graduate Center of the City University of New York.

Nelson Richardson worked as a staff writer and researcher for Poets & Writers. He is presently a computer programmer for Shearson-American Express in New York City.

Leonard Todd, the designer of this book, was formerly Design Director at Poets & Writers. He is also a writer and his first novel, *The Best Kept Secret of the War,* was published in 1984 by Alfred A. Knopf. He lives in New York.

Galen Williams is the founder and former Executive Director of Poets & Writers, Inc. She is now Chairman of the Board and continues as advisory editor to *Coda* while running "Galen Williams Landscape and Design" in East Hampton, New York.

Original publication date of *Coda* articles.

One: Getting Started
"Writer's Block: The Anxious Silence," June/July 1982, Volume 9 #5
"How to Get Out of the Slush Pile," June/July 1982, Volume 9 #5
"Over the Transom and Into Print—How to Give an Unsolicited Manuscript the Best Chance," June/July 1979, Volume 6 #5
"Self-Publishing: When a Writer Needs to go Public," November/December 1981, Volume 9 #2
"Vanity Press: Stigma or Sesame?" November/December 1976, Volume 4 #2
"The Chapbook: A Slender Volume of Poems," June/July 1983, Volume 10 #5
"Word Processors: Do They Help Writers?" February/March 1983, Volume 10 #3

Two: The Writer as Business Person
"Writers on Revision: Is Perfection the Death of Energy?" April/May 1982, Volume 9 #4
"Starting Your Own Small Press," September/October 1982, Volume 10 #1
"What Should a Writer Know About Book Design?" September/October 1981, Volume 9 #1

"The Rapid Evolution of the Paperback: All to the Writer's Good?" February/March 1984, Volume 11 #3
"The Blossoming of the Trade Paperback," April/May 1984, Volume 11 #4
"Major Paperback Publishers," April/May 1984, Volume 11 #4
"Behind the Blurb," February/March 1981, Volume 8 #3

Six: Nuts and Bolts

"On Cloud Nine: 21 Heavens for Writers," April/May 1983, Volume 10 #4
"Helping Writers Help Themselves: 10 Groups That Offer Information and Services to Writers," September/October 1983, Volume 11 #1
"Guide to Writers' Resources," June/July 1981, Volume 8 #5
"14 Major Magazines: What They Want and What They Pay," June/July 1983, Volume 10 #5
"A Writer's Guide to Reference Books," November/December 1983, Volume 11 #2
"A Checklist for Giving Readings," November/December 1983, Volume 11 #2

Publishers' Addresses

for books on Suggested Reading lists

R.R. Bowker
P.O. Box 1807
Ann Arbor, Michigan 48106

Coordinating Council of
 Literary Magazines
2 Park Avenue
New York, New York 10016

Dustbooks
P.O. Box 100
Paradise, California 95969

Harlo
50 Victor
Detroit, Michigan 48203

Harper & Row
10 East 53 Street
New York, New York 10022

Hawthorn/Dutton
E.P. Dutton, Inc.
2 Park Avenue
New York, New York 10016

Houghton Mifflin Company
One Beacon Street
Boston, Massachusetts 02108

IMS Press
426 Pennsylvania Avenue
Fort Washington,
Pennsylvania 19034

Mentor/New American
 Library
1633 Broadway
New York, New York 10019

New American Library
1633 Broadway
New York, New York 10019

Para Publishing
P.O. Box 4232Q
Santa Barbara, California
  93103

Poets & Writers, Inc.
201 West 54 Street
New York, New York 10019

Provision House
P.O. Box 5487
Austin, Texas 78763

Pushcart Press
P.O. Box 380
Wainscott, New York 11975

Trinity Press
Tomorrow Today Inc.
3279 20th Street
P.O. Box 5273
San Francisco, California
  94101

Wingbow Press
2940 Seventh Street
Berkeley, California 94710

Writer's Digest Books
9933 Alliance Road
Cincinnati, Ohio 45242